UNITED STATES
CORPORATION HISTORIES

GARLAND REFERENCE LIBRARY
OF SOCIAL SCIENCE
(Vol. 391)

UNITED STATES CORPORATION HISTORIES
A Bibliography, 1965–1985

Wahib Nasrallah

GARLAND PUBLISHING, INC. • NEW YORK & LONDON
1987

© 1987 Wahib Nasrallah
All rights reserved

Library of Congress Cataloging-in-Publication Data

Nasrallah, Wahib, 1945–
  United States Corporation histories.

  (Garland Reference Library of Social Science;
vol. 391)
  Includes index.
  1. Corporations–United States–History–
Bibliography. I. Title. II. Series: Garland Reference
Library of Social Science; v. 391.
Z7164.T87N37 1987 [HD2785] 016.3387'4'0973 86-33560
ISBN 0-8240-9847-1 (alk. paper)

Printed on acid-free, 250-year-life paper
Manufactured in the United States of America

CONTENTS

Introduction	vii
THE BIBLIOGRAPHY	3
Index by Industry	295
Index by Author	337

INTRODUCTION

Interest among various corporations to document progress over the years has recently increased. Corporations are finding new values in producing printed accounts of the company's history. The value of these accounts to the researcher is being supplemented by public relations benefits to the company's corporate image.

The great increase in corporate history literature has not been paralleled by a systematic bibliographic accounting of this important form. This bibliographic reference book bridges the gap in this area. It is an attempt to deal with this topic as comprehensively as possible.

The bibliography contains books, periodical articles, theses, dissertations, pamphlets and other company-produced literature, and corporate histories embedded in annual reports or fact sheets.

The focus of the time period is 1965 through 1985. Included are companies whose histories extended to 1965 or after. Excluded are companies whose histories did not extend to 1965 or beyond, even though they were published later than 1965.

The process of identifying those histories was a laborious and painstaking one. Bibliographic tools do not allow for direct access under the subject matter, i.e., corporation histories. It was necessary to search the literature using a company name approach to identify those histories in secondary sources. In addition, a direct mailing to the largest U.S. corporations was utilized to insure a wide and diversified method of collecting data.

The main body of the bibliography lists corporations alphabetically. A word-by-word approach is used, with hyphenated words treated as separate entities; acronyms are interfiled. Cross-references are used when the company's popular name is at variance with the official name. "See also" references are used to link name changes and other corporate family relationships. The index to U.S. corporations' histories by industry, which follows the main text, will aid researchers of industrial history. Collective histories of companies in one particular industry can often shed light on the whole industry.

The scope of this bibliography may be enlarged in future editions.

United States
Corporation Histories

A&P
See:
GREAT ATLANTIC AND PACIFIC TEA COMPANY

ABBOTT LABORATORIES

Abbott Laboratories. <u>Abbott: 1888-1979.</u> North Chicago: The Company, 1979. 4 p.

Kogan, Herman. <u>The Long White Line; The Story of Abbott Laboratories.</u> New York: Alexander Hamilton Institute, 1965. 327 p.

ABC
See:
AMERICAN BROADCASTING COMPANY

ABLE (RICHARD) AND COMPANY

Newlin, Lyman. "The Rise and Fall of Richard Able and Company, Inc." <u>Scholarly Publishing</u> 7 (January 1975): 55-61.

ACE HARDWARE CORPORATION

Ace Hardware Corporation. <u>Our 60th Anniversary.</u> Oak Brook, Ill.: The Company, 1984. 4 p.

ACCURAY CORPORATION

Kurstedt, Harold A. "AccuRay Puts Computers to Work." <u>IE News</u> 19 (Summer 1984): 1-3+.

ACME-CLEVELAND CORPORATION

Armstrong, Arthur S. The Persistence of Struggle: The Story of Acme-Cleveland Corporation. New York: Newcomen Society of North America, 1976. 24 p. (Newcomen Publication; no. 1040.)

ACME MARKETS, INC.

Nicholson, Arnold. Acme Markets, Inc., 1891-1967, From Corner Grocery to Supermarket Chain. Philadelphia: Acme Markets, 1967.

ADDRESSOGRAPH MULTIGRAPH CORPORATION

Addressograph Multigraph Corporation. Beginning with Imagination. Cleveland, Ohio: The Company, n.d. 11 p.

See also: Bruning (Charles) Company

AERO MAYFLOWER TRANSIT COMPANY, INC.

Floros, Leo. "The Mayflower Story." Public Relations Journal 39 (September 1983): 23-25.

AETNA LIFE AND CASUALTY

Post, James E. Risk and Response: Management and Social Change in the American Insurance Industry. Lexington, Mass.: Lexington Books, 1976. 206 p.

AFFILIATED FUND, INC.

Driscoll, Robert S. <u>The Story of Lord, Abbett and Company and Affiliated Fund, Inc.: A View of the Capital Needs of the U.S. Economy.</u> New York: Newcomen Society in North America, 1974. (Newcomen Publication; no. 999.)

AGWAY, INC.

Steel, George. <u>George Steel: Yesterdays (Sound Recordings).</u> West Chester, Pa.: Chester County District Library Center, 1979. 2 cassettes. (Recorded April 12, 1979.)

AIR FLORIDA

"Air Florida's Meteoric Rise." <u>Business Week</u> (10 November 1980): 141-142.

"Behind the Rise and Fall of Air Florida." <u>Business Week</u> (23 July 1984): 122-123+.

AIR PRODUCTS AND CHEMICALS, INC.

Air Products and Chemicals, Inc. <u>Who We Are.</u> Allentown, Pa.: The Company, 1982. 6 p.

"Air Products Begins in 1940 with 'A Better Idea.'" <u>Air Products Monthly News</u> (October 1975). (Special 35th anniversary issue.)

ALABAMA BANCORPORATION

Woods, John W. <u>Alabama Bancorporation: The Story of Alabama's Largest Banking Institution.</u> New York: Newcomen Society in North America, 1978. 26 p. (Newcomen Publication; no. 1070.)

ALACHUA GENERAL HOSPITAL, INC.

Rathbun, Frank F. <u>Proud of Our Past, Proud of Our Future: The Story of Alachua General Hospital, Inc.</u> Gainsville, Fla.: The Hospital, 1978. 79 p.

ALAGO SALES AND MANUFACTURING COMPANY

Persinos, John F. "East Side Story." <u>Inc.</u> 6 (July 1984): 61-64.

THE ALASKA AIRLINES, INC.

Satterfield, Archie. <u>The Alaska Airlines Story.</u> Anchorage: Alaska Northwest Publishing Company, 1981. 207 p.

ALBERT KAHN ASSOCIATES, INC.

King, Sol. <u>Creative--Responsive--Pragmatic. 75 Years of Professional Practice. Albert Kahn and Associates, Architects-Engineers.</u> New York: Newcomen Society in North America, 1970. 36 p. (Newcomen Address.)

ALCO STANDARD CORPORATION

Veale, Tinkham, and R.B. Mundt. Alco Standard Corporation, "The Corporate Partnership": A Commitment to Excellence. New York: Newcomen Society in North America, 1980. 29 p. (Newcomen Publication; no. 1131.)

ALCOA
See:
ALUMINUM COMPANY OF AMERICA

ALCON LABORATORIES, INC.

Alexander, Robert D. The Story of Alcon Laboratories, Inc.: Prescription for Success. New York: Newcomen Society in North America, 1969. 28 p. (Newcomen Address.)

ALEXANDER AIRCRAFT COMPANY

De Vries, John A. Alexander Eaglerock: A History of Alexander Aircraft Company. Colorado Springs: Century One Press, 1985. 126 p.

ALEXANDER AND BALDWIN, INC.

Alexander and Baldwin, Inc. Eighty-five Years a Corporation, 1900-1985. Honolulu: The Company, 1985. 66 p.

ALLEGHENY AIRLINES
See:
USAIR

ALLIED CORPORATION

Cunningham, Mary. *Powerplay: What Really Happened at Bendix.* New York: Linden Press/Simon & Schuster, 1984. 286 p.

Hennessy, Edward L. *Allied Corporation: Strength Through Diversification.* New York: Newcomen Society in North America, 1984. 24 p. (Newcomen Publication; no. 1218.)

ALLIED STORES CORPORATION

Macioce, Thomas M. *Allied Stores Corporation: 50 Years of Retail Growth.* New York: Newcomen Society in North America, 1979. (Newcomen Publication; no. 1100.)

ALLIS-CHALMERS CORPORATION

Peterson, Walter Fritio F. *An Industrial Heritage, Allis-Chalmers Corporation.* Milwaukee: Milwaukee County Historical Society, 1978. 448 p.

Scott, David Charles. *Managerial Vision and Craftsmanship: To Meet Human Needs: The Story of Allis-Chalmers Corporation.* New York: Newcomen Society in North America, 1979. 18 p. (Newcomen Publication; no. 1101.)

ALLSTATE INSURANCE COMPANY

Boe, Archie R. *Allstate: The Story of the Good Hands Company.* New York:

Newcomen Society in North America, 1981. 19 p. (Newcomen Publication; no. 1148.)

Seldow, Leona. *Allstate: A Study in Entrepreneurial Decision Making That Changed the Tradition-Bound Insurance Industry.* New York: Graduate School of Business Administration, New York University, 1976. 211 p.

See also: Sears, Roebuck and Company

ALLTEL CORPORATION

Case, Weldon W. *ALLTEL Corporation: Twenty-five Years of Growth and Dedication to Excellence.* New York: Newcomen Society in North America, 1985. 20 p. (Newcomen Publication; no. 1246.)

ALPHA BETA COMPANY

Cramer, Esther R. *The Alpha Beta Story; An Illustrated History of a Leading Western Food Retailer.* La Habra, Calif.: Alpha Beta Acme Markets, 1973. 436 p.

ALUMINUM COMPANY OF AMERICA (ALCOA)

"ALCOA Timeline: Significant Developments over the Past Decade." In *Aluminum Company of America Annual Report*, 10-11. Pittsburgh, Pa.: The Company, 1985.

AMARILLO NATIONAL BANK

Thompson, Thomas Hazzard. <u>The Ware Boys: The Story of a Texas Family Bank.</u> Canyon, Tex.: Staked Plains Press, 1978. 293 p.

AMAX, INC.

AMAX, Inc. <u>AMAX Today; What We Are, What We Do.</u> Greenwich, Conn.: The Company, 1984. 20 p.

Levinson, Harry, and Stuart Rosenthal. "Ian K. MacGregor." In <u>CEO: Corporate Leadership in Action,</u> 96-136. New York: Basic Books, 1984.

AMC CORPORATION
See:
AMERICAN MOTORS CORPORATION

AMCAST
See:
DAYTON MALLEABLE, INC.

AMDAHL CORPORATION

Amdahl Corporation. <u>The Amdahl Phenomenon.</u> Sunnyvale, Calif.: The Company, 1983. 13 p.

AMERICAN AIRLINES, INC.

American Airlines, Inc. <u>A Brief History of American Airlines.</u> Dallas: The Company, 1985. 17 p.

Cearley, George Walker, Jr. <u>American Airlines: An Illustrated History.</u> Dallas: G.W. Cearley, Jr., 1981. 100 p.

Serling, Robert J. <u>Eagle: The History of American Airlines.</u> New York: St. Martin's/Marek, 1985. 482 p.

AMERICAN BRASS COMPANY

<u>Brass Valley: The Story of Working People's Lives and Struggles in an American Industrial Region.</u> The Brass Workers History Project: Compiled and edited by Jeremy Brecher, Jerry Lombardi, and Jan Stakhouse. Philadelphia: Temple University Press, 1982. 284 p.

AMERICAN BROADCASTING COMPANY

American Broadcasting Company. <u>Historical Highlights.</u> New York: The Company, 1980. 12 p.

Quinlan, Sterling. <u>Inside ABC: American Broadcasting Company's Rise to Power.</u> New York: Hastings House, 1979. 290 p.

AMERICAN CRYSTAL SUGAR COMPANY

<u>Guide to the Records of the American Crystal Sugar Company.</u> Compiled by Lydia A. Lucas, and Marion E. Matters. St. Paul: Division of Archives and Manuscripts, Minnesota Historical Society, 1985. 100 p.

THE AMERICAN DISTILLING COMPANY

Brown, Russell R. The American Distilling Company: A Story of People, Products and Progress. New York: Newcomen Society in North America, 1965. 24 p. (Newcomen Address.)

AMERICAN ELECTRIC POWER COMPANY

White, W.S. American Electric Power: 75 Years of Meeting the Challenge. New York: Newcomen Society in North America, 1982. 23 p. (Newcomen Publication; no. 1175.)

AMERICAN EXPRESS COMPANY

American Express Company. Promises to Pay: The Story of American Express Company. New York: The Company, 1977. 283 p.

Carrington, Tim. The Year They Sold Wall Street. Boston: Houghton Mifflin, 1985. 384 p.

AMERICAN GENERAL INSURANCE COMPANY

Woodson, Benjamine W. "A Financial Services Supermarket": The American General Story. New York: Newcomen Society in North America, 1974. 32 p. (Newcomen Publication; no. 992.)

AMERICAN GREETINGS CORPORATION

American Greetings Corporation. *History of American Greetings Corporation.* Cleveland: The Company, 1985. 4 p.

Weiss, Morry. *American Greetings Corporation.* New York: Newcomen Society in North America, 1982. 20 p. (Newcomen Publication; no. 1164.)

AMERICAN HOSPITAL SUPPLY CORPORATION

Sturdivant, Frederick D. *Growth Through Service: The Story of American Hospital Supply Corporation.* Evanston, Illinois: Northwestern University Press, 1970. 382 p. (Northwestern University Studies in Business History.)

AMERICAN INSTITUTE OF STEEL CONSTRUCTION, INC.

Gillette, Leslie H. *The First 50 Years: The American Institute of Steel Construction, Inc., 1921-1980.* Chicago: The Institute, 1980. 179 p.

AMERICAN INTERNATIONAL GROUP, INC.

American International Group, Inc. *History of AIG.* New York: The Company, 1984. 10 p.

AMERICAN MOTORS CORPORATION

"AMC Looks Back on 25 Years." Automotive News (7 May 1979): 6+.

"The Story of American Motors." Wards Quarterly (Spring 1965): 1-40.

THE AMERICAN NATURAL RESOURCES COMPANY

Seder, Arthur R. The American Natural Resources Company. Seventy-five Years Old and Building for the future. New York: Newcomen Society in North America, 1977. 22 p. (Newcomen Publication; no. 1058.)

AMERICAN SHIP BUILDING COMPANY

Wright, Richard J. Freshwater Whales; A History of the American Ship Building Company and its Predecessors. Kent, Ohio: Kent State University Press, 1969. 299 p.

AMERICAN STOCK EXCHANGE

Sobel, Robert. Amex: A History of the American Stock Exchange, 1921-1971. New York: Weybright and Talley, 1972. 382 p.

Sobel, Robert. The Curbstone Brokers; The Origins of the American Stock Exchange. New York: Macmillan, 1970. 296 p.

AMERICAN TELEPHONE AND TELEGRAPH COMPANY

Bolling, George. *AT&T Aftermath of Antitrust: Preserving Positive Command and Control.* Washington, D.C.: National Defense University, 1983. 169 p.

Brooks, John. *Telephone: the First Hundred Years.* New York: Harper and Row, 1976. 369 p.

Goulden, Joseph C. *Monopoly.* New York: Putnam, 1968. 350 p.

Kahaner, Larry. *On the Line; The Men of MCI--Who Took on AT&T, Risked Everything, and Won.* New York: Random House, 1986. 327 p.

Kleinfield, Sonny. *The Biggest Company on Earth: A Profile of AT&T.* New York: Holt, Rinehart, and Winston, 1981. 321 p.

Phillips, John Patrick. *Ma Bell's Millions.* New York: Vantage Press, 1970. 141 p

Smith, George David. *Anatomy of a Business Strategy: Bell, Western Electric, and the Origins of the American Telephone Industry.* Baltimore: Johns Hopkins University Press, 1985. 208 p.

Toffler, Alvin. *The Adaptive Corporation.* New York: McGraw-Hill, 1984. 256 p.

See also: Western Electric Company

AMERICAN TOBACCO COMPANY

Cunningham, Bill. *On Bended Knees: the Night Rider Story.* Nashville: McClanahan Publishing House, 1983. 224 p.

AMERICAN ZINC COMPANY

Norris, James D. *AZN; A History of the American Zinc Company.* Madison: State Historical Society of Wisconsin, 1968. 244 p.

AMFAC, INC.

Simpich, Frederick, Jr. *Dynasty in the Pacific.* New York: McGraw-Hill, 1974. 270 p.

AMOSKEAG MANUFACTURING COMPANY

Hareven, Tamara K. *Amoskeag: Life and Work in an American Factory City.* New York: Pantheon Books, 1978.

Hareven, Tamara K. *Family Time and Industrial Time: the Relationship Between the Family and Work in a New England Industrial Community.* New York: Cambridge University Press, 1982. 474 p.

AMTORG TRADING CORPORATION

Amtorg Trading Corporation. <u>Amtorg Trading Corporation: Fiftieth Anniversary.</u> New York: The Corporation, 1974. 24 p.

Feinstein, J. M. Tather. <u>Fifty Years of U.S.-Soviet Trade.</u> New York: Symposium Press, 1974. 256 p.

AMTRAK

Bradley, Rodger. <u>Amtrak: The U.S. National Railroad Passenger Corporation.</u> Poole, Eng.: Blandford Press, 1985. 176 p.

Edmonson, Herald A. <u>Journey to Amtrak, The Year History Rode the Passenger Train.</u> Milwaukee, Wis.: National Railroad Passenger Corporation, 1972. 104 p.

Hilton, George Woodman. <u>Amtrak: The National Railroad Passenger Corporation.</u> Washington, D.C.: American Enterprise Institute for Public Policy Research, 1980. 80 p. (AEI Studies; no. 266.)

See also: Penn Central Company

AMWAY CORPORATION

Butterfield, Stephen. <u>Amway: Cult of Free Enterprise.</u> Boston: South End Press, 1985. 185 p.

Conn, Charles P. *The Possible Dream: A Candid Look at Amway.* Old Tappan, N.J.: Revell, 1977. 174 p.

Conn, Charles P. *Promises to Keep: The Amway Phenomenon and How It Works.* New York: Putnam, 1985. 128 p.

Conn, Charles P. *An Uncommon Freedom.* Old Tappan, N.J.: Revell, 1982. 160 p.

ANCHOR HOCKING GLASS CORPORATION

Gushman, John L. *Living Glass: The Story of the Anchor Hocking Glass Corporation.* New York: Newcomen Society in North America, 1965. 24 p. (Newcomen Address.)

ANDERSEN (ARTHUR) AND COMPANY

Arthur Andersen and Company. *70 Years of Superior Client Service, Innovative Use of New Technologies, Worldwide Expansion and Leadership in the Profession, 1913-1983.* New York: The Company, 1983. 26 p.

Arthur Andersen and Company, The First Sixty Years, 1913-1973. Chicago: The Company, 1974. 189 p.

ANDERSON, CLAYTON AND COMPANY

"Anderson, Clayton: Eight Decades of Progress." In *1984 Annual Report*, 4-9. Houston: The Company, 1984.

Fleming, Lamar. Growth of the Business of Anderson, Clayton and Company. Houston: Texas Gulf Coast Historical Association, 1966. 46 p.

ANDERSON CORPORATION

Ruble, Kenneth Dougls. The Magic Circle: A Story of the Men and Women Who Made Anderson the Most Respected Name in Windows. Bayport, Minn.: Ruble, 1978. 216 p.

ANDERSON ELECTRIC CORPORATION

Schuler, John Hamilton. The Anderson Story: A Profile of Growth. New York: Newcomen Society in North America, 1970. 28 p. (Newcomen Address.)

See also: Square D Company

ANDERSON-TULLY COMPANY

Heavrin, Charles A. Boxes, Baskets, and Boards: A History of Anderson-Tully Company. Memphis: Memphis State University Press, 1981. 178 p.

ANGLO AMERICAN CORPORATION OF SOUTH AFRICA, LTD.

Anglo American and the Rise of Modern South Africa. New York: Monthly Review Press, 1984. 352 p.

APPLE COMPUTER, INC.

Apple Computer, Inc. Press Background Information. Cupertino, Calif.: The Company, 1985. 5 p.

Moritz, Michael. Little Kingdom: The Private Story of Apple Computer. New York: Morrow, 1984. 336 p.

ARA SERVICES, INC.

Fishman, William S. ARA Services, Inc. Developing a New Industry: Service Management. New York: Newcomen Society in North America, 1977. 24 p. (Newcomen Publication; no. 1056.)

ARABIAN AMERICAN OIL COMPANY (ARAMCO)

Secret History of the Oil Companies in the Middle East. Edited by William J. Kennedy. Salisbury, N.C.: Documentary Publications, 1979. 2 vols. 466 p.

ARCHER DANIELS MIDLAND COMPANY

Archer Daniels Midland Company. Decatur, Ill.: The Company, 1984. 16 p.

ARDEN (ELIZABETH), INC.

Lewis, Alfred A., and Constance Woodworth. Miss Elizabeth Arden. New York: Coward, McCann & Geoghegan, 1972. 320 p.

THE ARIZONA BANK

Bean, G. Clarke. *The Spirit of the Arizona Bank.* New York: Newcomen Society in North America, 1972. 31 p. (Newcomen Address.)

ARIZONA PUBLIC SERVICE COMPANY

Reilly, William P. *Arizona Public Service Company: People, Power and Progress.* New York: Newcomen Society in North America, 1970. 32 p. (Newcomen Address.)

THE ARIZONA REPUBLIC

Pulliam, Eugene C. *Is There a Fighter in the House?* New York: Newcomen Society in North America, 1966. 24 p. (Newcomen Address.)

ARMCO STEEL CORPORATION

Verity, C. William. *Faith in Men: The Story of Armco Steel Corporation.* New York: Newcomen Society in North America, 1971. 28 p. (Newcomen Address.)

ARMOUR AND COMPANY

Shultz, George Pratt. *Strategies for the Displaced Worker: Confronting Economic Change.* Westport, Conn.: Greenwood Press, 1976, c1966. 221 p.

ARMSTRONG RUBBER COMPANY

Walsh James A. <u>The Armstrong Rubber Company: Seventy Years of Progress in the Tire Industry.</u> New York: Newcomen Society in North America, 1982. 19 p. (Newcomen Publication; no. 1155.)

ARMSTRONG WORLD INDUSTRIES, INC.

Armstrong World Industries, Inc. <u>Armstrong: A Historical Summary.</u> Lancaster, Pa.: The Company, 1985. 2 p.

Armstrong World Industries, Inc. <u>The Story of Armstrong.</u> Lancaster, Pa.: The Company, 1985. 11 p.

ART METAL, INC.

Yahn, Mildred L. <u>The Rise and Fall of a Corporation: The Story of Art Metal, Inc., 1888-1971.</u> Jamestown, N.Y.: M.L. Yahn, 1983. 170 p.

ARTHUR ANDERSEN AND COMPANY
See:
ANDERSEN (ARTHUR) AND COMPANY

ARVIN INDUSTRIES, INC.

Coons, Coke. <u>Arvin--The First Sixty Years History.</u> Columbus, Ind.: The Company, 1982. 263 p.

ASHLAND OIL AND REFINING COMPANY, INC.

Scott, Otto J. *The Exception; The Story of Ashland Oil and Refining Company.* New York: McGraw-Hill, 1968. 450 p.

ASSOCIATED GENERAL CONTRACTORS OF AMERICA

Mooney, Booth. *Builders for Progress, The Story of the Associated General Contractors of America.* New York: McGraw-Hill, 1965. 194 p.

ASSOCIATED GROCERS, INC.

"Fifty years of Excellence, 1934-1984." In *1984 Annual Report*, 4-10. Seattle, Wash.: The Company, 1984.

ASSOCIATES CORPORATION OF NORTH AMERICA

"The Associates History: 1918-1983." *Associates Magazine* (Summer 1983): 1-19. (Sixty-fifth anniversary issue.)

ASSOCIATES INVESTMENT COMPANY

Carmichael, O.C., Jr. *New Doors of Achievement: The Story of Associates Investment Company.* New York: Newcomen Society in North America, 1969. 24 p. (Newcomen Address.)

AT&T
See:
AMERICAN TELEPHONE AND TELEGRAPH COMPANY

ATARI, INC.

Cohen, Scott. <u>ZAP: The Rise and Fall of Atari.</u> New York: McGraw-Hill, 1984. 177 p.

ATLANTA BRAVES

Fields, Robert A. <u>Take Me Out to the Crowd; Ted Turner and the Atlanta Braves.</u> Huntsville, Ala.: Strodel, 1977. 256 p.

Onigman, Marc. <u>This Date in Braves History.</u> New York: Stein and Day, 1982. 194 p.

See also: Turner Broadcasting Systems, Inc.

ATLANTA GAS LIGHT COMPANY

Tate, James H. <u>Keeper of the Flame: The Story of Atlanta Gas Light Company, 1856-1985.</u> Atlanta: The Company, 1985. 342 p.

ATLANTA SAW COMPANY

Brown, Edmund D. <u>1594 Evans Drive, S.W.: A History of Southern Saw Service, Inc. and the Atlanta Saw Company.</u> Atlanta: Atlanta Saw Company, 1983. 213 p.

THE ATLANTIC AND PACIFIC TEA COMPANY
See:
GREAT ATLANTIC AND PACIFIC TEA COMPANY

ATLANTIC AVIATION CORPORATION

Grangier, M. "Atlantic Aviation: A Front Runner for 50 Years." Interavia 32 (September 1977): 897-899.

ATLANTIC MUTUAL INSURANCE COMPANY

Cosgrove, John N. Gray Days and Gold; A Character Sketch of Atlantic Mutual Insurance Company. New York: Doremus and Company, 1967. 142 p.

ATLANTIC RECORDING CORPORATION

Gillett, Charlie. Making Tracks; Atlantic Records and the Growth of a Multi-Billion-Dollar Industry. New York: E.P. Dutton, 1974. 305 p.

ATLANTIC RICHFIELD COMPANY

Jones, Charles S. From the Rio Grande to the Arctic: The Story of the Richfield Oil Corporation. Norman: University of Oklahoma Press, 1972. 364 p.

Shaner, J. Richard. "Arco Retreat a New Element in Normal Marketing Turmoil." National Petroleum News 77 (July 1985): 41-42.

ATLANTIC STEEL COMPANY

Kuniansky, Harry R. *A Business History of Atlantic Steel Company, 1901-1968.* New York: Arno Press, 1976. 395 p.

AUSTIN BRIDGE COMPANY

Miller, Shannon. *The First 50 Years, 1918-1968; Austin Bridge Company and Associated Companies.* Dallas: Taylor Publishing Company, 1974. 204 p.

THE AUSTIN COMPANY

Greif, Martin. *The New Industrial Landscape: The Story of the Austin Company.* Clinton, N.J.: Main Street Press, 1978. 192 p.

Shirk, Charles A. *The Austin Company: A Century of Results.* New York: Newcomen Society in North America, 1978. 23 p. (Newcomen Publication; no. 1085.)

AUTOMOBILE CLUB OF SOUTHERN CALIFORNIA

Mathison, Richard R. *Three Cars in Every Garage, a Motorist's History of the Automobile and the Automobile Club in Southern California.* New York: Doubleday, 1968. 257 p.

AVCO CORPORATION

Lawrence, Joanne T. *AVCO Corporation: The First Fifty Years.* Greenwich, Conn.: The Company, 1979. 106 p.

AVONDALE MILLS

Smith, James C. <u>Avondale's Third Generation.</u> New York: Newcomen Society in North America, 1972. 20 p. (Newcomen Address.)

THE BABCOCK AND WILCOX COMPANY

The Babcock and Wilcox Company. <u>The Babcock and Wilcox Story, 1867-1967, 100 Years of Service to Industry.</u> New York: The Company, 1967. 80 p.

Nielsen, M. <u>The Babcock and Wilcox Company 1867-1967: A Century of Progress.</u> New York: Newcomen Society in North America, 1967. 28 p. (Newcomen Address.)

BABSON (DAVID L.) AND COMPANY, INC.

Babson, David L. <u>David L. Babson and Company, Inc.</u> New York: Newcomen Society in North America, 1978. 22 p. (Newcomen Publication; no. 1094.)

BAKER INTERNATIONAL CORPORATION

Baker International Corporation. <u>The Baker Story.</u> Orange, Calif.: The Company, 1979. 33 p.

BALDWIN (D.H.) COMPANY

Thompson, Morley P. <u>D.H. Baldwin; The Multibank Music Company.</u> New York:

Newcomen Society in North America, 1974. 14 p.

BALDWIN-LIMA-HAMILTON CORPORATION

Dolzall, Gary W., and Stephen F. Dolzall. <u>Diesels from Eddystone: The Story of Baldwin Diesel Locomotives.</u> Milwaukee: Kalmbach Publishing Company, 1984. 152 p.

Kirkland, John F. <u>The Diesel Builders: Fairbanks-Morse and Lima-Hamilton.</u> Glendale, Calif.: Interurban Press, 1985. 111 p.

BALDWIN LOCOMOTIVE WORKS

Dolzall, Gary W., and S. F. Dolzall. <u>Diesels from Eddystone: the Story of Baldwin Diesel Locomotives.</u> Milwaukee: Kalmbach Publishing Company, 1984. 152 p.

Westing, Fred. <u>The Locomotives that Baldwin Built.</u> New York: Bonanza Books, 1966. 191 p.

BALTIMORE AND OHIO RAILROAD COMPANY

Baltimore and Ohio Railroad Company. <u>The Story So Far: The Birth and Growth of America's Railroads.</u> Cleveland: The Company, 1977. 32 p.

Bias, Charles V. "The Merger of the Chesapeake and Ohio Railway and the Baltimore and Ohio Railroad

Companies." *Journal of the West Virginia Historical Association* 4 (1980): 24-34.

Harwood, Herbert H. *Impossible Challenge: The Baltimore & Ohio Railroad in Maryland.* Baltimore: Barnard, Roberts, 1979. 497 p.

Mellander, Deane. *B & O Thunder in the Alleghenies.* Newton, N.J.: Carstens, 1983. 80 p.

Stoner, J.F. "America's Pioneer Railroad-- 150 Years of B&O." *Railway Age* 178 (25 April 1977): 46-52.

BALTIMORE ORIOLES

Hawkins, John C. *This Date in Baltimore Orioles and St. Louis Browns History.* New York: Stein and Day, 1983, c1982. 202 p.

Patterson, Ted. *Day by Day in Orioles History.* New York: Leisure Press, 1984. 207 p.

BANCOHIO CORPORATION

Searle, Philip F. *BancOhio Corporation Since 1929; Ohio's Leader in the Multibank Holding Company Concept.* New York: Newcomen Society in North America, 1974. 30 p. (Newcomen Publication; no. 980.)

BANCROFT (JOSEPH) AND SONS COMPANY

Booth, John M. "An Organizational History of the Joseph Bancroft & Company Textile Firm with References to the Chandler." Thesis, University of Pennsylvania, 1973. 239 p.

BANK OF BOSTON CORPORATION

Williams, Ben A. Bank of Boston 200: A History of New England's Leading Bank, 1784-1984. Boston: Houghton Mifflin, 1984. 480 p.

BANK OF NEW MEXICO

Clark, Wilfred A. History of the Bank of New Mexico: The Past is Prologue. New York: Newcomen Society in North America, 1972. 23 p. (Newcomen Address.)

BANK OF VIRGINIA

Bank of Virginia. Bank of Virginia: A Unique Heritage for the Future. Richmond: The Bank, 1981. 8 p.

Wessells, John H. The Bank of Virginia: A History. Charlottesville: University of Virginia Press, n.d.

BANKERS SECURITY LIFE INSURANCE SOCIETY

Schultz, Leslie P. Pioneering in Life Insurance: The Story of Bankers Security Life Insurance Society. New York: Newcomen Society in North

America, 1967. 28 p. (Newcomen Address.)

BANKERS TRUST COMPANY

Bankers Trust Company. <u>Bankers Trust Company: 75 Years.</u> New York: The Bank, 1978. 60 p.

BANTAM BOOKS, INC.

Peterson, Clarence. <u>The Bantam Story; Twenty-five Years of Paperback Publishing.</u> New York: Bantam Books, 1970. 118 p.

Peterson, Clarence. <u>The Bantam Story: Thirty Years of Paperback Publishing.</u> New York: Bantam Books, 1975. 167 p.

BARBER-GREENE COMPANY

Barber-Greene Company. <u>Our First Five Decades.</u> Aurora, Illinois: The Company, 1966. 63 p.

BARNETT BANK OF JACKSONVILLE

Barnett Bank of Jacksonville. Barnett: A <u>Century of Tradition.</u> Jacksonville, Fla: The Bank, 1977. 31 p.

BARRY (R.G.) CORPORATION

R.G. Barry Corporation. <u>Thirty Years of Progress Through People.</u> Columbus: The Company, 1977. 5 p. (Also published in

the 1977 March/April issue of <u>"It's
the Barry's,"</u> the company magazine.)

BATTELLE MEMORIAL INSTITUTE

Boehm, George A., and A. Groner. <u>Science
   in the Service of Mankind: The
   Battelle Story.</u> Lexington, Mass.:
   Lexington Books, 1972. 132 p.

Fawcett, Sherwood L. <u>Battelle Memorial
   Institute: On the Cutting Edge of the
   Future.</u> New York: Newcomen Society in
   North America, 1980. 28 p. (Newcomen
   Publication; no. 1113.)

BEAN (L.L.), INC.

Gorman, Leon A. <u>L.L. Bean, Inc.: Outdoor
   Specialties by Mail from Maine.</u> New
   York: Newcomen Society in North
   America, 1981. 23 p. (Newcomen
   Publication no. 1154.)

Montgomery, M.R. <u>In Search of L.L. Bean.</u>
   New York: New American Library, 1985,
   c1984. 244 p.

BEARINGS, INC.

Bruening, Joseph M. <u>Keeping Industry in
   Motion for Fifty Years: The Story of
   Bearings, Inc.</u> New York: Newcomen
   Society in North America, 1973. 15 p.

BEATRICE FOOD COMPANY

Beatrice Food Company. *The Beatrice Food Story.* Chicago: The Company, 1977. 16 p.

BECHTEL CORPORATION

Ingram, Robert Lockwood. *The Bechtel Story; Seventy Years of Accomplishment in Engineering and Construction.* San Francisco: The Company, 1968. 157 p.

THE BECK ENGRAVING COMPANY, INC.

Beck, George P. *The Economy of Excellence: The Story of the Beck Engraving Company.* New York: Newcomen Society in North America, 1966. 24 p. (Newcomen Address.)

BECKMAN INSTRUMENTS, INC.

Beckman, Arnold O. *Beckman Instruments, Inc.: "There Is No Satisfactory Substitute for Excellence".* New York: Newcomen Society in North America, 1976. 38 p. (Newcomen Publication; no. 1032.)

Stephens, Harrison. *Golden Past, Golden Future: The First Fifty Years of Beckman Instruments, Inc.* Claremont, Calif.: Claremont University Center, 1985. 144 p.

BEDFORD-STUYVESANT RESTORATION CORPORATION

Stein, Barry. Rebuilding Bedford-Stuyvesant: Community Economic Development in the Ghetto. Cambridge, Mass.: Center for Community Economic Development, 1975. 37 p.

BEECH AIRCRAFT CORPORATION

Hedrick, Frank E. Pageantry of Flight: The Story of Beech Aircraft Corporation. New York: Newcomen Society in North America, 1967. 34 p. (Newcomen Address.)

McDaniel, William Herbert. The History of Beech. Wichita, Kan.: McCormick-Armstrong Company, Publishing Division, 1971. 336 p.

BELL AND BECKWITH

Brickey, Homer. Master Manipulator. New York: AMACOM, 1985. 161 p.

BELL AND HOWELL COMPANY

Robinson, Jack Fay. Bell & Howell Company: A 75-Year History. Chicago: The Company, 1982. 175 p.

BELL TELEPHONE LABORATORIES, INC.

Gregor, Arthur. Bell Laboratories; Inside the World's Largest Communication

Center. New York: Scribner's, 1972. 125 p.

Morton, Jack Andrew. *Organizing for Innovation; A Systems Approach to Technical Management.* New York: McGraw-Hill, 1971. 171 p.

THE BENDIX CORPORATION

Cunningham, Mary. *Powerplay: What Really Happened at Bendix.* New York: Linden Press/Simon & Schuster, 1984. 286 p.

Fontaine, A.P. *Where Ideas Unlock the Future: The Story of the Bendix Corporation.* New York: Newcomen Society in North America, 1967. 28 p. (Newcomen Address.)

Hartz, Peter F. *Merger; The Exclusive Inside Story of the Bendix-Martin-Marietta Takeover War.* New York: Morrow, 1985. 418 p.

Lambert, Hope. *Till Death Do Us Part: Bendix vs Martin Marietta.* San Diego: Harcourt Brace Jovanovich, 1983. 264 p.

Sloan, Allan. *Three Plus One Equals Billions: The Bendix-Martin Marietta War.* New York: Arbor House, 1983. 270 p.

BENEFICIAL CORPORATION

Williams, George M. *You're Good for More: The Story of Beneficial Corporation, 1913-1975.* S.l.: Haddon Craftsmen, 1977. 338 p.

BENHAM-BLAIR AND AFFILIATES, INC.

Benham, David Blair. *One Good Job Leads to Another: The Story of Benham-Blair and Affiliates, Inc.* New York: Newcomen Society in North America, 1979. 24 p. (Newcomen Publication; no. 1108.)

BENIHANA NATIONAL CORPORATION

McCallum, Jack. *Making it in America: The Life and Times of Rocky Aoki, Benihana's Pioneer.* New York: Dodd, Mead and Company, 1985. 165 p.

BENTON AND BOWLES, INC.

Danzig, Fred. "Benton & Bowles, at 50, Likes Quiet Consistency." *Advertising Age* 50 (16 July 1979): 3+.

BERRY (L.M.) AND COMPANY

Berry, Loren M. *L.M. Berry and Company 1910-1971: A People Company.* New York: Newcomen Society in North America, 1971. 24 p. (Newcomen Address.)

BESSEMER AND LAKE ERIE RAILROAD COMPANY

Beaver, Roy C. *Bessemer & Lake Erie Railroad, 1819-1969.* San Marino, Calif.: Golden West Books, 1969. 184 p.

BETHLEHEM STEEL CORPORATION

Bethlehem Steel Corporation. *A Brief History of Bethlehem Steel Corporation.* Bethlehem, Pa.: The Company, 198? 17 p.

Bethlehem Steel Corporation. *Recollections: in Celebration of 75 Years.* Bethlehem, Pa.: The Company, 1979. 33 p.

Martin, Edmund F. *Promise for the Future.* New York: Newcomen Society in North America, 1967. 16 p. (Newcomen Address.)

BIG SKY OF MONTANA, INC.

Thompson, Layton S. *Increased Tax Base and Increased Costs of Public Services Resulting Directly from Economic Development: A Case Study Involving Big Sky of Montana, Inc.* Bozeman: Montana Agricultural Experiment Station, Montana State University, 1976. 34 p.

THE *BIRMINGHAM NEWS*

Hanson, Clarence B., Jr. *The Story of the Birmingham News: A Good Newspaper.* New York: Newcomen Society in North America, 1967. 24 p. (Newcomen Address.)

BLACK AND DECKER MANUFACTURING COMPANY

Black and Decker Manufacturing Company. *Highlights of Progress.* Towson, Md.: The Company, 1981. 30 p.

Scott, Otto J. *The Powered Hand: History of the Black and Decker Manufacturing Company.* New York: McGraw-Hill, 1972.

BLACK AND VEATCH, INC.

Robinson, Thomas B. *Black and Veatch: Consulting Engineers; A Back-sight at 63 Years of Growth.* New York: Newcomen Society in North America, 1970. 31 p (Newcomen Address.)

BLACK CLAWSON COMPANY

Landegger, Karl F. *Growing with the Paper Industry Since 1853...: The Parsons and Whittemore Organization and the Black Clawson Company.* New York: Newcomen Society in North America, 1968. 24 p. (Newcomen Address.)

BLISS AND LAUGHLIN INDUSTRIES

Robbins, Frederic J. "The Performance of Change": The Story of Bliss and Laughlin Industries. New York: Newcomen Society in North America, 1968. 28 p. (Newcomen Address.)

BLOOMINGDALE'S

Brady, Maxine. Bloomingdale's. New York: Harcourt Brace Jovanovich, 1980. 229 p.

Stevens, Mark. "Like No Other Store in the World": The Inside Story of Bloomingdale's. New York: Crowell, 1979. 224 p.

BLOUNT, INC.

Blount, Winton M. The Blount Story: "American Enterprise at Its Best". New York: Newcomen Society in North America, 1980. 23 p. (Newcomen Publication; no. 1114.)

BLUE CROSS AND BLUE SHIELD CORPORATION
See:
HOSPITAL CORPORATION OF AMERICA

BOB EVANS FARMS

Bob Evans Farms. The Bob Evans Story. Columbus, Ohio: The Company, 1985. 4 p.

BOBBS-MERRILL COMPANY

O'Bar, Jack. *Origins and History of the Bobbs-Merrill Company.* Urbana: Graduate School of Library and Information Science, University of Illinois, 1985.

BODINE CORPORATION

Bodine, Richard P. *A Man and His Machines: The Story of Alfred Van Sante Bodine and the Bodine Corporation.* New York: Newcomen Society in North America, 1982. 34 p. (Newcomen Publication; no. 1183.)

THE BOEING COMPANY

The Boeing Company. *Background Information.* Seattle: The Company, 1984. 31 p.

Hardy, Michael John. *Boeing.* New York: Beufort Books, 1984, c1982. 86 p.

Mansfield, Harold. *Vision, The Story of Boeing; A Saga of the Sky and the New Horizons of Space.* New York: Popular Library, 1966. 383 p.

Munson, Kenneth G. *Boeing.* New York: Arco Publishing Company, 1971. 144 p.

Norris, William. *Willful Misconduct: An Untold Story.* New York: Norton, 1984. 290 p.

BOISE CASCADE CORPORATION

Boschken, Herman L. Corporate Power and the Mismarketing of Urban Development: Boise Cascade Recreation Communities. New York: Praeger, 1974. 283 p.

BORMAN'S, INC.

Borman's, Inc. Farmer Jack's 50th Birthday, 1927-1977. Detroit: The Company, 1977. 12 p.

BOSTON CELTICS

Henshaw, Tom. The Boston Celtics: A Championship Tradition. Englewood Cliffs, N.J.: Prentice-Hall, 1974. 127 p.

THE **BOSTON GLOBE**

Lyons, Louis M. Newspaper Story: One Hundred Years of the Boston Globe. Cambridge, Massachusetts: Belknap Press, 1971. 482 p.

BOSTON RED SOX

Clark, Ellery H. Boston Red Sox: Seventy-fifth Anniversary History, 1901-1975. Hicksville, N.Y.: Exposition Press, 1975. 168 p.

Frommer, Harvey. Baseball's Greatest Rivalry: The New York Yankees and Boston Red Sox. New York: Atheneum, 1982. 159 p.

Valenti, Dan. *From Florida to Fenway.* Pittsfield, Mass.: Literations, 1982. 141

Walton, Ed. *Red Sox Triumphs and Tragedies: A Continuation of Day by Day Listings and Events in the History of the Boston American League Baseball Team.* New York: Stein and Day, 1980. 380 p.

BOVAY ENGINEERS, INC.

Bovay, Harry E., Jr. *Bovay Engineers, Inc.: The Cutting Edge of Technology.* New York: Newcomen Society in North America, 1982. 23 p. (Newcomen Publication; no. 1166.)

BOWERY SAVINGS BANK

Schisgall, Oscar. *The Bowery Savings Bank of New York; A Social and Financial History.* New York: AMACOM, 1984. 402 p.

Schisgall, Oscar. *Out of One Small Chest: A Social and Financial History of the Bowery Savings Bank.* New York: AMACOM, 1975. 312 p.

BOYERTOWN AUTO BODY WORKS

Hafer, Erminie Shaeffer. *A Century of Vehicle Craftsmanship.* Boyertown, Pa.: Hafer Foundation, 1972. 264 p.

BRADLEY (MILTON) COMPANY

Shea, James J., Jr. The Milton Bradley Story. New York: Newcomen Society in North America, 1973. 24 p. (Newcomen Address.)

BRANIFF AIRWAYS

Nance, John J. Splash of Colors: The Self-destruction of Braniff International. New York: Morrow, 1984. 426 p.

BRIGGS AND STRATTON CORPORATION

Briggs and Stratton Corporation. The History of Briggs & Stratton Corporation. Milwaukee: The Company, 197? 10 p.

BROADMOOR HOTEL, INC.

Tutt, William Thayer. The Broadmoor Story. New York: Newcomen Society in North America, 1969. 24 p. (Newcomen Address.)

BROCKWAY GLASS COMPANY, INC.

Brockway Glass Company, Inc. A History of Brockway, Inc. Brockway, Pa.: The Company, 1985. 14 p.

Brockway Glass Company, Inc. Brockway: Serving Growth Industries for 75 Years. Brockway, Pa.: The Company, 1982. 17 p.

BROWN (K.J.) AND COMPANY

Geelhoed, E. Bruce. <u>Bringing Wall Street to Main Street: The Story of K.J. Brown and Company, Inc., 1931-1981.</u> Muncie, Ind.: Bureau of Business and Research, College of Business, and Department of History, Ball State University, 1981. 59 p. (Ball State University Business History Series; no. 1.)

BROWN BROTHERS, HARRIMAN AND COMPANY

Kouwenhoven, John A. <u>Partners in Banking, an Historical Portrait of a Great Private Bank, Brown Brothers, Harriman and Company.</u> New York: Doubleday, 1968. 248 p.

BROWN-FORMAN DISTILLERS CORPORATION

Lucas, William F. <u>"Nothing Better in the Market": Brown-Forman's Century of Quality 1870-1970.</u> New York: Newcomen Society in North America, 1970. 32 p. (Newcomen Address.)

Pearce, John E. <u>Nothing Better in the Market.</u> Louisville: The Company, 1970. 96 p. (Double golden 100th anniversary.)

BROWN GROUP, INC.

Brown Group, Inc. *The First Hundred Years.* St. Louis: The Company, 1978. 72 p.

BROWNING-FERRIS INDUSTRIES

Browning-Ferris Industries. *50 Years of People.* Houston: The Company, 1975. 4 p.

Browning-Ferris Industries. *BFI Corporate History.* Houston: The Company, 1985. 6 p.

BRUNING (CHARLES) COMPANY

Addressograph Multigraph Corporation. *Today at Bruning.* Mt. Prospect, Ill.: Charles Bruning Company, 1966. 14 p.

See also: Addressograph Multigraph Corporation

BRUNSWICK CORPORATION

Murphy, H. Lee. "Oldest Sporting-Goods Maker Builds on its Athletic Foundation." *Illinois Business* (Autumn 1984): 62-63.

BRYAN FOODS, INC.

Bryan, George W. *The Bryan Foods Story.* New York: Newcomen Society in North America, 1983. 17 p. (Newcomen Publication; no. 1193.)

BUCKEYE FEDERAL SAVINGS AND LOAN ASSOCIATION

Guthrie, William S. The Buckeye; A Community Institution. New York: Newcomen Society in North America, 1970. 31 p.

BUCKEYE INTERNATIONAL

Blackford, Mansel G. A Portrait Cast in Steel: Buckeye International and Columbus, Ohio, 1881-1980. Westport, Conn: Greenwood Press, 1982. 225 p.

BUCYRUS-ERIE COMPANY

Anderson, George. One Hundred Booming Years: A History of Bucyrus-Erie Company, 1880-1980. South Milwaukee: The Company, 1980. 303 p.

THE BUDD COMPANY

Richard, Gilbert F. "Budd on the Move": Innovation for a Nation on Wheels. New York: Newcomen Society in North America, 1975. 20 p. (Newcomen Publication; no. 1008.)

BUFFALO SAVINGS BANK

Harder, William H. The Life and Times of Buffalo Savings Bank Through 125 Years. New York: Newcomen Society in North America, 1971. 24 p. (Newcomen Address.)

BUILDINGS; THE CONSTRUCTION AND BUILDING MANAGEMENT JOURNAL

"Our First 75 Years." *Buildings* 75 (September 1981): 50-63.

BURLINGTON INDUSTRIES, INC.

Burlington Industries, Inc. *A Portrait of the World's Largest and Most Diversified Textile Company.* New York: The Company, 1966. 49 p.

BURLINGTON NORTHERN, INC.

Dorin, Patrick C. *Everything West: The Burlington Route.* Seattle: Superior Publishing Company, 1976. 171 p.

BURNETT (LEO) COMPANY

"Special Report: 50 Years of Reaching for the Stars - Leo Burnett, 1935-1985." *Advertising Age* 56 (1 August 1985): 15-48.

BURROUGHS CORPORATION

MacDonald, Ray W. *Strategy for Growth: The Story of Burroughs Corporation.* New York: Newcomen Society in North America, 1978. 28 p. (Newcomen Publication; no. 1076.)

BURROUGHS WELLCOME COMPANY

Coe, Fred A. *Burroughs Wellcome Company, 1880-1980: Pioneer of Pharmaceutical Research.* New York: Newcomen Society in North America, 1980. 24 p. (Newcomen Publication; no. 1127.)

BUSINESS MEN'S ASSURANCE COMPANY OF AMERICA

Grant, William Downing. *Aiming High: The 75-Year Story of Business Men's Assurance Company of America.* New York: Newcomen Society of the United States, 1984. 28 p. (Newcomen Publication; no. 1217.)

Grant, W.D. *From Jalopies to Jets - Sixty Exciting Years of Growth: The Story of Business Men's Assurance Company.* New York: Newcomen Society in North America, 1969. 28 p. (Newcomen Address.)

BUTCHER AND COMPANY

Butcher, Jonathan. *Butcher and Company: Serving the American Investment Community for 75 Years.* New York: Newcomen Society of the United States, 1985. 20 p. (Newcomen Publication; no. 1235.)

CABOT CORPORATION

"Cabot Centennial." In *Cabot Corporation Annual Report*, 2-22. Boston: The Company, 1982.

Cabot Corporation. *Cabot 100.* Boston: The Company, 1982. 16 p.

CALDWELL AND COMPANY.

McFerrin, John Berry. *Caldwell and Company, A Southern Financial Empire.* Nashville: Vanderbilt University Press, 1969. 284 p.

CALDWELL (J.E.) AND COMPANY

Green, Joseph Hugh. *Jewelers to Philadelphia and the World: 125 Years on Chestnut Street.* New York: Newcomen Society in North America, 1965. 24 p. (Newcomen Address.)

THE CALIFORNIA AERO COMPANY

Cull, George E. "The LARK-95." *American Aviation Historical Society Journal* 25, no. 4 (1980): 277-280.

CALIFORNIA ANGELS

Newhan, Ross. *The California Angels.* New York: Simon and Schuster, 1982. 191 p.

CALIFORNIA FEDERAL SAVINGS AND LOAN ASSOCIATION

Edgerton, J. Howard. The Story of California Federal Savings. New York: Newcomen Society in North America, 1969. 24 p. (Newcomen Address.)

CALUMET AND HECLA, INC.

Robson, Paul W. Calumet and Hecla: Pioneer, Producer, and Pacemaker. New York: Newcomen Society in North America, 1966. 28 p. (Newcomen Address.)

CAMP DRESSER AND MCKEE, INC.

Lawler, Joseph C. Camp Dresser and McKee, Inc.: 30 Years of Environmental Consulting. New York: Newcomen Society in North America, 1977. 26 p. (Newcomen Publication; no. 1057.)

CAMPBELL SOUP COMPANY

Campbell Soup Company. Chronology. Camden, N.J.: The Company, 1985. 7 p.

CARBORUNDUM COMPANY

Wendel, William H. The Scratch Heard 'Round the World: The Story of the Carborundum Company. New York: Newcomen Society in North America, 1965. 24 p.

CARGILL, INC.

Cargill, Inc. <u>Cargill.</u> Minneapolis: The Company, 1977. 26 p.

CARNATION COMPANY

Weaver, John Downing. <u>Carnation: The First 75 Years. 1899-1974.</u> Los Angeles: The Company, 1974. 253 p.

CARRIER CORPORATION

Mellow, Craig. "The Coolest Company in America." <u>Across the Board</u> 22 (July-August 1985): 11-14.

CASCO NORTHERN BANK, N.A.

Daigle, John M. <u>Casco Northern Bank, N.A. The Chronicle of a Bank.</u> New York: Newcomen Society in North America, 1984. 28 p. (Newcomen Publication; no. 1224.)

CASTLE AND COOKE, INC.

Castle and Cooke, Inc. <u>Castle and Cooke, Incorporated: From Land and Sea.</u> Honolulu: The Company, 1966.

Taylor, Frank J. <u>From Land and Sea: The Story of Castle and Cooke of Hawaii.</u> San Francisco: Chronicle Books, 1976. 288 p.

See also: Standard Fruit and Steamship Company

CATERPILLAR TRACTOR COMPANY

Benjamin Holt: The Story of the Caterpillar Tractor. Edited by Walter A. Payne. Stockton, Calif.: University of the Pacific, 1982. 102 p.

Century of Change. Caterpillar World Special Historical Edition. Peoria, Ill.: The Company, 1984. 59 p.

Naumann, William L. The Story of Caterpillar Tractor Company. New York: Newcomen Society in North America, 1977. 23 p. (Newcomen Publication; no. 1060.)

CBS
See:
COLUMBIA BROADCASTING COMPANY

CELANESE CORPORATION OF AMERICA

Hall, Richard W. Putting Down Roots, Twenty-five Years of Celanese in Mexico. New York: Vantage Press, 1969. 128 p.

CENTEX CORPORATION

Centex Corporation. Centex Corporation. Dallas: The Company, n.d. 16 p.

CENTRAL HUDSON GAS AND ELECTRIC CORPORATION

Central Hudson Gas and Electric Corporation. <u>Central Hudson's 75 Years of Service.</u> Poughkeepsie, N.Y.: The Company, 1975. 15 p.

CENTRAL ILLINOIS PUBLIC SERVICE COMPANY

Central Illinois Public Service Company. <u>It Started with a Streetcar; Central Illinois Public Service Company, 1902-1979.</u> Springfield, Ill.: The Company, 1979. 20 p.

CENTRAL NATIONAL BANK OF CLEVELAND

Jollie, Rose Marie. <u>On the Grow with Cleveland.</u> Cleveland: The Bank, 1965. 110 p.

CENTRAL PACIFIC RAILWAY COMPANY

Best, Gerald M. <u>Iron Horses to Promontory Railroad: Central Pacific-Union Pacific.</u> San Marino, Calif.: Golden West Books, 1969. 207 p.

CENTRAL POWER AND LIGHT COMPANY

Central Power and Light Company. <u>CPL 60th Anniversary: From Ice to Atoms.</u> Corpus Christi: The Company, 1977. 17 p.

Central Power and Light Company. <u>The First 50 Years.</u> Corpus Christi: CPL, 1967. 38 p.

CENTRAL SOYA COMPANY, INC.

Central Soya Company, Inc. <u>Central Soya: People and Perspective--Fifty Years of Growth and a Future to Share.</u> Fort Wayne, Ind.: The Company, 1984. 21 p.

McMillan, Harold W. <u>Mr. Moe and Central Soya: The Foodpower Story.</u> New York: Newcomen Society in North America, 1967. 28 p. (Newcomen Address.)

CENTRAL VERMONT PUBLIC SERVICE CORPORATION

Cree, Albert A. <u>The Story of Central Vermont Public Service Corporation.</u> Rutland, Vt.: The Company, 1966.

CERTAIN-TEED CORPORATION

Meyer, Malcolm. <u>Total Committment to a Better Environment: The Story of Certain-Teed Products Corporation.</u> New York: Newcomen Society in North America, 1972. 16 p. (Newcomen Address.)

CF&I STEEL CORPORATION

Scamehorn, Howard Lee. <u>Pioneer Steelmaker in the West: The Colorado Fuel and Iron Company, 1872-1903.</u> Boulder, Colo.: Pruett Publishing Company, 1976. 231 p. (The latter part of the book includes an update of current history.)

CHAMPION BRIDGE COMPANY

Miars, David H. <u>A Century of Bridges; The History of the Champion Bridge Company and the Development of Industrial Manufacturing in Wilmington, Ohio.</u> Wilmington, Ohio: Cox Print Company, 1972. 47 p.

CHAMPION HOME BUILDERS COMPANY

Champion Home Builders Company. <u>The Story of Champion Home Builders.</u> Dryden, Mich.: The Company, 1971. 21 p.

CHANCE (A.B.) COMPANY

Chance, F. Gano. <u>The Ideas That Guide Us: The Story of the A.B. Chance Company, Centralia, Missouri.</u> New York: Newcomen Society in North America, 1968. 20 p. (Newcomen Address.)

CHARLOTTE PIPE AND FOUNDRY COMPANY

Smith, Beth Laney. <u>A Foundry Volume 1: Being the Story of Charlotte Pipe and Foundry Company, Founded November 1, 1907.</u> Charlotte, N.C.: Laney-Smith, 1977. 86 p.

THE CHARTER COMPANY

Mason, Raymond K. <u>The History of the Charter Company: Its Challenges and Opportunities.</u> New York: Newcomen

Society in North America, 1983. 13 p. (Newcomen Publication; no. 1189.)

CHASE MANHATTAN CORPORATION

"History of Chase, 1799-1982." Chase News 25 (March 1982): 1-8. (Special Edition.)

CHEMICAL BANK

Chemical Bank. Chemical Bank, 1823-1983. New York: The Bank, 1983. 20 p. (Special edition of the Chemical Chronicle.)

Glasberg, Davita Silfen. "Corporate Power and Control: The Case of Leascp Corporation Versus Chemical Bank." Social Problems 29 (December 1981): 104-116.

THE CHESAPEAKE AND OHIO RAILWAY

Bias, Charles V. "The Merger of the Chesapeake and Ohio Railway and the Baltimore and Ohio Railroad Companies." Journal of the West Virginia Historical Association 4 (1980): 24-34.

THE CHESAPEAKE AND POTOMAC TELEPHONE COMPANY OF MARYLAND

Cromwell, Joseph H. The C&P Story: Service in Action: Maryland. Washington, D.C.: The Company, 1981. 241. 65 p.

THE CHESAPEAKE AND POTOMAC TELEPHONE COMPANY OF VIRGINIA

Cromwell, Joseph H. *The C&P Story: Service in Action: Virginia.* Washington, D.C. The Company, 1981. 201, 65 p.

THE CHESAPEAKE AND POTOMAC TELEPHONE COMPANY OF WASHINGTON, D.C.

The C&P Story: Service in Action: Washington. Washington, D.C.: The Company, 1981. 144, 82 p.

THE CHESAPEAKE AND POTOMAC TELEPHONE COMPANY OF WEST VIRGINIA

The C&P Story: Service in Action: West Virginia. Washington, D.C.: The Company, 1981. 110, 65 p.

THE CHESAPEAKE CORPORATION OF VIRGINIA

Dill, Alonzo Thomas. *Chesapeake: Pioneer Papermaker; A History of the Company and Its Community.* Charlottesville: University Press of Virginia, 1968. 356 p.

CHESEBROUGH-POND'S, INC.

Chesebrough-Pond's, Inc. *The First Hundred Years.* Greenwich, Conn: The Company, 1980. 6 p. (Special centennial issue of *Chesebrough-Pond's World*.)

THE CHESSIE SYSTEM, INC.

Bias, Charles V. "Chessie's Growth: Success and Failure, 1966-1973." West Virginia History 44 (January 1982): 41-53.

CHEVRON CHEMICAL COMPANY - ORTHO DIVISION

Gardner, Leo R. The First Thirty Years: The Early History of the Company Now Known as Ortho Division, Chevron Chemical Company. San Francisco: The Company, 1978. 45 p.

CHICAGO BEARS

Whittingham, Richard. The Chicago Bears: An Illustrated History. Chicago: Rand McNally, 1982. 268 p.

CHICAGO, BURLINGTON AND QUINCY RAILROAD COMPANY

Dorin, Patrick C. Everything West: The Burlington Route. Seattle: Superior Publishing Company, 1976. 171 p.

CHICAGO CUBS

Ahrens, Art, and Eddie Gold. Day by Day in Chicago Cubs History. El Cerrito, Calif.: Leisure Press, 1982. 352 p.

Langford, Jim. The Game Is Never Over: An Appreciative History of the Chicago

Cubs. 2nd, rev. ed. South Bend, Ind.: Icarus Press, 1982. 264 p.

CHICAGO, INDIANAPOLIS AND LOUISVILLE RAILWAY

Hilton, George Woodman. Monon Route. Berkeley, Calif.: Howell North Books, 1978. 323 p.

CHICAGO TRIBUNE

Geis, Joseph. The Colonel of Chicago. New York: Dutton, 1979. 261 p.

Wendt, Lloyd. Chicago Tribune: The Rise of a Great American Newspaper. Chicago: Rand McNally, 1979. 861 p.

CHICAGO WHITE SOX

Berke, Art, and Paul Schmitt. This Date in Chicago White Sox History. Briarcliff Manor, N.Y.: Stein and Day, 1982. 177 p.

Lindberg, Richard. Who's on Third: The Chicago White Sox Story. South Bend, Ind.: Icarus Press, 1983. 287 p.

Vanderberg, Bob. Sox: From Lane & Fain to Zisk & Fisk. 2nd ed. Chicago: Chicago Review Press, 1984. 384 p.

CHISOS MINING COMPANY

Ragsdale, Kenneth Baxter. Quicksilver: Terlingua and the Chisos Mining

Company. Foreword by Joe B. Frantz.
College Station: Texas A&M University
Press, 1976. 327 p.

CHRYSLER CORPORATION

Abodaher, David J. Iacocca. New York:
Macmillan, 1982. 319 p.

Dammann, George H. Seventy Years of
Chrysler. Glen Ellyn, Ill.: Crestline
Publications, 1974. 382 p.

Gallaway, Edward A. Accountability.
Philadelphia: Dorrance, 1975. 99 p.

Gordon, Maynard M. Iacocca Management
Technique; A Profile of the Chrysler
Chairman's Unique Key to Business
Success. New York: Dodd, Mead, 1985.
154 p.

Iacocca, Lee A., and W. Novak. Iacocca:
An Autobiography. New York: Bantam
Books 1984. 352 p.

Langworth, Richard M., and Jan P. Norbye.
The Complete History of Chrysler
Corporation, 1924-1985. New York:
Beekman House, 1985. 384 p.

Moritz, Michael, and B. Seaman. Going for
Broke: The Chrysler Story. Garden
City, N.Y.: Doubleday, 1981. 374 p.

Reich, Robert B., and John D. Donahue.
New Deals: The Chrysler Revival and

the American System. New York: Times Books, 1985. 352 p.

Stuart, Reginald. Bailout: The Story Behind America's Billion Dollar Gamble on the New Chrysler Corporation. South Bend, Ind.: Icarus Books, 1980. 210 p.

CHRYSLER CORPORATION, DODGE DIVISION

Pitrone, Jean M., and J.P. Elwart. The Dodges, the Auto Family Fortune and Misfortune. South Bend, Ind.: Icarus Press, 1981. 316 p.

CIANBRO CORPORATION

Cianchette, Ival R. Cianbro: The Constructors. New York: Newcomen Society in North America, 1984. 20 p. (Newcomen Publication; no. 1199.)

CINCINNATI BELL, INC.

Cincinnati Bell, Inc. Cincinnati Bell Centennial, 1873-1973. Cincinnati: Cincinnati Bell, Inc., 1973.

CINCINNATI BENGALS

Collett, Ritter. Super Stripes: Paul Brown & the Super Bowl Bengals. Dayton: Landfall Press, 1982. 221 p.

Snyder, John, and Floyd Conner. Day by Day in Cincinnati Bengals History. New York: Leisure Press, 1984. 368 p.

THE CINCINNATI COUNTRY CLUB

The Cincinnati Country Club, 1903-1965.
  Cincinnati: The Club, 1965. 76 p.

THE CINCINNATI ENQUIRER

Pale, Francis L. The Cincinnati Enquirer:
  The Shadows of Its Publishers. New
  York: Newcomen Society in North
  America, 1966. 28 p. (Newcomen
  Address.)

CINCINNATI FINANCIAL CORPORATION

Curry, Robert P. Prospectus Fulfilled:
  The Cincinnati Financial Corporation.
  Cincinnati: The Company, 1984. 73 p.

Schiff, John J. Cincinnati Financial
  Corporation: Keeping Every Promise.
  New York: Newcomen Society in North
  America, 1978. 20 p. (Newcomen
  Publication; no. 1083.)

CINCINNATI GAS AND ELECTRIC COMPANY

Cincinnati Gas and Electric Company.
  History. Cincinnati: The Company,
  1984. 11 p.

CINCINNATI MILACRON

Cincinnati Milacron. Cincinnati Milacron,
  1884-1984; Finding Better Ways.
  Cincinnati, The Company, 1984. 288 p.

CINCINNATI POST

Stevens, George E. "A History of the Cincinnati Post." Thesis, University of Minnesota, 1968. 422 p.

THE CINCINNATI REDS

Anderson, Sparky. The Main Spark: Sparky Anderson and the Cincinnati Reds. Garden City, N.Y.: Doubleday, 1978. 239 p.

Collett, Ritter. The Cincinnati Reds: A Pictorial History of Professional Baseball's Oldest Team. Virginia Beach: Jordan-Powers Corp., 1976. 192 p.

Conner, Floyd, and John Snyder. Day by Day in Cincinnati Reds History. New York: Leisure Press, 1983. 300 p.

Rathgeber, Bob. Cincinnati Reds Scrapbook. Virginia Beach: JCP Corp. of Virginia, 1982. 151 p.

C.I.T. FINANCIAL CORPORATION

Wilson, William L. Full Faith and Credit: The Story of C.I.T. Financial Corporation, 1908-1975. New York: Random House, 1976. 376 p.

CITICORP

Cleveland, Harold Van B. Citibank, 1812-1970. Cambridge: Harvard University

Press, 1986. 512 p. (Harvard Studies in Business History; no. 37.)

Levinson, Harry, and Stuart Rosenthal. "Walter B. Wriston." In <u>CEO: Corporate Leadership in Action, 56-95.</u> New York: Basic Books, 1984.

"The First Sixteen Decades." <u>Citicorp Magazine</u> no.2 (1972): 17-27. (160th anniversary issue.)

Hutchinson, Robert A. <u>Off the Books. Citibank and the World's Biggest Money Game.</u> New York: Morrow, 1986. 416 p.

CITIZENS FEDERAL SAVINGS AND LOAN ASSOCIATION OF DAYTON

Kerby, Jerry L. <u>"Where Rainbows Begin" The Story of Citizens Federal Savings and Loan Association of Dayton.</u> New York: Newcomen Society in North America, 1984. 32 p. (Newcomen Publication; no. 1214.)

CITIZENS GAS AND COKE UTILITY

Rumer, Thomas A. "Corporate History--One Company's Approach." <u>Public Utilities Fortnightly</u> 114 (19 July 1984): 19-22.

CITY NATIONAL BANK AND TRUST COMPANY OF ROCKFORD

Garson, Bill. <u>The Knight on Broadway: The Story of City National Bank and Trust Company of Rockford and Sir Greenback--</u>

The Bank's Financial Symbol.
Rockford, Ill.: City National Bank and Trust Company of Rockford, 1978. 171 p.

THE CLARK COUNTY STATE BANK

Haffner, Gerald O., and Albert M. Helzer. "The Clark County State Bank and Its Years of Service." Unpublished paper, 1983. 15 p. (On file at the CommerceAmerica Corporation, Jeffersonville, Ind.)

CLARK EQUIPMENT COMPANY

French, Robert W. *Living Together, Buchanan and Clark 1904-1975.* 1976. 194 p.

Phillips, Bert E. *Plus Faith Unlimited: The Story of Clark Equipment Company.* New York: Newcomen Society in North America, 1978. 32 p. (Newcomen Publication; no. 1087.)

CLARK (J.L.) MANUFACTURING COMPANY

Nelson, William C. *Clark Manufacturing Company: A Model of American Enterprise.* New York: Newcomen Society in North America, 1981. 20 p. (Newcomen Publication; no. 1136.)

CLEVELAND BROWNS

Clary, Jack T. *Cleveland Browns.* New York: Macmillan, 1973. 191 p.

Eckhouse, Morris. *Day by Day in Cleveland Browns History.* New York: Leisure Press, 1984. 528 p.

Levy, William V. *Sam, Sipe & Company: The History of the Cleveland Browns.* Cleveland: J.T. Zubal and P.D. Dole, Publishers, 1981. 237 p.

THE CLEVELAND-CLIFFS IRON COMPANY

Harrison, H. Stuart. *The Cleveland-Cliffs Iron Company.* New York: Newcomen Society in North America, 1974. 32 p. (Newcomen Publication; no. 1004.)

THE CLEVELAND INDIANS

Eckhouse, Morris. *Day by Day in Cleveland Indians History.* New York: Leisure Press, 1983. 400 p.

CLOROX COMPANY

Shetterly, Robert B. *Renaissance of the Clorox Company.* New York: Newcomen Society in North America, 1973. 16 p. (Newcomen Address.)

CLOW CORPORATION

Rinehart, Raymond G. *Clow Corporation: 100 years of Service to the Water and Waste Water Industries.* New York: Newcomen Society in North America, 1978. 24 p. (Newcomen Publication; no. 1092.)

CLUETT, PEABODY AND COMPANY, INC.

Cluett, Peabody and Company, Inc. <u>The Cluett Experience: A History of Cluett, Peabody & Company, Inc.</u> New York: The Company, 1976. (Leaflet.)

COACHMEN INDUSTRIES, INC.

Coachmen Industries, Inc. <u>An Overview.</u> Middlebury, Ind.: The Company, 1983? 14 p.

Coachmen Industries, Inc. <u>Milestones.</u> Middlebury, Ind.: The Company, 1984. 3 p.

COCA-COLA BOTTLING COMPANY OF CHATTANOOGA

Harrison, Desales. <u>"Footprints on the Sands of Time": A History of Two Men and the Fulfillment of a Dream.</u> New York: Newcomen Society in North America, 1969. 24 p. (Newcomen Address.)

COCA-COLA BOTTLING COMPANY OF WEST POINT-LAGRANGE, GEORGIA

Henry, Waights G. <u>Tributary to a Golden Stream: The Story of the Coca-Cola Bottling Company of West Point-LaGrange, Georgia.</u> New York: Newcomen Society in North America, 1982. 22 p. (Newcomen Publication; no. 1182.)

COCA-COLA COMPANY

Coca-Cola Company. *Portrait of a Business, the Coca-Cola Bottling Company.* Atlanta: Coca-Cola Company, 1968. 19 p.

Louis, J.C. *The Cola Wars.* New York: Everest House, 1980. 386 p.

Watters, Pat. *Coca-Cola.* Garden City, N.Y.: Doubleday, 1978. 288 p.

COLD SPRING GRANITE COMPANY

Dominik, John J. *Cold Spring Granite: A History.* Cold Spring, Minn.: Cold Spring Granite Company, 1982. 123 p.

COLDWELL BANKER REAL ESTATE GROUP, INC.

Levy, Jo Ann L. *Behind the Western Skyline: Coldwell Banker: The First 75 Years.* Los Angeles: The Company, 1981. 210 p.

COLECO INDUSTRIES, INC.

Coleco Industries, Inc. *Coleco, 1932-1982.* Hartford, Conn.: The Company, 1982. 53 p.

Hoffman, William. *Fantasy: the Incredible Cabbage Patch Phenomenon.* Dallas: Taylor Publishing Company, 1984. 217 p.

COLEMAN COMPANY, INC.

Jones, Lawrence M. *The Coleman Story: The Ability to Cope with Change.* New York: Newcomen Society in North America, 1975. 28 p. (Newcomen Publication; no. 1010.)

COLGATE-PALMOLIVE COMPANY

Foster, David R. *The Story of Colgate-Palmolive: One Hundred and Sixty-nine Years of Progress.* New York: Newcomen Society in North America, 1975. 40 p. (Newcomen Publication; no. 1022.)

COLLINS RADIO COMPANY

Braband, Ken C. *The First 50 Years: A History of Collins Radio Company and the Collins Divisions of Rockwell International.* Cedar Rapids, Iowa: Communications Dept., Avionics Group, Rockwell International, 1983. 218 p.

COLT INDUSTRIES, INC.

Wilson, Robert Laurence. *The Colt Heritage: The Official History of Colt Firearms from 1836 to the Present.* New York: Simon & Schuster, 1979. 358 p.

Wilson, Robert Laurence. *The Rampant Colt: The Story of a Trademark.* Spencer, Ind.: T. Haas, 1969. 107 p.

COLUMBIA BROADCASTING SYSTEM, INC.

Metz, Robert. CBS: Reflections in a Bloodshot Eye. Chicago: Playboy Press, 1975. 428 p.

COLUMBIA GAS SYSTEM SERVICE CORPORATION

Columbia Gas System Service Corporation. A History of the Columbia Gas System: The First 50 Years. Wilmington, Del.: The Company, 1976. 22 p.

COLUMBIA PICTURES INDUSTRIES

McClintick, David. Indecent Exposure: A True Story of Hollywood and Wall Street. New York: Morrow, 1982. 544 p.

COLUMBUS AND SOUTHERN OHIO ELECTRIC COMPANY

Columbus and Southern Ohio Electric Company. A Brief History. Columbus: The Company, 1978? 24 p.

COLUMBUS MUTUAL LIFE INSURANCE COMPANY

Gingher, Paul R. Running Mates: The Story of State Automotive Mutual Insurance Company and Columbus Mutual Life Insurance Company. New York: Newcomen Society in North America, 1978. 30 p. (Newcomen Publication; no. 1090.)

COMAIR, INC.

Comair, Inc. <u>History of Comair.</u>
   Cincinnati: The Company, 1985. 3 p.

COMBINED INSURANCE COMPANY OF AMERICA

Shook, Robert L. "W. Clement Stone" in
   <u>The Entrepreneurs,</u> 19-39. New York:
   Harper & Row, 1980.

COMBUSTION ENGINEERING, INC.

Santry, Arthur J. <u>Combustion Engineering
   Today, A Presentation at the Luncheon
   Meeting of the Security Analysts of
   San Francisco.</u> San Francisco: The
   Company, 1967.

COMMAND-AIRE CORPORATION

Davisson, Budd. "Forgotten Success; the
   Command-Aire Aircraft Company." <u>Air
   Progress</u> 46 (October 1984): 70-75.

COMMERCE TRUST COMPANY

Kemper, James M. <u>A Bank and Its
   Community: The Story of Commerce Trust
   Company.</u> New York: Newcomen Society in
   North America, 1966. 24 p. (Newcomen
   Address.)

COMMUNICATIONS SATELLITE CORPORATION

Communication Satellite Corporation.
   <u>Twenty Years via Satellite: a
   Chronology of Events of Communications</u>

Satellite Corporation, 1962-1985. Washington, D.C.: The Company, 1985. 32 p.

COMPUTER SCIENCES CORPORATION

"CSC: the First 25 Years, 1959-1984; Excellence in Action." CSC News 15, no.3 (April 1984). (Anniversary issue.)

CONFEDERATION LIFE INSURANCE COMPANY

Davidson, J. Craig. The Confederation Life People Story. New York: Newcomen Society in North America, 1971. 24 p. (Newcomen Address.)

CONNECTICUT MUTUAL LIFE INSURANCE COMPANY

Cahn, William. A Matter of Life and Death: The Connecticut Mutual Story. New York: Random House, 1970. 309 p.

CONOCO
See:
CONTINENTAL OIL COMPANY

CONSOLIDATED AIRCRAFT CORPORATION

Wagner, William. Reuben Fleet: and The Story of Consolidated Aircraft. Fallbrook, Calif.: Aero Publishers, 1976. 324 p.

CONSOLIDATED EDISON COMPANY OF NEW YORK, INC.

Axelrod, Regina S. <u>Conflict Between Energy and Urban Environment: Consolidated Edison versus the City of New York.</u> Washington, D.C.: University Press of America, 1982. 198 p.

Luce, Charles F. <u>155 Years of Technological Excellence.</u> New York: Newcomen Society in North America, 1978. 24 p. (Newcomen Publication; no. 1095.)

Talbot, Allan R. <u>Power Along the Hudson, the Storm King Case and the Birth of Environmentalism.</u> New York: Dutton, 1972. 244 p.

CONSOLIDATED FOODS

Cummings, Nathan. <u>Consolidated Foods: Blueprint for the Construction of a Diversified Company.</u> New York: Newcomen Society in North America, 1965. 24 p. (Newcomen Address.)

CONSOLIDATED FREIGHTWAYS, INC.

Consolidated Freightways, Inc. <u>Consolidated Freightways, Inc.: Fact Book and Financial Review 1961-1970.</u> San Francisco: The Company, 1970.

Consolidated Freightways, Inc. <u>Consolidated Freightways, Inc.: The First 50 Years, 1929-1979.</u> Researched

and written by Mirriam Stein; edited
by W.J. Grant. San Francisco: The
Company, 1979. 64 p.

CONSOLIDATED NATURAL GAS COMPANY

Tankersley, G.J. The Story of
Consolidated Natural Gas Company:
Innovation, Ingenuity, and
Accomplishment. New York: Newcomen
Society in North America, 1980. 23 p.
(Newcomen Publication; no. 1118.)

CONSUMERS POWER COMPANY

Bush, George. Future Builders: The Story
of Michigan's Consumers Power Company.
New York: McGraw-Hill, 1973. 603 p.

CONTEXT MANAGEMENT CORPORATION

Berger, Harvey. "Success Story: Context
Management Corporation." Computers &
Electronics 22 (April 1984): 52-53+.

CONTINENTAL AIRLINES CORPORATION

Davies, Ronald E.G. Continental Air
Lines: The First Fifty Years, 1934-
1984. The Woodlands, Texas: Pioneer
Publications, Inc., 1984. 191 p.

Serling, Robert J. Maverick: The Story of
Robert Six and Continental Airlines.
Garden City, N.Y.: Doubleday, 1974.
351 p.

Wagner, William. *Continental; Its Motors and Its People.* Fallbrook, Calif.: Aero Publishers, 1983. 256 p.

CONTINENTAL INSURANCE COMPANY

Kelchburg, Ann, and Ronald G. Mullins. *A History of the Continental Insurance Company.* New York: Corporate Communications Dept., Continental Corporation, 1979. 126 p.

CONTINENTAL MOTORS CORPORATION

Wagner, William. *Continental: Its Motors and Its People.* Washington, D.C.: Armed Forces Journal International; Fallbrook, Calif.: Aero Publishers, 1983. 240 p.

CONTINENTAL OIL COMPANY

CONOCO: The First One Hundred Years: Building on the Past for the Future. New York: Special Marketing Division, Dell Publishing Company, 1975. 238 p.

Continental Oil Company. *Historical Brief--Continental Oil Company, 1875-1970.* Stamford, Conn.: The Company, 1970.

CONTINENTAL TELEPHONE CORPORATION

"A Special Report; the Talking Machine and Bit Streams." In *Continental Telephone Corporation. Annual Report*, 9-14. Atlanta: The Corporation, 1978.

COOPER INDUSTRIES

Keller, David N. *Cooper Industries, 1833-1983.* Athens: Ohio University Press, 1983. 400 p.

COOPER TIRE AND RUBBER COMPANY

Cooper Tire and Rubber Company. *A History of Cooper.* Findlay, Ohio: The Company, 1985. 7 p.

COORS (ADOLPH) COMPANY

Adolph Coors Company. *The Adolph Coors Story.* Golden, Colo.: The Company, 1984. 32 p.

COPPER RANGE COMPANY

Boyd, James. *Copper Range Company: The Story of Man's Oldest and Newest Metal.* New York: Newcomen Society in North America, 1970. 24 p. (Newcomen Address.)

CORNELL HOTEL AND RESTAURANT ADMINISTRATION QUARTERLY

"A History of the *Quarterly.*" *Cornell Hotel and Restaurant Administration Quarterly* 26 (May 1985): 102-103.

CORPORATION FOR ENTERTAINMENT AND LEARNING

"20 Years of Entertainment and Learning." Broadcasting 105 (25 July 1983): 95-96.

COWARD, MCCANN AND GEOGHEGAN

Weyr, Thomas. "Coward, McCann & Geoghegan: Fifty Years in the Business of Books." Publishers Weekly 213 (3 April 1978): 33-36.

COX BROADCASTING CORPORATION

Cox Broadcasting Corporation. Cox Broadcasting Corporation: General Information. Atlanta: Cox Broadcasting Corporation, 1979. 14 p.

Howard, Herbert H. "Cox Broadcasting Corporation: A Group-ownership Case Study [History of One of the Oldest and Largest of the Group Owners in Radio and Television, which Maintains Headquarters in Atlanta]." Journal of Broadcasting 20 (Spring 1976): 209-232.

CROWN ZELLERBACH CORPORATION

Crown Zellerbach. It's a Beginning: Crown Zellerbach's First One Hundred Years. San Francisco: The Company, 1970. 10 p.

CUMMINGS AND LOCKWOOD

Drake, Philip M. *Cummings & Lockwood: A 75-year Reputation of Hard-earned Excellence.* New York: Newcomen Society in North America, 1984. 22 p. (Newcomen Publication; no. 1225.)

CUNA MUTUAL INSURANCE SOCIETY

Eikel, Charles F. *The Debt Shall Die with the Debtor; the CUNA Mutual Insurance Society Story.* New York: Newcomen Society in North America, 1972. 47 p. (Newcomen Address.)

CUNARD STEAMSHIP COMPANY, LTD.

Hyde, Francis Edwin. *Cunard and the North Atlantic, 1840-1973: A History of Shipping and Financial Management.* Atlantic Highlands, N.J.: Humanities Press, 1975, c1974.

CURTIS PUBLISHING COMPANY

Ackerman, Martin S. *The Curtis Affair.* Los Angeles: Nash, 1970. 202 p.

Culligan, Mathew J. *The Curtis-Culligan Story; from Cyrus to Horace, to Joe.* New York: Crown Publishing, 1970. 224 p.

Friedrich, Otto. *Decline and Fall: The Struggle for Power at a Great American Magazine, the Saturday Evening Post.* New York: Harper & Row, 1970. 499 p.

Goulden, Joseph C. *The Curtis Caper.* New York: G.P. Putnam's Sons, 1965. 281 p.

Wood, James Playsted. *The Curtis Magazines.* New York: Ronald Press Company, 1971. 297 p.

CUTLER-HAMMER, INC.

Cutler-Hammer, Inc. *A History of Cutler-Hammer, Inc., 1892-1967.* Milwaukee: Cutler-Hammer, Inc., 1967. 82 p.

DALLAS COWBOYS

Meyers, Jeff. *Dallas Cowboys.* New York: Macmillan, 1974. 192 p.

Stowers, Carlton. *Journey to Triumph: 110 Dallas Cowboys Tell Their Stories.* Dallas: Taylor Publishing Company, 1982. 260 p.

Whittingham, Richard. *The Dallas Cowboys: An Illustrated History.* New York: Harper & Row, 1981. 224 p.

DAN RIVER, INC.

Cross, Malcolm A. *Dan River Runs Deep: An Informal History of a Major Textile Company, 1950-1981.* New York: The Total Book, 1982. 293 p.

DANA CORPORATION

McPherson, Rene C. *Dana: Toward the Year 2000.* New York: Newcomen Society in North America, 1973. 24 p.

DARLING-DELAWARE COMPANY, INC.

Dainty, Ralph B. *Darling-Delaware Centenary, 1882-1982.* Chicago: The Company, 1981. 229 p.

DARTNELL CORPORATION

Lewis, Leslie L., and R.S. Minor. *The Dartnell Story.* Chicago: The Company, 1984. 148 p.

DATA GENERAL CORPORATION

Kidder, Tracy. *The Soul of a New Machine.* Boston: Little, Brown, 1981. 292 p.

DAY AND ZIMMERMANN, INC.

Day and Zimmermann, Inc. *Sixty Five Years with the Men of Day and Zimmermann.* Philadelphia: The Company, 1966. 44 p.

Yoh, Harold L. *Day & Zimmermann, Inc.: Dedicated to Excellence for Eighty Years, 1901-1981.* New York: Newcomen Society in North America, 1981. 27 p. (Newcomen Publication; no. 1144.)

DAYCO CORPORATION

Fisher, David G. Dayco History. Springfield, Mo.: The Company, 1984. 26 p.

DAYTON, COVINGTON, AND PIQUA TRACTION COMPANY

Gordon, William Reed, and Richard M. Wagner. The Overlook Route: the Dayton, Covington and Piqua Traction Company. Wyoming, Ohio: Trolley Talk, 1972. 52 p.

DAYTON MALLEABLE, INC.

Miske, Jack C. "Amcast--New Company with a 117-year History." Foundry Management and Technology 112 (April 1984): 52-55.

Miske, Jack C. "Dayton Malleable Inc.--A Company Shaping Change." Foundry Management and Technology 109 (November 1981): F1-F16.

Torley, John F. Dayton Malleable, Inc.: A Story of Progress. New York: Newcomen Society in North America, 1976. 20 p. (Newcomen Publication; no. 1037.)

DE LOREAN MOTOR COMPANY

DeLorean, John Z. DeLorean. Grand Rapids, Mich.: Zondervan Publishing House, 1985. 349 p.

Fallon, Ivan, and J. Strodes. <u>Dream Maker: The Rise and Fall of John Z. De Lorean.</u> New York: Putnam, 1983. 455 p.

Haddad, William F. <u>Hard Driving: My Years with John De Lorean.</u> New York: Random House, 1985. 193 p.

Lamm, John, and M. Knepper. <u>De Lorean: Stainless Steel Illusion.</u> Santa Ana, Calif.: Newport Press, 1983. 160 p.

Levin, Hillel. <u>Grand Delusions; The Cosmic Career of John De Lorean.</u> New York: Viking Press, 1983. 336 p.

Levin, Hillel. <u>John De Lorean: The Maverick Mogul.</u> London: Orbis Publishing Company, 1983. 268 p.

Shook, Robert L. "John Z. De Lorean." In <u>The Entrepreneurs</u>, 157-171. New York: Harper & Row, 1980.

DEAK-PERERA GROUP

Deak, Nicholas L. <u>Deak-Perera Group: Story of the Nation's Oldest and Largest Foreign Money Exchange Firm.</u> New York: Newcomen Society in North America, 1975. 24 p. (Newcomen Publication; no. 1015.)

DEERE AND COMPANY

Broehl, Wayne G. <u>John Deere's Company; A History of Deere & Company and Its</u>

Times. New York: Doubleday, 1984. 880 p.

DEL MONTE CORPORATION

Braznell, William. <u>California's Finest: The History of Del Monte Corporation and the Del Monte Brand.</u> San Francisco: Del Monte, 1982. 168 p.

Eames, Alfred W. <u>"The Business of Feeding People": The Story of Del Monte Corporation.</u> New York: Newcomen Society in North America, 1974. 22 p. (Newcomen Publication; no. 985.)

DELAWARE AND HUDSON RAILROAD

Zimmermann, Karl R. <u>A Decade of D&H.</u> Oradell, N.J.: Delford Press, 1978. 79 p.

DELTA AIRLINES, INC.

Delta Air Lines, Inc. <u>Delta--Highlights of our History.</u> Atlanta: The Company, 1983. 5 p.

Lewis, Walter David, and Wesley Phillips Newton. <u>Delta: The History of an Airline.</u> Athens: University of Georgia Press, 1979. 503 p.

Lewis, Walter David, and Wesley Phillips Newton. "The Delta-C&S Merger:A Case Study in Airline Consolidation and Federal Regulation." <u>Business History Review</u> 53 (Summer 1979): 161-179.

DELTA NATURAL GAS COMPANY, INC.

Delta Natural Gas Company, Inc. *Historical Summary. Annual Report*, 1-4. Winchester, Ky.: The Company, 1984.

THE DELTA QUEEN STEAMBOAT COMPANY

August Perez and Associates. *The Delta Queen: Last of the Paddlewheel Palaces.* Gretna, La.: Pelican Publishing Company, 1973. 96 p.

Greene, Letha C. *Long Live the Delta Queen.* New York: Hastings House, 1973. 174 p.

DELTA STEAMSHIP LINES

Beargie, T. "Delta Steamship Lines: 1919-1985." *American Shipping* 27 (March 1985): 48.

DENVER BRONCOS

Connor, Dick. *The Denver Broncos.* Englewood Cliffs, N.J.: Prentice-Hall, 1974. 127 p.

The Denver Broncos. Denver: R.R. Donnelley & Sons, 1982. 111 p.

DENVER TRAMWAY CORPORATION

Luskey, Sam. *101 Years Young; The Tramway Saga.* Denver: Printed by A.B. Hirschfeld Press, 1968. 95 p.

DEPOSIT GUARANTEE BANK AND TRUST COMPANY
OF JACKSON

McMullan, W.P. *From Mississippi Soil--A People and a Bank. The Story of Deposit Guarantee Bank and Trust Company of Jackson.* New York: Newcomen Society in North America, 1965. 24 p. (Newcomen Address.)

DEPOSITORS CORPORATION

Haselton, Wallace M. *Busy Building Maine: The Story of Depositors Corporation.* New York: Newcomen Society in North America, 1971. 24 p.

DETROIT BANK AND TRUST COMPANY

Woodford, Arthur. *Detroit and Its Bank; The Story of Detroit Bank and Trust Company.* Detroit: Wayne State University Press, 1974. 298 p.

DETROIT EDISON COMPANY

McCarthy, Walter J. "*Detroit Edison Generates More Electricity.*" New York: Newcomen Society in North America, 1983. 24 p. (Newcomen Publication; no. 1180.)

Miller, Raymond Curtis. *The Force of Energy: A Business History of the Detroit Edison Company.* East Lansing: Michigan State University Press, 1971. 363 p.

DETROIT TIGERS

Falls, Joe. <u>Detroit Tigers.</u> New York: Macmillan, 1975. 192 p.

Hawkins, John C. <u>This Date in Detroit Tigers History: A Day by Day Listing of the Events in the History of the Detroit Tigers Baseball Team.</u> New York: Stein and Day, 1981. 239 p.

Sullivan, George. <u>The Detroit Tigers: The Complete Record of Detroit Tigers Baseball.</u> New York: Collier Books, 1985. 432 p.

DEXTER CORPORATION

Coffin, David Linwood. <u>The History of the Dexter Corporation, 1767-1967.</u> New York: Newcomen Society in North America, 1967. 24 p. (Newcomen Address.)

DI GIORGIO FRUIT CORPORATION

Galarza, Ernesto. <u>Spiders in the House and Workers in the Field.</u> South Bend, Indiana: University of Notre Dame Press, 1970. 306 p.

DIAMOND MATCH COMPANY

Stephens, Kent. <u>Matches, Flumes, and Rails: The Diamond Match Company in the High Sierra.</u> 2nd ed. Corona Del

Mar, Calif.: Trans-Anglo Books, 1981. 176 p.

DIAMOND SHAMROCK

Bricker, William H. *Partners by Choice and Fortune: The Story of Diamond Shamrock.* New York: Newcomen Society in North America, 1977. 27 p. (Newcomen Publication; no. 1064.)

DICKERSON (CHARLES W.) FIELD MUSIC, INC.

Boddie, David L. *We've Come a Long Way Together: The Story of a Drum Corps.* New Rochelle, N.Y.: The Company, 1981. 135 p.

DIGITAL EQUIPMENT CORPORATION

Olsen, Kenneth H. *Digital Equipment Corporation, The First Twenty-five Years.* New York: Newcomen Society in North America, 1983. 19 p. (Newcomen Publication; no. 1179.)

DISNEY (WALT) PRODUCTIONS

Mosley, Leonard. *Disney's World: A Biography.* New York: Stein & Day, 1985. 330 p.

Thomas, Bob. *Walt Disney: An American Original.* New York: Simon and Schuster, 1976. 379 p.

DIXON (JOSEPH) CRUCIBLE COMPANY

"History of a By-product of the Joseph Dixon Crucible Company." *New Jersey Business* 13 (June 1967): 34-38.

DONNELLEY (R.R.) AND SONS

Donnelley, Gaylord. *To Be a Good Printer: Our Commitments.* Chicago: Lakeside Press, 1977. 110 p.

DORSEY LABORATORIES

Lavin, Joseph J. *Dorsey Laboratories: People--The Key to Growth and Success.* New York: Newcomen Society in North America, 1984. 28 p. (Newcomen Publication; no. 1216.)

DOUGLAS AIRCRAFT COMPANY

Ingells, Douglas J. *The Plane that Changed the World, A Biography of the DC-3.* Fallbrook, Calif.: Aero Publishers, Inc., 1966. 256 p.

DOW CHEMICAL COMPANY

Duerksen, Christopher J. *Dow vs. California: A Turning Point in the Envirobusiness Struggle.* Washington, D.C.: Conservation Foundation, 1982. 151 p.

Seward, William. *East from Brozosport.* Midland, Mich.: Dow Chemical Company, 1974. 191 p.

Sorey, Gordon Kent. The Foreign Policy of a Multinational Enterprise: An Analysis of the Policy Interactions of Dow Chemical Company and the United States. New York: Arno Press, 1980, c1976. 156 p.

Thompson, Stanley J. The S/B Latex Story: Recollections of "Can Do" at Dow. Midland, Mich.: The Company, 1980. 326 p.

Whitehead, Don. The Dow Story: the History of Dow Chemical Company. New York: McGraw-Hill, 1968. 298 p.

See also: Merrell Dow Pharmaceuticals

DOW, JONES AND COMPANY

Caliam, Carnegie Samuel. The Gospel According to the Wall Street Journal. Atlanta: John Knox Press, 1975. 114 p.

"Celebrating Our First Century." In Dow Jones Annual Report, 5-15. New York: The Company, 1981.

Neilson, Winthrop, and Frances Neilson. What's News--Dow Jones: Story of the Wall Street Journal. Radnor, Pa.: Chilton Book Company, 1973. 171 p.

Rosenberg, Jerry M. Inside the Wall Street Journal: The History and the Power of Dow Jones & Company and

America's Most Influential Newspaper. New York: Macmillan, 1982. 328 p.

Wendt, Lloyd. *The Wall Street Journal: The Story of Dow Jones & the Nation's Business Newspaper.* Chicago: Rand McNally, 1982. 448 p.

DR. PEPPER COMPANY

Ellis, Harry E. *Dr. Pepper, King of Beverages.* Dallas: The Company, 1979. 268 p.

Dr. Pepper Company. *Dr. Pepper's Phos-Ferrates.* Dallas: The Company, 1972. 18 p.

Jabbonsky, Larry. "Still Out of the Ordinary After All These Years." *Beverage World* 103 (October 1984): 59-64.

Morgan, Monty Brown. *The Dr. Pepper Company: A Case Study.* Austin: University of Texas at Austin, 1981. 121 p. (M.B.A. Report.)

DRAVO CORPORATION

A Company of Uncommon Enterprise: The Story of Dravo Corporation, 1891-1966. Pittsburgh, Pa.: The Company, 1974. 176 p.

DRESSER INDUSTRIES, INC.

Payne, Darwin. Initiative in Energy: Dresser Industries, Inc., 1880-1978. New York: Simon & Schuster, 1979. 415 p.

DREXEL BURNHAM LAMBERT

Drexel Burnham Lambert. Fiftieth Anniversary. New York: The Company, 1984. 68 p.

DU PONT DE NEMOURS (E.I.) AND COMPANY

Chandler, Alfred D., and Stephen Salsbury. Pierre S. Du Pont and the Making of the Modern Corporation. New York: Harper and Row, 1971. 722 p.

Colby, Gerald. Du Pont Dynasty: Behind the Nylon Curtain. Secaucus, N.J.: Lyle Stuart, 1984. 960 p.

Duke, Marc. The Du Ponts: Portrait of a Dynasty. New York: Saturday Review Press/E.P.Dutton, 1976. 340 p.

Moseley, Leonard. Blood Relations: The Rise and Fall of the Du Ponts of Delaware. New York: Atheneum, 1980. 426 p.

Munyan, Mary G. Du Pont--The Story of a Company Town. Puyallup, Wash.: Valley Press, 1972. 240 p.

Taylor, Graham D. Du Pont and the
    International Chemical Industry.
    Boston Twayne Publishers, 1984. 251 p.

Williams, Jon M., and D.T. Muir.
    Corporate Images: Photography and the
    Du Pont Company, 1865-1972.
    Wilmington, Del.: Hagley Museum and
    Library, 1984. 72 p.

Wingate, Phillip Jerome. The Colorful Du
    Pont Company. Wilmington, Del.:
    Serendipity Press, 1982. 213 p.

Zilg, Gerald C. Du Pont: Behind the Nylon
    Curtain. Englewood Cliffs, N.J.:
    Prentice-Hall, 1974. 623 p.

DUKE POWER COMPANY

Horn, Carol. The Duke Power Story 1904-
    1973. New York: Newcomen Society in
    North America, 1973. 17 p. (Newcomen
    Publication; no. 969.)

DULUTH, MISSABLE AND IRON RANGE RAILWAY COMPANY

King, Frank A. The Missable Road: The
    Duluth, Missable and Iron Range
    Railway. San Marino, Calif.: Golden
    West Books, 1972. 224 p.

EAST AUGUSTA MUTUAL FIRE INSURANCE COMPANY

East Augusta Mutual Fire Insurance
    Company. Centennial: The East Augusta

Mutual Fire Insurance Company: Organization and Growth, 1870-1970. Verona, Va.: McClure Printing Company, 1970. 111 p.

EAST RIVER SAVINGS BANK

Murphy, Austin S. East River Savings Bank: 125 Years of Service to the People and the City of New York. New York: Newcomen Society in North America, 1973. 26 p. (Newcomen Address.)

EAST TEXAS CHAMBER OF COMMERCE

The First Fifty Years: A History of Commerce. Edited by Howard W. Rosser. Longview, Tex.: East Texas Magazine, 1976. 213 p.

EASTERN AIRLINES, INC.

Cearley, George Walker, Jr. Eastern Air Lines: An Illustrated History. Dallas: G.W. Cearely, Jr., 1985. 96 p.

Hall, Floyd D. Sunrise at Eastern: Rebirth of a Pioneer Airline. New York: Newcomen Society in North America, 1965. 32 p.

Serling, Robert J. From the Captain to the Colonel: An Informal History of Eastern Airlines. New York: Dial Press, 1980. 535 p.

Smith, Frank K. *Legacy of Wings: The Story of Harold F. Pitcairn.* New York: Jason Aronson, 1981. 371 p.

THE EASTERN COMPANY

McMillen, Russell G. *The Eastern Company since 1858: From Farm Tools to Yachting Instruments.* New York: Newcomen Society in North America, 1971. 24 p.

EASTERN GAS AND FUEL ASSOCIATES

"50 Years : A Retrospective." In *Eastern Gas and Fuel Associates. Annual Report,* Special Section. Boston: The Company, 1979.

EASTMAN KODAK COMPANY
See:
KODAK (EASTMAN) COMPANY

EATON CORPORATION

Scobel, Donald N. *Creative Worklife.* Houston: Gulf Publishing Company, 1981. 244 p.

EATON YALE AND TOWNE, INC.

Ludvigsen, E.L. *Eaton Yale and Towne: A Corporate Portrait.* New York: Newcomen Society in North America, 1968. 20 p. (Newcomen Address.)

ECHLIN, INC.

Mancheski, Frederick J. <u>The Echlin Manufacturing Company: Its First Fifty Years.</u> New York: Newcomen Society in North America, 1975. 18 p. (Newcomen Publication; no. 1024.)

ECONOMICS LABORATORY, INC.

Lanners, Fred T. <u>"Products and Services for a Cleaner World: The Story of Economics Laboratory, Inc."</u> New York: Newcomen Society in North America, 1981. 24 p. (Newcomen Publication; no. 1152.)

ELANO CORPORATION

Nutler, Ervin J. <u>The Elano Story: An Engineer's Free Enterprise Dream.</u> New York: Newcomen Society in North America, 1982. 24 p. (Newcomen Publication; no. 1168.)

ELECTRONIC DATA SYSTEMS CORPORATION

Sorge, M., and M. Krebs "23 Years of EDS." <u>Automotive News</u> (18 March 1985): 28.

ELECTRONIC NEWS

"25th Anniversary Issue." <u>Electronic News</u> 28 (25 January 1982): Sec. 2, 1-95.

ELLAM (PATRICK), INC.

Ellam, Patrick. *Wind Song: Our Ten Years in the Yacht Delivery Business.* Camden, Maine: International Marine Publishing Company, 1976. 222 p.

EMERSON ELECTRIC COMPANY

Snead, William Scott. *Emerson Electric Company, 1890-1965: The History of an Industrial Pioneer.* New York: Newcomen Society in North America, 1965. 28 p. (Newcomen Address.)

EMERY AIR FREIGHT CORPORATION

"Landmarks in Emery History." In *Emery Air Freight Corporation 1984 Factbook*, 16. Wilton, Conn.: The Company, 1984.

EMPLOYERS INSURANCE OF WAUSAU MUTUAL COMPANY

Schlueter, Clyde F. *The Wausau Story of Employers Insurance of Wausau.* New York: Newcomen Society in North America, 1974. 24 p. (Newcomen Publication; no. 998.)

ENDICOTT JOHNSON CORPORATION

White, Eli G. *The Awakening of a Company: The Story of Endicott Johnson Corporation.* New York: Newcomen Society in North America, 1967. 24 p. (Newcomen Address.)

EQUIFAX, INC.

Equifax, Inc. <u>A History of Equifax, Inc.</u>
   Atlanta: The Company, 1985. 2 p.

EQUITABLE LIFE ASSURANCE SOCIETY OF THE UNITED STATES

Burley, Roscoe Carlyle. <u>The Equitable Life Assurance Society of the United States, 1859-1964.</u> New York: Appleton-Century-Crofts, 1967. 2 vols. 1475 p.

Equitable Life Assurance Society of the United States. <u>The Equitable Story.</u> New York: The Society, 197? 20 p.

EQUITABLE LIFE INSURANCE COMPANY OF IOWA

Pease, George Sexton. <u>Patriarch of the Prairie, The Story of Equitable of Iowa, 1867-1967.</u> New York: Appleton-Century-Crofts, 1967. 260 p.

ERIE INSURANCE EXCHANGE

Hirt, A. Orth. <u>The Story of Erie Insurance Exchange.</u> New York: Newcomen Society in North America, 1971. 32 p. (Newcomen Address.)

ESTEE LAUDER
See:
LAUDER (ESTEE)

ETHYL CORPORATION

Robert, Joseph C. *Ethyl: A History of the Corporation and the People who Made It.* Charlottesville: University Press of Virginia, 1983. 448 p.

THE EVENING GAZETTE (WORCHESTER, MASS.)

Stoddard, Robert W. *The Evening Gazette: 100 Years--A Consistent Story.* New York: Newcomen Society in North America, 1966. 24 p. (Newcomen Address.)

EX-CELL-O CORPORATION

Giblin, Edward J., and E.P. Casey. *Innovative Products Through People: The Story of Ex-Cell-O Corporation.* New York: Newcomen Society in North America, 1982. 28 p. (Newcomen Publication; no. 1162.)

EXXON CORPORATION

Exxon Corporation. *The Other Dimensions of Business: A Report on Exxon's Participation in Areas of Public Interest.* New York: The Company, 1977. 44 p.

"Milestones in 90 Years of Company History." *Lamp* 54 (Winter 1972): 24-27.

FAIRBANKS-MORSE CORPORATION

Kirkland, John F. *The Diesel Builders: Fairbanks-Morse and Lima-Hamilton.* Glendale, Calif.: Interurban Press, 1985. 111 p.

THE FAMOUS AMOS CHOCOLATE CHIP COOKIE COMPANY

Amos, Wally, and Leroy Robinson. *The Famous Amos Story: The Face that Launched a Thousand Chips.* Garden City, N.Y.: Doubleday, 1983. 201 p.

FANSTEEL, INC.

Tennyson, Jon R. *$2500 and a Dream: The Fansteel Story.* Chicago: The Company, 1982. 118 p.

FARMERS AND MECHANICS NATIONAL BANK, FREDERICK, MD.

Cahn, Louis F. *Sesqui Centennial History, 1817-1967, Farmers and Mechanics National Bank, Frederick, Maryland.* Frederick, Md.: Farmers and Mechanics National Bank, 1967. 48 p.

FARMERS AND MERCHANTS BANK OF LOS ANGELES

Cleland, Robert Glass, and Frank B. Putnam. *Isais W. Hellman and the Farmers and Merchants Bank.* San Marino, Calif.: Huntington Library, 1965. 136 p.

FARMLAND INDUSTRIES, INC.

Anderson, John F. "Make No Little Plans--" : The Story of Farmland Industries, Inc. New York: Newcomen Society in North America, 1980. 20 p. (Newcomen Publication; no. 1120.)

Farmland Industries, Inc. This is Farmland Industries; the Story of a Farmer-owned Business. Kansas City, Mo.: The Company, 1984. 12 p.

Fite, Gilbert Courtland. Beyond the Fence Rows: A History of Farmland Industries, Incorporated, 1929-1978. Columbia: University of Missouri Press, 1978. 404 p.

FEDERAL DEPOSIT INSURANCE CORPORATION

Waddell, Harry. "The FDIC's Fifty Years." ABA Bank Journal 75 (October 1983): 38-52.

FEDERAL EXPRESS CORPORATION

Feldman, Joan M. "Federal Express: Big, Bigger and Biggest." Air Transport 22 (November 1985): 46-54.

Kanner, Barbara. "Story of a Brilliant Commercial." New York 14 (26 October 1981): 19-20+.

Ponder, Ronny. Federal Express: The Small Package Airline. Memphis: The Company, 1977. 17 p.

FEDERAL PAPER BOARD COMPANY, INC.

Kennedy, John R. *No Room for Discouragement: The Story of Federal Paper Board Company.* New York: Newcomen Society in North America, 1967. 24 p. (Newcomen Address.)

FEDERATED DEPARTMENT STORES

Gottschalk, Alfred. *Fred Lazarus, Jr., 1884-1973.* Cincinnati: Hebrew Union College Press, 1973. 55 p.

THE FELLOWS GEAR SHAPER COMPANY

Miller, Edward W. *Ingenuity and Courage: A Personalized History of the Fellows Gear Shaper Company.* New York: Newcomen Society in North America, 1966 24 p. (Newcomen Address.)

FERRACUTE MACHINE COMPANY

Cox, Arthur J., and Thomas Malim. *Ferracute: The History of an American Enterprise.* Bridgeton, N.J.: A.J. Cox, 1985. 197 p.

FIDELITY-PHILADELPHIA TRUST COMPANY

Fidelity-Philadelphia Trust Company. *A Tribute to the Year 1866.* Philadelphia: The Company, 1966. 26 p.

FIDELITY UNION LIFE INSURANCE COMPANY

Fidelity Union Life Insurance Company.
   Dallas: Fidelity Union Life Insurance
   Company, 1972.

Neville, Dorothy. Carr P. Collins: Man on
   the Move. Dallas: Park Press, 1963.
   185 p.

FIDUCIARY TRUST COMPANY OF NEW YORK

Fowler, Harry W. Fiduciary Trust Company
   of New York: Investment Management
   Specialists--for Individuals,
   Corporations, Institutions. New York:
   Newcomen Society in North America,
   1974. 23 p. (Newcomen Publication; no.
   1013.)

FIELD ENTERPRISES EDUCATIONAL CORPORATION

Phalin, Howard V. The Pursuit of
   Excellence. Chicago: The Company,
   1968. 190 p.

FIELDCREST MILLS, INC.

Fieldcrest Mills, Inc. Fieldcrest:
   Promise and Pride; Challenge and
   Achievement. Eden, N.C.: The Company,
   1978. 59 p.

FIGGIE INTERNATIONAL HOLDINGS, INC.

"Reflections." In Figgie International
   Holdings, Inc. Annual Report, 4-23.
   Willoughby, Ohio: The Company, 1983.

FINANCIAL GENERAL BANKSHARES, INC.

Olmsted, George Hamden. *The Story of Financial General Bankshares and the Importance of Financial Institutions in a Free Enterprise Society.* New York: Newcomen Society in North America, 1976. 20 p. (Newcomen Publication; no. 1042.)

FIRESTONE TIRE AND RUBBER COMPANY

Firestone Tire and Rubber Company. *Historical Highlights of the Firestone Tire and Rubber Company.* Akron: The Company, 1984. 7 p.

FIRST ALABAMA BANCSHARES

Plummer, Frank. *First Alabama Bankshares: An Outstanding Record of Performance.* New York: Newcomen Society in North America, 1984. 24 p. (Newcomen Publication; no. 1202.)

FIRST AND MERCHANTS NATIONAL BANK, RICHMOND

Williams, Frances Leigh. *A Century of Service; Prologue to the Future, A History of the First & Merchants National Bank.* Richmond: The Bank, 1965. 141 p.

FIRST BANK SYSTEM, INC.

First Bank System, Inc. <u>A History of First Bank System, Inc.</u> Minneapolis: The System, 1985. 3 p.

First Bank System, Inc. <u>The First Fifty Years.</u> Minneapolis: The System, 1979. 14 p.

FIRST FEDERAL SAVINGS AND LOAN ASSOCIATION OF JACKSON

Scott, Tom B. <u>Making Change: The Story of First Federal Savings and Loan Association of Jackson.</u> New York: Newcomen Society in North America, 1970. 24 p. (Newcomen Address.)

FIRST FEDERAL SAVINGS AND LOAN ASSOCIATION OF MINNEAPOLIS

Lund, Doniver Adolph. <u>50 Years, A History of First Federal, Minneapolis.</u> Minneapolis: First Federal Savings and Loan Association, 1976. 95 p.

FIRST FEDERAL SAVINGS AND LOAN ASSOCIATION OF ST. PETERSBURG

Thomson, Lila. <u>The Biography of Business.</u> St. Petersburg, Fla.: The Company, 1969. 174 p.

FIRST FIDELITY BANCORPORATION

First Fidelity Bancorporation. *History of First Fidelity Bancorporation.* Newark: The Company, 1985. 4 p.

FIRST HAWAIIAN BANK

"First Hawaiian Bank: 125 years." In *First Hawaiian, Inc. Annual Report.* Honolulu: The Bank, 1983.

FIRST MISSISSIPPI CORPORATION

Williams, J. Kelly. *First Mississippi Corporation: The First Twenty Five Years.* New York: Newcomen Society in North America, 1982. 24 p. (Newcomen Publication; no. 1174.)

FIRST NATIONAL BANK AND TRUST COMPANY OF WYOMING

Dowdy, Auburn W. *The First 100 Years: The First National Bank and Trust Company of Wyoming.* New York: Newcomen Society in North America, 1982. 24 p. (Newcomen Publication; no. 1166.)

FIRST NATIONAL BANK IN HOUSTON

Kirkland, William A. *Old Bank-New Bank: The First National Bank, Houston, 1866-1956.* Houston: Pacesetter Press, 1975. 115 p.

FIRST NATIONAL BANK OF BELLEVILLE

First National Bank of Belleville. <u>The First 100 Years.</u> Belleville, Ill.: The Bank, 1974. 95 p.

FIRST NATIONAL BANK OF BILOXI

Holt, Hazel. <u>75th Anniversary; First National Bank of Biloxi, 1893-1968.</u> Biloxi, Miss.: The Bank, 1968. 56 p.

FIRST NATIONAL BANK OF COMMERCE

White, Joseph C. <u>Eulogies in Bronze: The Story of First National Bank of Commerce.</u> New Orleans: The Bank, 1983. 79 p.

FIRST NATIONAL BANK OF DENVER

Adams, Eugene H. <u>The Pioneer Western Bank: First of Denver, 1860-1980.</u> Denver, Colo.: First Interstate Bank of Denver; State Historical Society of Colorado, Colorado Heritage Center, 1984.

FIRST NATIONAL BANK OF FARGO

First National Bank of Fargo, N.D. <u>First National Bank of Fargo, 1878-1978: A Century of Service to the Community.</u> Fargo, N.D.: The Bank, 1978. 8 p.

FIRST NATIONAL BANK OF FORT WORTH

Mason, Paul. The First: The Story of Fort Worth's Oldest National Bank. New York: Newcomen Society in North America, 1977. 23 p. (Newcomen Publication; no. 1062.)

FIRST NATIONAL BANK OF GENEVA

Wood, William C. The First 65 years. Geneva, Ill.: The Bank, 1972. 49 p.

FIRST NATIONAL BANK OF GRAND ISLAND

Lund, Doniver. A Great Tradition: The Centennial History of the First National Bank of Grand Island. Grand Island, Neb.: The Bank, 1980. 140 p.

FIRST NATIONAL BANK OF MOBILE

Mathews, Charles Elijah. Highlights of 100 Years in Mobile. Mobile, Ala.: The Bank, 1965. 169 p.

FIRST NATIONAL BANK OF PLATTEVILLE

Dobson, Linda. The First National Bank of Platteville, Eighty-one Years of Progress. Platteville, Wis.: The Bank, 1972. 16 p.

FIRST NATIONAL BANK OF TUSCALOOSA

The First National Bank of Tuscaloosa. The First National Bank of Tuscaloosa:

Growing with You, Caring for You.
Tuscaloosa, Ala.: The Bank, 1971. 12 p.

FIRST NATIONAL CITY BANK

First National City Bank. *Citibank, Nader and the Facts.* New York: Citibank, 1974. 92 p.

Leinsdorf, David, and Donald Etra. *Citibank; Ralph Nader's Study Group Report on First National City Bank.* New York: Grossman Publishers, 1973. 406 p.

FIRST PENNSYLVANIA BANK, N.A.

First Pennsylvania Bank, N.A. *The Bank, 1781-1976: A Short History of First Pennsylvania Bank.* Philadelphia: The Bank, 1976. 96 p.

Foltz, N. "200 Years Ago, America Needed a Bank." *Banking* 67 (March 1975): 102+.

FIRST SECURITY CORPORATION

Eccles, George S. *First Security Corporation: The First Fifty Years, 1928-1978.* New York: Newcomen Society in North America, 1978. 21 p. (Newcomen Publication; no. 1089.)

Hyman, Sidney. *Challenge and Response: The First Security Corporation's First*

Fifty Years, 1928-1978. Salt Lake City: Graduate School of Business, University of Utah, 1978. 462 p.

FIRST TRUST AND DEPOSIT COMPANY, SYRACUSE, N.Y.

Schramm, Henry W. The Dynamic Years: A History of First Trust and Deposit Company. Syracuse: The Company, 1976. 131 p.

FIRST UNION CORPORATION

Cameron, Charles Clifford. First Union Corporation, A Bank Holding Company: A Tradition of Leadership. New York: Newcomen Society in North America, 1980. 30 p. (Newcomen Publication; no. 1111.)

FLORIDA POWER CORPORATION

Parsons, Al. Lightning in the Sun; A History of Florida Power Corporation, 1899-1974. St. Petersburg: The Company, 1974. 199 p.

FLOUR CORPORATION

Flour, J. Robert. Flour Corporation: A 65-Year History. New York: Newcomen Society in North America, 1978. 30 p. (Newcomen Publication; no. 1074.)

FLUKE (JOHN) MANUFACTURING COMPANY, INC.

"Thumbnail History of the John Fluke Mfg. Co., Inc." In <u>John Fluke Mfg. Co., Inc. General Information</u>, 16. Everett, Wash.: The Company, 1985.

FORBES MAGAZINE

Jones, Arthur. <u>Malcolm Forbes: Peripatetic Millionaire.</u> New York: Harper & Row, 1977. 211 p.

FORD, BACON AND DAVIS, INC.

Ford, Bacon and Davis, Inc. <u>For Human Needs: The Story of Ford, Bacon & Davis.</u> New York: The Company, 1967. 223 p.

FORD MOTOR COMPANY

Beynon, H. <u>Working for Ford.</u> London: Allen Lane, 1973. 336 p.

Friedman, Henry, and Sander Meredeen. <u>The Dynamics of Industrial Conflict: Lessons from Ford.</u> London: Croom Helm, 1980. 386 p.

Gawronski, F.W. "By Land, Air, Sea; Automotive Transportation is not the Only Mode at Ford." <u>Automotive News</u> (16 June 1978): 196-201.

Gordon, Maynard M. <u>Iacocca Management Technique; A Profile of the Chrysler</u>

Chairman's Unique Key to Business Success. New York: Dodd, Mead, 1985. 154 p.

Herndon, Booton. *Ford; An Unconventional Biography of the Men and Their Times.* New York: Weybright and Talley, 1969. 408 p.

Lasky, Victor. *Never Complain, Never Explain: The Story of Henry Ford II.* New York: R. Marek Publishers, 1981. 307 p.

"75 Years of Ford Motor Company." *Automotive News* (16 June 1978): 1-275. (Special issue.)

Sorenson, Lorin. *The American Ford: From the Fordiana Series.* St. Helena, Calif.: Silverado Publishing Company, 1975. 263 p.

Strobel, Lee Patrick. *Reckless Homicide?: Ford's Trial.* South Bend, Ind.: And Books, 1980. 286 p.

FOREMOST-MCKESSON, INC.

Morison, William W. *The Story of Foremost-McKesson, Inc.* New York: Newcomen Society in North America, 1978. 30 p. (Newcomen Publication; no. 1086.)

FORT WORTH NATIONAL BANK

Bond, Lewis H. <u>Century One: 1873-1973: A City ... and the Bank that Bears Its Name. The Story of the Fort Worth National Bank</u>. New York: Newcomen Society in North America, 1973. 21 p. (Newcomen Publication; no. 976.)

FORT WORTH STAR-TELEGRAM

Meek, Phillip J. Fort Worth Star-Telegra<u>m: "Where the West Begins."</u> New York: Newcomen Society in North America, 1981. 28 p. (Newcomen Publication; no. 1145.)

FOSTER WHEELER CORPORATION

Azzato, Louis E. <u>Foster Wheeler Corporation: Meeting Industrial Change Worldwide.</u> New York: Newcomen Society in the United States, 1985. 24 p. (Newcomen Publication; no. 1237.)

Foster Wheeler Corporation. <u>Foster Wheeler History.</u> The Company, n.d. 4 p.

THE FOURTH NATIONAL BANK AND TRUST COMPANY

Kincade, Arthur W. <u>"Ad Astra per Aspera,"</u> <u>"To the Stars Through Difficulties": The Story of the Fourth National Bank and Trust Company, Wichita, Kansas.</u>

New York: Newcomen Society in North America, 1969. 32 p. (Newcomen Address.)

FRANKLIN NATIONAL BANK

Spero, Joan Edelman. <u>The Failure of the Franklin National Bank: Challenge to the International Banking System.</u> New York: Columbia University Press, 1980. 235 p. (Published for the Council on Foreign Relations.)

FREESE AND NICHOLS, INC.

Nichols, James R. <u>Freese and Nichols, Inc.: An Engineering Institution.</u> New York: Newcomen Society in North America, 1983. 28 p. (Newcomen Publication; no. 1171.)

FRONTIER AIRLINES

Frontier Airlines. <u>Frontier Airlines: Historical Highlights.</u> Denver: The Company, 1985. 4 p.

FRUEHAUF CORPORATION

Fruehauf Corporation. <u>Fruehauf's History.</u> Detroit: The Company, 1983. 7 p.

FUQUA INDUSTRIES, INC.

Fuqua, J.B. <u>The Story of Fuqua Industries, Inc.</u> New York: Newcomen Society in North America, 1973. 18 p.

GAF CORPORATION

Marder, William. *Anthony, The Man, The Company, The Cameras; An American Photographic Pioneer: 140 Year History of a Company from Anthony to Ansco to GAF.* Plantation, Fla.: Pine Ridge Publishing Company, 1982. 384 p.

GALBREATH (JOHN W.) AND COMPANY

Shook, Robert L. "John W. Galbreath." In *The Enterpreneurs,* 1-17. New York: Harper & Row, 1980.

THE GARLOCK PACKING COMPANY

Waples, R.M., Sr., and R.M. Waples, Jr. *Garlock: The First Eighty-eight Years, 1887-1975.* Palmyra, N.Y.: Garlock, Inc., 1976. 105 p.

GARRETT (ROBERT) AND SONS, INC.

Williams, Harold A. *Robert Garrett and Sons, Inc.; Origin and Development, 1840-1965.* Baltimore: The Company, 1965. 102 p.

GARRETT CORPORATION

Schoneberger, William A., and Robert R.H. Scholl. *Out of Thin Air: Garrett's First 50 Years.* Los Angeles: The Company, 1985.

GASTON, SNOW AND ELY, BARTLETT

Gaston, Snow & Ely, Bartlett. <u>A Brief History.</u> New York: Newcomen Society in North America, 1979. 32 p. (Newcomen Publication; no. 1103.)

GATX (GENERAL AMERICAN TRANSPORTATION CORPORATION)

Scanlin, J.R. <u>GATX (General American Transportation Corporation): Meeting the Changing Needs of Industry.</u> New York: Newcomen Society in North America, 1970. 32 p. (Newcomen Address.)

Ruderman, Gary S. "Truck Innovation Marks 50 Years." <u>Automotive News</u> (13 August 1984): 16+.

GELCO CORPORATION

"Historical Highlights." In <u>Gelco Corporation. 1982 Fact Book</u>, 4-5. Eden Prairie, Minn.: The Company, 1982.

GENERAL DYNAMICS CORPORATION

Goodwin, Jacob B. <u>Brotherhood of Arms: General Dynamics and the Business of Defending America.</u> New York: Times Books, 1985. 384 p.

Boulware, Lemuel R. <u>The Truth about Boulwarism; Trying to Do Right Voluntarily.</u> Washington, D.C.: BNA, 1969. 180 p.

GENERAL ELECTRIC COMPANY

General Electric Company. *GE 100, 1878-1978.* Fairfield, Conn.: The Company, 1978. 52 p.

Greenwood, Ronald G. *Managerial Decentralization; A Study of the General Electric Philosophy.* Lexington, Mass.: Lexington Books, 1974. 176 p.

Levinson, Harry, and Stuart Rosenthal. "Reginald H. Jones." In *CEO: Corporate Leadership in Action*, 16-55. New York: Basic Books, 1984.

Liebhafsky, H.A. *Silicones Under the Monogram: A Story of Industrial Research.* New York: Wiley, 1978. 381 p.

Schatz, Ronald W. *The Electrical Workers: A History of Labor at General Electric and Westinghouse, 1923-1960.* Urbana: University of Illinois Press, 1983. 279 p.

Wise, George Willis R. *Whitney, General Electric and the Origins of U.S. Industrial Research.* New York: Columbia University Press, 1985. 400 p.

GENERAL FOODS CORPORATION

Ferguson, James Leonard. General Foods Corporation: A Chronicle of Consumer Satisfaction. New York: Newcomen Society in North America, 1985. 24 p. (Newcomen Publication; no. 1238.)

GENERAL FOODS CORPORATION, JELL-O DIVISION

Whitman, Edmund S. Plant Relocation; A Case Study of a Move. New York: American Management Association, 1966. 158 p.

GENERAL MILLS, INC.

General Mills, Inc. General Mills: A Collected History. Minneapolis: The Company, 1980. 9 p.

Kennedy, Gerald S. Minutes and Moments in the Life of General Mills. Minneapolis: The Company, 1971. 270 p.

GENERAL MOTORS CORPORATION

Berry, Bryan H. "GM at 75: The Making of a Giant." Chilton's Iron Age 226 (5 December 1983): 28-50.

Cray, Ed. Chrome Colossus: General Motors and Its Times. New York: McGraw-Hill, 1980. 615 p.

De Lorean, John Z. On a Clear Day You Can See General Motors: John Z. De

Lorean's Look Inside the Automotive Giant. Grosse Pointe, Mich.: Wright Enterprises, 1979. 237 p.

El-Messidi, Kathy Groehn. The Story Behind the 30-Year Honeymoon of GM and the UAW. New York: Nellon Publishing Company, 1980. 120 p.

Fleming, Al. "Lund Looks Back on 40 Years at GM." Automotive News (29 October 1984): 6+.

General Motors, the First 75 Years. New York: Crown Publishers, 1983. 223 p.

"GM 75th Anniversary Issue." Automotive News (16 September 1983): 1-434.

General Motors, The First 75 Years of Transportation Products. Princeton, N.J.: Automobile Quarterly Publications, 1983. 223 p.

Guston, L.R. "From Recklessness to Global Auto Dominance in 75 Years." Wards Auto World 19 (November 1983): 21-24.

"Reminiscing with GM's Retiring Bob Lund." Wards Automotive World 20 (December 1984): 21.

Serrin, William. The Company and the Union; The "Civilized Relationship" of the General Motors Corporation and the United Automobile Workers. New York: Knopf, 1973, c1972. 308 p.

Smith, Roger B. Building on 75 Years of
Excellence: The General Motors Story.
New York: Newcomen Society in North
America, 1984. 22 p. (Newcomen
Publication; no. 1208.)

GENERAL MOTORS CORPORATION, BUICK MOTOR DIVISION

Dunham, Terry B., and Lawrence R. Gustin.
The Buick: A Complete History.
Princeton, N.J.: Princeton Publishing,
1985. 444 p.

Gawronski, Francis. "The Car that Built
a City." Automotive News (16 September
1983): 107-114.

GENERAL MOTORS CORPORATION, CADILLAC MOTOR DIVISION

Gawronski, Frank. "Detroit's Oldest Auto
Manufacturer." Automotive News (16
September 1983): 97-106.

GENERAL MOTORS CORPORATION, CHEVROLET MOTOR DIVISION

Dammann, George H. Sixty Years of
Chevrolet. Glen Ellyn, Ill.: Crestline
Publishing, 1972. 319 p.

King, Jenny L. "A Bow Tie for Everyman."
Automotive News (16 September 1983):
127-142.

GENERAL MOTORS CORPORATION, DELCO ELECTRONICS DIVISION

Rowand, Roger. "From Radios to Rockets." Automotive News (16 September 1983): 289-290.

GENERAL MOTORS CORPORATION, FISHER BODY DIVISION

Fleming, Al. "Body by Fisher." Automotive News (16 September 1983): 143-154.

GENERAL MOTORS CORPORATION, GMC TRUCK AND CAR DIVISION

Walsh, Jack. "They Just Keep Trucking Along." Automotive News (16 September 1983): 259-260.

GENERAL MOTORS CORPORATION, OLDSMOBILE DIVISION

Kimes, Beverly Rae. Oldsmobile; The First Seventy Five Years. New York: Automotive Quarterly, 1972. 72 p.

Sorge, Marjorie. "Ransome's Merry Oldsmobile." Automotive News (16 September 1983): 81-95.

THE GENERAL RADIO COMPANY

Sinclair, Donald B. The General Radio Company: 1915-1965. New York: Newcomen Society in North America, 1965. 32 p.

Thiessen, Arthur E. <u>A History of the General Radio Company.</u> West Concord, Mass.: The Company, 1965. 116 p.

GENERAL TELEPHONE COMPANY OF FLORIDA

Cooper, Dennis R. <u>The People Machine; An Illustrated History of the Telephone on the Central West Coast of Florida.</u> Tampa: The Company, 1971. 301 p.

GENERAL TELEPHONE DIRECTORY COMPANY

Briggs, Don F. <u>WES: Portrait of a Man in Motion.</u> St. Petersburg Beach, Fla.: Briggs, 1978. 179 p.

GENERAL TIRE AND RUBBER COMPANY

O'Neill, Dennis J. <u>A Whale of a Territory: The Story of Bill O'Neill.</u> New York: McGraw-Hill Company, 1966. 249 p.

GENESCO, INC.

Genesco, Inc. <u>Genesco's Business Past and Present.</u> Nashville: The Company, n.d. 5 p. (History through 1982.)

Jarman, W. Maxey. <u>The Genesco: Formula for Growth--People--Products.</u> New York: Newcomen Society in North America, 1969. 22 p. (Newcomen Address.)

GEORGIA-PACIFIC CORPORATION

Cheatham, Owen R. *The Georgia-Pacific Story.* New York: Newcomen Society in North America, 1966. 28 p. (Newcomen Address.)

Ross, John R. *Maverick, the Story of Georgia-Pacific.* Portland: The Company, 1978, c1980. 318 p.

GERBER PRODUCTS COMPANY

Gerber Products Company. *Fifty Years of Caring: Our Golden Anniversary Year, 1928-1978.* Fremont, Mich.: The Company, 1978. 26 p.

GETTY OIL COMPANY

Getty, Jean Paul. *As I See It: The Autobiography of J. Paul Getty.* London: W.H. Allen, 1976. 361 p.

Getty Oil Company. *Getty Oil Company.* Los Angeles: Petroleum Information Corporation, 1971.

Lenzner, Robert. *The Great Getty: The Life and Loves of J. Paul Getty, Richest Man in the World.* New York: Crown Publishers, 1985. 283 p.

Miscellaneous Pamphlets on the Company Compiled at Normandale Community College. Bloomington, Minn.: Normandale Community College, 1977.

GIBBS AND HILL, INC.

Johnson, Barclay G. Before the Colors Fade: A Personal History of Gibbs & Hill, Inc., 1911-1971. New York: Gibbs & Hill, 1975. 110 p.

GIBRALTAR SAVINGS AND LOAN ASSOCIATION

"A History of Gibraltar Savings; A Federal Savings and Loan Association." Gibraltar Journal 4 (September 1982): 1-8.

GIBSON GREETING CARDS, INC.

Gibson Greeting Cards, Inc. Gibson, 1850-1975: Our 125th Anniversary. Cincinnati: The Company, 1975. 16 p.

GIFFORD-HILL AND COMPANY, INC.

Gifford, P.W. The Gifford-Hill Story. New York: Newcomen Society in North America, 1968. 20 p. (Newcomen Address.)

"So We've Made 200 Years--Now What?" Gifford-Hill Times 8, no.7 (July 1976): 1-3.

GILBERT AND BENNETT MANUFACTURING COMPANY

Miller, Raymond Curtis, and Phillip H. Knowles. Gilbert and Bennett Manufacturing Company, 1818-1968, 150th Anniversary. Georgetown, Conn.: The Company, 1968. 93 p.

GILLETTE COMPANY

Adams, Russell B. King C. Gillette, The Man and His Wonderful Shaving Device. Boston: Little, Brown, 1978. 311 p.

Gillette Company. The Gillette Company, 1901-1976. Boston: The Company, 1977. 32 p.

GILPIN (HENRY B.) COMPANY

Allen, James Elbert. The Story of the Henry B. Gilpin Company. New York: Newcomen Society in North America, 1977. 24 p. (Newcomen Publication; no. 1063.)

GLEN RAVEN MILLS, INC.

Gant, Margaret Elizabeth. The Raven's Story. S.l.: The Company, 1979. 225 p.

GLENDALE FEDERAL

Edwards, Raymond D. Glendale Federal: A One-stop Financial Services Center: Now in Our 50th Year. New York: Newcomen Society in North America, 1984. 20 p. (Newcomen Publication; no. 1219.)

GOODRICH TRANSIT COMPANY

Elliot, James L. Red Stacks over the Horizon; The Story of the Goodrich

Steamboat Line. Grand Rapids, Mich.: William B. Erdman Publishing Company, 1967. 314 p.

GOODYEAR TIRE AND RUBBER COMPANY

O'Reilly, Maurice. The Goodyear Story. Edited by James T. Keating. Elmsford, N.Y.: Benjamin Company, 1983. 223 p.

GOULD, INC.

Ylvisaker, William T. Integrated Technology: The Story of Gould, Inc. New York: Newcomen Society in North America, 1972. 16 p. (Newcomen Address.)

GOVERNMENT EMPLOYEES INSURANCE COMPANY

Byrne, John J. Government Employees Insurance Company, The First Forty Years. New York: Newcomen Society in North America, 1981. 27 p. (Newcomen Publication; no. 1125.)

Davidson, Lorimer A. The Government Employees Insurance Company, 1936-1966: A Brief History. New York: Newcomen Society in North America, 1966. 32 p. (Newcomen Address.)

GRACE (W.R.) AND COMPANY

Grace (W.R.) and Company. What is Grace? New York: The Company, 1982. 3 p. (Reprinted from Chemical Week [29 September, 1982].)

GRAINGER (W.W.), INC.

W.W. Grainger, Inc. <u>50 Years of Growth, 1927-1977.</u> Chicago: The Company, 1977. 16 p.

GRAND HOTEL

Woodfill, W. Stewart. <u>Grand Hotel: The Story of an Institution.</u> New York: Newcomen Society in North America, 1969. 28 p. (Newcomen Address.)

GREAT ATLANTIC AND PACIFIC TEA COMPANY

Mueller, Robert W. <u>A&P; Past, Present and Future.</u> New York: Progressive Grocer Magazine, 1971. 173 p. (Based on the A&P study written by the editors of <u>Progressive Grocer Magazine</u> in cooperation with the Great Atlantic and Pacific Tea Company.)

Hoyt, Edwin P. <u>That Wonderful A&P!</u> New York: Hawthorn Books, 1969. 279 p.

GREEN BAY PACKERS

Torinus, John B. <u>The Packer Legend: An Inside Look.</u> Neshkoro, Wis.: Landmark Press, 1982. 251 p.

GREENWOOD MILLS

Wideman, Frank J. <u>"Fabric with the Character of Quality": The Story of</u>

Greenwood Mills. New York: Newcomen Society in North America, 1980. 24 p. (Newcomen Publication; no. 1126.)

THE GRENADA BANK

Kennington, Robert E. Grenada Bank: The Story of a $180,000,000 Small Town Bank. New York: Newcomen Society in North America, 1975. 23 p. (Newcomen Publication; no. 996.)

GREYHOUND CORPORATION

Greyhound Corporation. An Era of Excellence: The History of Greyhound. Chicago: Greyhound Corporation, 1967. 18 p.

Jackson, Carlton. Hounds of the Road: A History of the Greyhound Bus Company. Bowling Green: Bowling Green University Popular Press, 1984. 214 p.

Schisgall, Oscar. The Greyhound Story; from Hibbing to Everywhere. New York: Doubleday, 1985. 309 p.

GROLIER, INC.

Grolier, Inc. A Brief History of Grolier. Danbury, Conn.: The Company, 1984. 4 p.

GROSS, KELLY AND COMPANY, INC.

Kelly, Daniel T. The Buffalo Head; A Century of Mercantile Pioneering in the Southwest. Santa Fe, N.M.: Vergara Publishing Company, 1972. 288 p.

GROVE FARM COMPANY, INC.

Krauss, Bob. Grove Farm Plantation; The Biography of a Hawaiian Sugar Plantation. Palo Alto, Calif.: Pacific Books, 1965. 400 p.

GRUMMAN CORPORATION

Grumman Corporation. Grumman: 50 Years. Bethpage, N.Y.: The Company, 1978. 32 p.

Thruelsen, Richard. The Grumman Story. New York: Praeger, 1976. 401 p.

GS&A GROUP, INC.

Shook, Robert L. "Joseph Sugarman." In The Entrepreneurs, 115-125. New York: Harper & Row, 1980.

GUARANTEE MUTUAL LIFE COMPANY

Conley, Eugene A. Guarantee Mutual Life Company: A Promise Fulfilled During 75 Years, 1901-1976. New York: Newcomen Society in North America, 1976. 20 p. (Newcomen Publication; no. 1038.)

GULF AND WESTERN INDUSTRIES

Bluhdorn, Charles G. The Gulf+Western Story. New York: Newcomen Society in North America, 1973. 23 p.

GULF OIL CORPORATION

Gulf Oil Corporation: A Capsule History. Pittsburgh, Pa.: The Corporation, 1980. 25 p.

McCloy, John Jay. The Great Oil Spill: The Inside Report, Gulf Oil's Bribery and Political Chicanery. New York: Chelsea House Publishers, 1976. 374 p.

National Council of Churches of Christ in the United States of America. Corporate Information Center. Gulf Oil: Portuguese Ally in Angola. New York: The Council, 1972. 26 p.

United Church of Christ. Ohio Conference. Background Information Passed at the Seventh Annual Meeting. Columbus, Ohio, 1970. 45 p.

HACKENSACK WATER COMPANY

Leiby, Adrian Coulter. Hackensack Water Company: 1869-1969. River Edge, N.J.: Bergen County Historical Society, 1969. 231 p.

HAGERSTOWN AND FREDERICK RAILWAY COMPANY

Harwood, Herbert H., Jr. Blue Ridge Trolley: The Hagerstown and Frederick Railway. San Marino, Calif.: Golden West Books, 1970. 144 p.

HALCON INTERNATIONAL, INC.

Landau, Ralph. *Halcon International, Inc.: An Enterpreneurial Chemical Company.* New York: Newcomen Society in North America, 1978. 32 p. (Newcomen Publication; no. 1088.)

HALLMARK CARDS, INC.

Hall, Joyce C. *When You Care Enough.* Kansas City, Mo.: The Company, 1979. 269 p.

HAMILTON COUNTY STATE BANK

"Hamilton County State Bank: A Dream Realized." *NIP* (April 1984): 36+.

HAMMERMILL PAPER COMPANY

Hammermill Paper Company. *Hammermill: An Industrial Pioneer with Ongoing Pride in Quality and Innovation.* Erie, Pa.: The Company, 1982. 17 p.

Laslie, Donald S. *Hammermill: A Revolution in Papermaking.* New York: Newcomen Society in North America, 1965. 24 p. (Newcomen Address.)

McQuillen, Michael J., and William P. Garvey. *The Best Known Name in Paper: Hammermill, A History of the Company.* Erie, Pa.: The Company, 1985. 206 p.

HARBERT CORPORATION

Harbert, John M., III. Harbert: "A Story of Continuous Beginnings." New York: Newcomen Society in North America, 1982. 24 p. (Newcomen Publication; no. 1161.)

HARLEY-DAVIDSON MOTOR COMPANY

Wright, David. The Harley-Davidson Motor Company: An Official Eighty-year History. Osceola, Wis.: Motorbooks International, 1983. 288 p.

HARNISCHFEGER CORPORATION

Harnischfeger Corporation. A Centennial History. New York: Newcomen Society of the United States, 1985. 24 p. (Newcomen Publication; no. 1234.)

Harnischfeger Corporation. A Centennial History of the Harnischfeger Corporation. Milwaukee: The Company, 1984. 30 p.

HARPER AND ROW, PUBLISHERS, INC.

Exman, Eugene. The House of Harper: One Hundred and Fifty Years of Publishing. New York: Harper & Row, 1967. 31 p.

Nevins, Allan. The Price of Survival. New York: Harper & Row, 1967. 31 p.

HARRIS TRUST AND SAVINGS BANK

Harris Trust and Savings Bank. *History*. Chicago: The Bank, 1979. 2 p.

THE HARTER BANK AND TRUST COMPANY

Root, John B. *One Hundred Years of the Harter Bank and Trust Company.* New York: Newcomen Society in North America, 1967. 24 p. (Newcomen Address.)

HARTFORD NATIONAL BANK AND TRUST COMPANY

Enders, Ostrom. *Hartford National Bank and Trust Company: Three Stories of Its One Hundred and Seventy-five Years.* New York: Newcomen Society in North America, 1967. 24 p. (Newcomen Address.)

HARTFORD STEAM BOILER INSPECTION AND INSURANCE COMPANY

Wilde, Wilson. *"--In the Pursuit of Greater Safety, Reliability, and Efficiency": The Story of the Hartford Steam Boiler Inspection and Insurance Company.* New York: Newcomen Society in North America, 1978. 24 p. (Newcomen Publication; no. 1067.)

HARZA ENGINEERING COMPANY

Harza Engineering Company: Developing Water Resources Worldwide, 1920-1983.

New York: Newcomen Society in North America, 1984. 24 p. (Newcomen Publication; no. 1213.)

HASKINS AND SELLS

Foye, Arthur B. <u>Haskins and Sells, Our First Seventy Five Years; 1895-1970.</u> New York: The Company, 1970. 192 p.

HEARST CORPORATION

Chaney, Lindsay, and Michael Cieply. <u>The Hearsts: Family and Empire: The Later Years.</u> New York: Simon & Schuster, 1981. 416 p.

HEDERMAN BROTHERS

Hederman, Robert M., Jr. <u>The Hederman Story: A Saga of the Printed Word in Mississippi.</u> New York: Newcomen Society in North America, 1966. 28 p. (Newcomen Address.)

HEILEMAN (G.) BREWING COMPANY, INC.

G. Heileman Brewing Company, Inc. <u>The House of Heileman Story: A Short History.</u> La Crosse, Wis.: The Company, 1985. 8 p.

HEINZ (H.J.) COMPANY

Alberts, Robert C. <u>The Good Provider: H.J. Heinz and His 57 Varieties.</u> Boston: Houghton Mifflin, 1973. 297 p.

THE HENNEGAN COMPANY

Hennegan & Company. *Hennegan & Company: Lithographers, Engineers, Printers, Designers.* Cincinnati: The Company, 1975. 14 p.

HENNINGSON, DURHAM AND RICHARDSON

Durham, Charles W. *Henningson, Durham and Richardson: Offering Professional Design Services Since 1917.* New York: Newcomen Society in North America, 1978. 32 p. (Newcomen Publication; no. 1082.)

HERCULES, INC.

Brown, Werner C. *Hercules, Inc.* New York: Newcomen Society in North America, 1977. 24 p. (Newcomen Publication; no. 1078.)

HERSHEY FOODS CORPORATION

Hershey Foods Corporation. *Hershey Foods Corporation: A Profile.* Hershey, Pa.: The Company, 1983. 14 p.

HEXCEL CORPORATION

Hexcel Corporation. *Background Information.* Dublin, Calif.: The Company, 1975. 6 p.

HILLENBRAND INDUSTRIES
See:
HILL-ROM COMPANY

HILL-ROM COMPANY

Dalglish, Garven. <u>Of This Man: The Biography of William A. Hillenbrand.</u> Canaan, N.H.: Phoenix Publishing Company, 1982. 250 p.

HILLS BROTHERS COFFEE, INC.

Wilson, Thomas Carroll. <u>A Background Story of Hills Bros. Coffee, Inc., As Presented by T. Carroll Wilson, Philadelphia District Sales Meeting, September 9, 1966.</u> San Francisco: Printed by the James H. Barry Co., 1967. 80 p.

HOE (R.) AND COMPANY

Comparato, Frank E. <u>Chronicles of Genius and Folly: R. Hoe & Company and the Printing Press as a Service to Democracy.</u> Culver City, Calif.: Labyrinthos, 1979. 846 p.

HOLIDAY HOUSE

Freedman, Russell. <u>Holiday House: The First Fifty Years.</u> New York: Holiday House, 1985. 152 p.

HOLIDAY INNS OF AMERICA, INC.

Wilson, Kemmons. The Holiday Inn Story. New York: Newcomen Society in North America, 1968. 24 p. (Newcomen Address.)

HOLLINS (WILLIAM) AND COMPANY, LTD.

Wells, Frederick Arthur. Hollins and Viyella; A Study in Business History. New York: A.M. Kelly, 1968. 264 p.

THE HOME INSURANCE COMPANY

Tullis, Robert H. The Home Insurance Company: Men of Vision During 125 Years. New York: Newcomen Society in North America, 1978. 24 p. (Newcomen Publication; no. 1081.)

HOME-STAKE PRODUCTION COMPANY

McClintick, David. Stealing from the Rich: The Home-Stake Oil Swindle. New York: M. Evans, 1977. 338 p.

HOMESTAKE MINING COMPANY

Cash, Joseph H. Working the Homestake. Ames: Iowa State University Press, 1973. 141 p.

Fielder, Mildred. The Treasure of Homestake Gold. Aberdeen, S.D.: North Plains Press, 1970. 478 p.

Johnson, Jerry W. *Regional Impact via Multiplier Analysis of Primary Industries: A Case Study: Homestake Mining Company, Lead, South Dakota.* Vermillion: Business Research Bureau, School of Business, University of South Dakota, 1974. 38 p.

HONEYWELL, INC.

Honeywell, Inc. *The First 100 Years.* Minneapolis: The Company, 1985. 36 p.

THE HOOVER COMPANY

The Hoover Company. *A Proud Past--An Exciting Future.* North Canton, Ohio: The Company, n.d. 10 p.

THE HORCHOW COLLECTION

Shook, Robert L. "S. Roger Horchow." In *The Entrepreneurs*, 67-79. New York: Harper & Row, 1980.

HORMEL (GEORGE A.) AND COMPANY

Dougherty, Richard. *In Quest of Quality: Hormel's First 75 Years.* Austin, Minn.: The Company, 1966. 357 p.

HORSMAN DOLLS, INC.

Gibbs, Patikii. *Horsman Dolls, 1950-1970.* Paducah, Ky.: Collector Books, 1985. 263 p.

HOSPITAL CORPORATION OF AMERICA

Hospital Corporation of America. *Fifteen Years of Growing Through Caring.* Nashville: The Company, 1983. 5 p.

HOUGHTON MIFFLIN COMPANY

Ballou, Ellen B. *The Building of the House of Houghton.* Boston: Houghton Mifflin Company, 1970. 695 p.

Miller, Harold T. *Houghton Mifflin Company.* New York: Newcomen Society in North America, 1984. 19 p. (Newcomen Publication; no. 1211.)

HOUSEHOLD FINANCE CORPORATION

Kogan, Herman. *Lending is Our Business; The Story of Household Finance Corporation.* Chicago: Household Finance Corporation, 1965. 147 p.

HOWARD SHIP YARD AND DOCK COMPANY

Fishbaugh, Charles Preston. *From Paddle Wheels to Propellers; The Howard Ship Yard of Jeffersonville in the Story of Steam Navigation on the Western Rivers.* Indianapolis: Indiana Historical Society, 1970. 240 p.

HUBBARD CONSTRUCTION COMPANY

Powers, Ormund. *One Man, One Mule, One Shovel.* Winter Park, Fla.: Anna Publications, 1982. 314 p.

HUDEPOHL BREWING COMPANY

Hudepohl Brewing Company. *Brewing in Cincinnati, 1885-1985: 100 Years of the Hudepohl Brewing Company.* Cincinnati: The Company, 1985. 20 p.

HUDSON OIL COMPANY

Shook, Robert L. "Mary Hudson." In *The Entrepreneurs*, 41-52. New York: Harper & Row, 1980.

HUGHES AIRCRAFT COMPANY

Bain, Trevor. *Defense Manpower and Contract Termination.* Tucson: Division of Economic and Business Research, College of Business and Public Administration, University of Arizona, 1968. 59 p.

Davenport, Joe. *The Empire of Howard Hughes.* San Francisco: Peace and Pieces Foundation, 1975. 81 p.

Drosnin, Michael. *Citizen Hughes.* New York: Holt, Rinehart and Winston, 1985. 532 p.

Smith, George F. "The Early Laser Years at Hughes Aircraft Company." *IEEE Journal of Quantum Electronics* 20 (June 1984): 577-584.

HUGHES TOOL COMPANY

"Historical Issue." *Hughes Rigway* 14 (Fall 1976): 1-24.

HUMMEL INDUSTRIES, INC.

Baird, Nancy Disher. *Tradition and Progress; A History of Hummel Industries, Inc.* Cincinnati: The Company, 1981. 98 p.

HUNT INTERNATIONAL RESOURCES CORPORATION

Hurt, Harry. *Texas Rich: The Hunt Dynasty, from the Early Oil Days Through the Silver Crash.* New York: W.W. Norton, 1981. 446 p.

Tuccille, Jerome. *Kingdom: The Story of the Hunt Family of Texas.* Ottawa, Ill.: Jameson Books, 1984. 384 p.

HUNTINGTON BANCSHARES, INC.

Fultz, Claire E. *Huntington: A Family and a Bank.* Columbus, Ohio: The Bank, 1985. 92 p.

HUNTINGTON NATIONAL BANK OF COLUMBUS

Fultz, Clair E. *"The Huntington": A Story of the Huntington National Bank of Columbus.* New York: Newcomen Society in North America, 1966. 32 p. (Newcomen Address.)

HUSKY OIL COMPANY

Harlow, Howard Reed. "A Profile of Growth: Husky Oil Ltd. Strategy and Tactics from 1938-1972." Ph.D. diss., University of Nebraska, 1973. 329 p.

IBM
See:
INTERNATIONAL BUSINESS MACHINES CORPORATION

IC INDUSTRIES

Johnson, William B. IC Industries. New York: Newcomen Society in North America, 1973. 27 p. (Newcomen Publication; no. 971.)

IDAHO FIRST NATIONAL BANK

Idaho First National Bank. A National Bank 100 Years: 1867-1967. Boise, Idaho: The Bank, 1967.

ILLINOIS CENTRAL INDUSTRIES
See:
IC INDUSTRIES

ILLINOIS CENTRAL RAILROAD

Stover, John F. History of the Illinois Central Railroad. New York: Macmillan Publishing Company, 1975. 575 p.

ILLINOIS POWER COMPANY

Illinois Power Company. <u>A History of Illinois Power Company.</u> Decatur, Ill.: The Company, 1972. 6 p.

<u>Punch, Counterpunch: 60 Minutes vs. Illinois Power Company.</u> Washington D.C.: The Media Institute, 1981. 46 p.

ILLINOIS TOOL WORKS, INC.

Illinois Tool Works, Inc. <u>History.</u> Chicago: The Company, 1982. 5 p.

INDEPENDENT LIFE AND ACCIDENT INSURANCE COMPANY

Bryan, Jacob F. <u>The First Fifty Years of Independent Life.</u> New York: Newcomen Society in North America, 1970. 28 p. (Newcomen Address.)

INDIANA GAS COMPANY

Heiney, J.W. <u>The Story of Indiana Gas Company, Inc.</u> New York: Newcomen Society in North America, 1972. 28 p. (Newcomen Address.)

INDIANAPOLIS POWER AND LIGHT COMPANY

Todd, Zone G. <u>Electrifying Indianapolis: The Story of Indianapolis Power and Light Company.</u> New York: Newcomen Society in North America, 1977. 30 p. (Newcomen Publication; no. 1077.)

INDIANAPOLIS WATER COMPANY

Giffin, Marjie G. Water Runs Downhill: A History of the Indianapolis Water Company and Other Centenarians. New York: Newcomen Society in North America, 1981. 66 p. (Newcomen Publication; no. 1149.)

INDUSTRIAL NATIONAL BANK OF RHODE ISLAND

Weston, Frank. The Passing Years, 1791-1966. Text by Frank Weston. Presidential portrait by Stacy Tolman and others. Providence: The Bank, 1966. 144 p.

INDUSTRIAL SERVICES OF AMERICA, INC.

Industrial Services of America, Inc. History. Louisville: The Company, 1985. 2 p.

INGERSOLL-RAND COMPANY

Koether, George. The Building of Men, Machines, and a Company. Woodcliff Lake, N.J.: Ingersoll-Rand, 1971. 107 p.

INLAND STEEL COMPANY

Rowand, Roger. "Inland's Always Been a Technological Pioneer." Automotive News (26 November 1979): 8+.

See also: General Motors Corporation

INSURANCE COMPANY OF NORTH AMERICA

Carr, William H.A. *Perils: Named and Unnamed, The Story of the Insurance Company of North America.* New York: McGraw-Hill, 1967. 424 p.

INTER-CONTINENTAL HOTELS

Hampton, Max. *Throw Away the Key.* Indianapolis: Bobbs-Merrill, 1966. 256 p.

INTERCO, INC.

Interco, Inc. *Interco, 1911-1980.* St. Louis: The Company, 1980. 8 p.

INTERNATIONAL BUSINESS MACHINES CORPORATION

Applied Management Services. *Inside IBM.* Medford, N.Y.: AMS, 1983. 135 p.

Fisher, Franklin M. *IBM and the U.S. Data Processing Industry; An Academic History.* New York: Praeger, 1983. 532 p.

Fisher, Franklin M. *Folded, Spindled, and Mutilated: Economic Analysis and U.S. vs IBM.* Cambridge, Mass.: MIT Press, 1983. 443 p.

Fishman, Katherine Davis. *The Computer Establishment.* New York: Harper and Row, 1981. 468 p.

Foy, Nancy S. *The Sun Never Sets on IBM.* New York: W. Morrow, 1975. 218 p.

Levinson, Harry, and Stuart Rosenthal. "Thomas J. Watson, Jr." In *CEO: Corporate Leadership in Action*, 178-218. New York: Basic Books, 1984.

Malik, Rex. *And Tomorrow--The World: Inside IBM.* London: Millington, 1975. 496 p.

Rodgers, William. *Think, A Biography of the Watsons and IBM.* New York: Stein and Day, 1969. 320 p.

Sobel, Robert. *IBM. Colossus in Transition.* New York: Times Books, 1981. 360 p.

Weil, Ulric. *Computer Company Valuations: IBM and Its Major Competitors.* New York: Morgan Stanley & Company, 1979, c1980. 28 p.

INTERNATIONAL HARVESTER COMPANY

Marsh, Barbara. *A Corporate Tragedy: The Agony of International Harvester Company.* Garden City, N.Y.: Doubleday, 1985. 312 p.

Ozanne, Robert. *A Century of Labor-Management Relations at McCormick and International Harvester.* Madison: University of Wisconsin Press, 1967. 300 p.

Wendel, C.H. <u>150 Years of International Harvester.</u> Sarasota, Fla.: Crestline Publishers, 1981. 416 p.

INTERNATIONAL MINERALS AND CHEMICAL CORPORATION

Ware, Thomas M. <u>So Little Soil--So Little Time: The Story of International Minerals and Chemical Corporation.</u> New York: Newcomen Society in North America, 1967. 24 p. (Newcomen Address.)

INTERNATIONAL SILVER COMPANY

International Silver Company. <u>Sketch of the International Silver Company.</u> Meriden, Conn.: The Company, 1969.

INTERNATIONAL TELEPHONE AND TELEGRAPH CORPORATION

Burns, Thomas S. <u>Tales of ITT; An Insider's Report.</u> Boston: Houghton Mifflin, 1974. 246 p.

Goolrick, Robert M. <u>Public Policy Toward Corporate Growth: The ITT Merger Cases.</u> Foreword by John V. Tunney. Port Washington, N.Y.: Kennikat Press, 1978. 212 p.

National Council of Churches of Christ in the United States of America. Corporate Information Center. <u>IT&T:</u>

Apartheid and Business in Southern Africa. New York: The Council, 1972. 37 p.

Sampson, Anthony. *The Sovereign State of ITT.* New York: Stein and Day, 1973. 323 p.

Schoenberg, Robert J. *Geneen.* New York: Norton, 1985. 429 p.

Sobel, Robert. *ITT: The Management of Opportunity.* New York: Times Books, 1982. 421 p.

United States Congress. Senate Committee on Foreign Relations. Subcommittee on Multinational Corporations. *The International Telephone and Telegraph Company and Chile, 1970-71: Report to the Committee on Foreign Relations, United States Senate.* Washington, D.C.: U.S. Government Printing Office, 1973. 20 p. (93rd Congress, 1st Session Committee Print.)

INTERNATIONAL UTILITIES CORPORATION

Seabrook, John M. *International Utilities Corporation: A Binational Past and a Multinational Future.* New York: Newcomen Society in North America, 1969. 28 p. (Newcomen Address.)

INVESTORS OVERSEAS SERVICES

Cantor, Bert. *The Bernie Cornfeld Story.* New York: L. Stuart, 1970. 320 p.

Raw, Charles, B. Page, and G. Hodgson. *"Do You Sincerely Want to Be Rich?" The Full Story of Bernard Cornfeld and IOS.* New York: Viking Press, 1971. 400 p.

IOWA BEEF PROCESSORS, INC.

Tinstman, Dale C., and R.L. Peterson. *Iowa Beef Processors, Inc.: An Entire Industry Revolutionized.* New York: Newcomen Society in North America, 1981. 17 p. (Newcomen Publication; no. 1137.)

IRWIN UNION BANK AND TRUST COMPANY

Irwin Union Bank and Trust Company. *History.* Columbus, Ind.: The Company, 1985. 3 p.

ITHACA STREET RAILWAY COMPANY

Kerr, Richard D. *Ithaca Street Railway Company.* Forty Fort, Pa.: Printed and sold by H.E. Cox, 1972. 48 p.

ITT
See:
INTERNATIONAL TELEPHONE AND TELEGRAPH CORPORATION

IVEY (J.B.) AND COMPANY

Ivey, George M. J.B. Ivey and Company: A 75th Anniversary Address, 1900-1975. New York: Newcomen Society in North America, 1975. 18 p. (Newcomen Publication; no. 1016.)

J.C. PENNEY COMPANY, INC.
See:
PENNEY (J.C.) COMPANY, INC.

JACOBS ENGINEERING GROUP, INC.

Jacobs, Joseph J. Jacobs Engineering Group, Inc.: A Story of Pride, Reputation and Integrity. New York: Newcomen Society in North America, 1980. 22 p. (Newcomen Publication; no. 1122.)

JERGENS (ANDREW) COMPANY

Erwin, Paul F. With Lotions of Love. Cincinnati: The Author, 1965. 107 p.

JIM WALTERS CORPORATION
See:
WALTERS (JIM) CORPORATION

JITNEY JUNGLE STORES OF AMERICA

Holman, William H. "Save a Nickel on a Quarter": The Story of Jitney Jungle Stores of America. New York: Newcomen Society in North America, 1974. 30 p.

JOHNS-MANVILLE COMPANY
See:
MANVILLE CORPORATION

JOHNSON AND JOHNSON, INC.

Johnson & Johnson, Inc. *Brief History of Johnson & Johnson.* New Brunswick, N.J.: The Company, 1981. 8 p.

Johnson & Johnson Company. *Update.* Washington, D.C.: Investor Responsibility Research Center, 1984. 18 p.

JONES (J.A.) CONSTRUCTION COMPANY

Jones, Edwin L. *J.A. Jones Construction Company: 75 Years' Growth in Construction.* New York: Newcomen Society in North America, 1965. 28 p. (Newcomen Address.)

JONESBORO, LAKE CITY AND EASTERN RAILROAD

Drew, Lee A. *The JLC&E: The History of an Arkansas Railroad.* State University: Arkansas State University Press, 1968. 121 p.

JOY LINE

Dunbaugh, Edwin. *The Era of the Joy Line: A Saga of Steamboating on Long Island Sound.* Westport, Conn.: Greenwood Press, 1981.

JOY MANUFACTURING COMPANY

"A Tribute to Joseph Francis Joy; Born September 13, 1883." <u>Communique</u> (September 1983). 15 p. (Special Commemorative Issue.)

Drain, James A. <u>Machines that Change the Way the World Works: A Tale of Joy.</u> New York: Newcomen Society in North America, 1968. 24 p. (Newcomen Address.)

K MART
See:
KRESGE (S.S.) COMPANY

KAISER INDUSTRIES CORPORATION

Kaiser Industries Corporation. <u>The Kaiser Story.</u> Oakland: The Company, 1968. 72 p.

KAMAN CORPORATION

Kaman, Charles H. <u>Kaman: Our Early Years.</u> Indianapolis: Curtis Publishing Company, 1985. 175 p.

Kaman, Charles H. <u>Kaman Corporation: An American Story.</u> New York: Newcomen Society in North America, 1983. 24 p. (Newcomen Publication; no. 1200.)

KANSAS CITY CHIEFS

Connor, Dick. <u>Kansas City Chiefs.</u> New York: Macmillan, 1974. 192 p.

KANSAS CITY POWER AND LIGHT COMPANY

Olson, Robert A. *Kansas City Power and Light Company: the First Ninety Years.* New York: Newcomen Society in North America, 1972. 24 p. (Newcomen Address.)

KANSAS CITY SOUTHERN RAILWAY COMPANY

Bryant, Keith L. *Arthur E. Stilwell: Promoter with a Hunch.* Nashville: Vanderbilt University Press, 1971. 256 p.

KANSAS CITY STAR

Kansas City Star. The First 100 Years: A Man, A Newspaper and a City; Centennial Sections, Sunday, September 14, 1980. Kansas City, Mo.: *Kansas City Star*, 1980. 192 p.

KANSAS POWER AND LIGHT COMPANY

Jeffrey, Balfour S. *The Kansas Power and Light Company: Through Fifty Years to the Electric Economy.* New York: Newcomen Society in North America, 1975. 29 p. (Newcomen Publication; no. 1005.)

KAUFMAN AND BROAD, INC.

"Two Decades as a Public Company; Special Report." *Spectrum* (September 1981): 7-10

KELLER MANUFACTURING COMPANY

Kaufman, Charles N. The History of the Keller Manufacturing Company. New York: Arno Press, 1976, c1966.

KELLOGG COMPANY

Kellogg Company. The History of Kellogg's. Battle Creek, Mich.: The Company, 1982. 3 p.

THE KELLOGG (L.D.) LUMBER COMPANY

Kellogg, Walter W. The Kellogg Story: 50 Years in Southern Hardwoods. Monroe, La.: The Company, 1969. 179 p.

THE KELLWOOD COMPANY

The Kellwood Company. Kellwood: A History. St. Louis: The Company, 1981. 20 p.

THE KEMPER GROUP

The Kemper Group. Presenting the Kemper Group. Long Grove, Ill.: The Company, 1983. 20 p.

KENNAMETAL, INC.

McKenna, Donald C. The Roots of Kennametal: Or Philip McKenna and How He Grew. Latrobe, Pa.: The Company, 1974. 32 p.

KENRICK (ARCHIBALD) AND SONS

Church, Roy A. Kenricks in Hardware; A Family Business, 1791-1966. New York: A.M. Kelley Publishers, 1969. 340 p.

KENTUCKY CENTRAL LIFE INSURANCE COMPANY

"Kentucky Central, State's Oldest Life Insurer, Now One of the Nation's Largest." Kincaid Towers (1980): 16-21.

KENTUCKY FINANCE COMPANY, INC.

"Kincaid Started Kentucky Finance Company from Scratch." Kincaid Towers (1980): 36-39.

KENTUCKY FRIED CHICKEN

Pearce, John E. The Colonel: The Captivating Biography of the Dynamic Founder of Fast-Food Empire. Garden City, N.Y.: Doubleday, 1982. 225 p.

Sanders, Harland. The Incredible Colonel. Carol Stream, Ill.: Creation House, 1974. 144 p.

Sanders, Harland. Life as I Have Known It Has Been Finger Lickin' Good. Carol Stream, Ill.: Creation House, 1974. 144 p.

KENTUCKY HILLS INDUSTRIES

Ross, Smith G. Come Go With Me. Pine Knot, Ky.: The Company, 1977. 152 p.

KERITE COMPANY

Rudd, Theodore O. A Century of Cable Making: The Kerite Company, 1854-1966. New York: Newcomen Society in North America, 1966. 28 p. (Newcomen Address.)

KERR-MCGEE CORPORATION

Ezell, John Samuel. Innovations in Energy: The Story of Kerr-McGee. Norman: University of Oklahoma Press, 1979. 542 p.

McGee, Dean A. Evolution into Total Energy: The Story of Kerr-McGee Corporation. New York: Newcomen Society in North America, 1971. 24 p. (Newcomen Address.)

KERR-MCGEE NUCLEAR CORPORATION

Kohn, Howard. Who Killed Karen Silkwood? New York: Summit Books, 1981. 462 p.

Rashke, Richard L. The Killing of Karen Silkwood: The Story Behind the Kerr-McGee Plutonium Case. Boston: Houghton Mifflin, 1981. 407 p.

KEWANEE OIL COMPANY

Kewanee Oil Company. *Kewanee Oil Company, 1871-1971: 100 Years of Beginning.* Bryn Mawr, Pa.: The Company, 1971. 34 p.

KEY BANKS, INC.

Key Banks, Inc. *Key Banks, Inc.: A Short History.* Albany, N.Y.: The Bank, 1985. 4 p.

Key Banks, Inc. *Key Banks, Inc.: Milestones.* Albany, N.Y.: The Company, 1985. 3 p.

KIDDER, PEABODY, AND COMPANY

Carosso, Vincent P. *More than a Century of Investment Banking: The Kidder, Peabody & Company Story.* New York: McGraw-Hill, 1979. 212 p.

KIEWIT (PETER) SONS, INC.

Limprecht, Hollis. *The Kiewit Story: Remarkable Man, Remarkable Company.* Omaha: H.J. Limprecht; Omaha World-Herald Company, 1981. 294 p.

KNOX INDUSTRIAL SUPPLIES

"Knox celebrates 50 years of teamwork." *Industrial Distribution* 72 (November 1982): 81+.

KODAK (EASTMAN) COMPANY

Eastman Kodak Company. *A Brief History.* Rochester, N.Y.: The Company, 1983. 11 p.

Eastman Kodak Company. *Kodak Milestones.* Rochester, N.Y.: The Company, 1982. 32 p.

KRESGE (S.S.) COMPANY

Kresge, Stanley Sebastian. *The S.S. Kresge Story.* Racine, Wis.: Western Publishing Company, 1979. 373 p.

THE KROGER COMPANY

Laycock, George. *The Kroger Story: A Century of Innovation.* Cincinnati: The Company, 1983. 143 p.

"The Kroger Story." *Dallas Times Herald Sunday Magazine* (18 June 1967): 1-16.

KRUEGER (W.A.) COMPANY

Wells, Robert W., and Robert A. Klaus. *We Have with Us Today: W.A. Krueger Company, 1934-1974.* Scottsdale, Ariz.: The Company, 1974. 219 p.

KUHN, LOEB AND COMPANY

Kuhn, Loeb and Company. *A Century of Investment Banking.* New York: The Company, 1967. 52 p.

KWIK-KOPY CORPORATION

Palmer, Peggy. *An American Original: The Story of Kwik-Kopy Printing.* Houston: D. Armstrong Co., 1981. 138 p.

LAKER AIRWAYS

Banks, Howard. *The Rise and Fall of Freddie Laker.* Winchester, Mass.: Faber and Faber, 1982. 155 p.

Eglin, Roger, and B. Ritchie. *Fly Me, I'm Freddie!: The Life and Times of the Man Who Broke the Airline Cartel and Made Air Travel Available to Everyone.* New York: Rawson, Wade, 1980. 238 p.

LAMSON AND SESSIONS COMPANY

Case, George S., Jr. *Lamson and Sessions-- Starting a Second Century of Industrial Fastener Development and Production.* New York: Newcomen Society in North America, 1965. 24 p. (Newcomen Address.)

LANCE, INC.

Van Every, Philip Lance. *The History of Lance.* New York: Newcomen Society in North America, 1974. 16 p. (Newcomen Publication; no. 1002.)

LAND O'LAKES CREAMERIES, INC.

Ruble, Kenneth Douglas. *Land O'Lakes: Farmers Make It Happen.* Minneapolis: The Company, 1973. 205 p.

LANE PUBLISHING COMPANY

Holt, Patricia. "Lane Publishing Company Celebrates a Half-Century in the West." *Publishers Weekly* 215 (12 March 1979): 37+.

Lane, L.W., Jr. *The Sunset Story: "To Serve the Westerner--and No One Else."* New York: Newcomen Society in North America, 1973. 29 p. (Newcomen Address.)

LASKY COMPANY

Lasky Company. *The First 50 Years.* Newark, N.J.: The Company, 1967. 32 p.

LAUDER (ESTEE)

Lauder, Estee. *Estee: A Success Story.* New York: Random House, 1985. 222 p.

LEA AND FEBIGER

Bussy, R. Kenneth. *Two Hundred Years of Publishing: A History of the Oldest Publishing Company in the United States, Lea & Febiger, 1785-1985.* Philadelphia: Lea & Febiger, 1985. 126 p.

LEAR SIEGLER, INC.

Brooks, John G. <u>Planning for Growth and Profit: The Success Story of Lear Siegler, Inc.</u> New York: Newcomen Society in North America, 1970. 28 p. (Newcomen Address.)

LEASCO DATA PROCESSING EQUIPMENT CORPORATION

Glasberg, Davita Silfen. "Corporate Power and Control: The Case of Leasco Corporation Versus Chemical Bank." <u>Social Problems</u> 29 (December 1981): 104-116.

LEAVELL COMPANY

Lynde, Bill. <u>The Leavell Story: The Man and His Work, 1933-1983.</u> El Paso, Tex.: Guynes Print Company, 1983. 83 p.

LEE AND SHEPARD, PUBLISHERS

Kilgour, Raymond Lincoln. <u>Lee and Shepard, Publishers for the People.</u> Hamden, Conn.: Shoe String Press, 1965. 306 p.

LEHMAN BROTHERS KUHN LOEB

Auletta, Ken. <u>Greed and Glory on Wall Street: The Fall of the House of Lehman.</u> New York: Random House, 1986. 253 p.

LEISY BREWING COMPANY

Leisy, Bruce R. A History of the Leisy Brewing Companies. North Newton, Kan.: Mennonite Press, 1975. 106 p.

LEPAGE (F.R.) BAKERY, INC.

Lepage, Regis A. Seventy Years of Quality: The F.R. Lepage Bakery, Inc. Story. New York: Newcomen Society in North America, 1973. 20 p.

LEVI STRAUSS AND COMPANY

Cray, Ed. Levi's. Boston: Houghton Mifflin, 1978. 286 p.

Grether, E.T. "Four Men and a Company: Levi Strauss Since World War I." California Management Review 20 (Fall 1977): 14-20.

LEVITZ FURNITURE CORPORATION

Martindale, Wight. We Do It Every Day: The Story Behind the Success of Levitz Furniture. New York: Fairchild Publications, 1972. 150 p.

LEWIS GROCER COMPANY

Lewis, Morris, Jr. Wholesaler--Retailer: The Story of Lewis Grocer Company and Sunflower Food Stores. New York: Newcomen Society in North America, 1975. 21 p. (Newcomen Publication; no. 1021.)

THE LIBERTY CORPORATION

Hipp, Francis M. *The Liberty Corporation: A Success Story of the Changing South.* New York: Newcomen Society in North America, 1982. 20 p. (Newcomen Publication; no. 1157.)

LIFE INSURANCE COMPANY OF VIRGINIA

Sanford, James K., and Robert B. Lancaster. *Century One, One Hundred Years of the Life Insurance Company of Virginia.* Richmond: The Company, 1971. 120 p.

LIGGERT GROUP, INC.

Liggert Group. *The Companies of Your Pleasure.* Montvale, N.J.: The Company, 1977. 32 p.

LILLY (ELI) AND COMPANY

Kahn, E.J. *All in a Century: The First 100 Years of Eli Lilly and Company.* West Cornwall, Conn.: Kahn, 1975. 211 p.

THE LIMITED, INC.

The Limited, Inc. *The Pursuit of Excellence.* Columbus, Ohio: The Company, 1985. 4 p.

THE LINCOLN TELEPHONE AND TELEGRAPH COMPANY

Geist, James E. The Lincoln Telephone and Telegraph Company: The Great Independent. New York: Newcomen Society in North America, 1979. 21 p. (Newcomen Publication; no. 1104.)

LING-TEMCO-VOUGHT, INC.

Brown, Stanley H. Ling: The Rise, Fall and Return of a Texas Titan. New York: Atheneum, 1972. 308 p.

Jacobs, Donald. "An Account and Evaluation of James Ling's Rise and Fall with Ling-Temco-Vought." Ph.D. diss., University of Nebraska, 1977. 208 p.

LIONEL TRAIN COMPANY

Hollander, Ron. All Aboard!: The Story of Joshua Lionel Cowen and His Lionel Train Company. New York: Workman Pub., 1981. 253 p.

LIPPINCOTT (J.B) COMPANY

J.B. Lippincott Company. The Author and His Audience; With a Chronology of Major Events in the Publishing History of J.B. Lippincott. Philadelphia: The Company, 1967. 79 p.

THE LITTLETON SAVINGS BANK

McLaughlin, Ambrose P. *To Rise Above a Village We Need a Bank!: The Story of the Littleton Savings Bank, 1868-1968.* New York: Newcomen Society in North America, 1968. 24 p. (Newcomen Address.)

LITTON INDUSTRIES, INC.

Lay, Beirne. *Someone Has to Make It Happen: The Inside Story of Tex Thornton, The Man Who Built Litton Industries.* Englewood Cliffs, N.J.: Prentice-Hall, 1969. 204 p.

LOCKHEED AIRCRAFT CORPORATION

Anderson, Roy A. *A Look at Lockheed.* New York: Newcomen Society in North America, 1983. 52 p. (Newcomen Publication; no. 1186.)

Boulton, David. *The Grease Machine.* New York: Harper & Row, 1978. 289 p.

"A History of Lockheed." *Lockheed Horizons* 12 (1983) 1-156. (Special Issue.)

LOCKHEED-GEORGIA COMPANY

Rice, Berkely. *The C-5A Scandal; An Inside Story of the Military-Industrial Complex.* Boston: Houghton Mifflin, 1971. 238 p.

LOCTITE CORPORATION

Grant, Ellsworth S. *Drop by Drop: The Loctite Story, 1953-1980.* Newington, Conn.: The Company, 1983. 156 p.

LONE STAR GAS COMPANY

The Lone Star Gas Company. *The First Seventy-five Years: A Pictorial History of the Lone Star Gas Company, 1909-1984.* Dallas: The Company, 1984. 116 p.

LORD, ABBET AND COMPANY

Driscoll, Robert S. *The Story of Lord, Abbet and Company and Affiliated Fund, Inc.: A View of the Capital Needs of the U.S. Economy.* New York: Newcomen Society in North America, 1974. (Newcomen Publication; no. 999.)

LORD CORPORATION

Lord, Thomas. *Lord Corporation: A Story of Innovation, Invention, and Learning.* New York: Newcomen Society in North America, 1974. 34 p. (Newcomen Publication; no. 982.)

LOS ANGELES DODGERS

Gewecke, Clifford George. *Day by Day in Dodgers History.* New York: Leisure Press, 1984. 336 p.

Schoor, Gene. *A Pictorial History of the Dodgers: Brooklyn to Los Angeles.* New York: Leisure Press, 1985.

Whittingham, Richard. *The Los Angeles Dodgers: An Illustrated History.* New York: Harper & Row, 1982. 256 p.

LOS ANGELES RAMS

Bisheff, Steve. *Los Angeles Rams.* New York: Macmillan, 1973. 192 p.

LOS ANGELES TIMES

Gottlieb, Robert, and Irene Wolt. *Thinking Big: The Story of the Los Angeles Times, Its Publishers and Their Influence on Southern California.* New York: Putnam, 1977. 603 p.

Hart, Jack R. *The Information Empire: The Rise of the Los Angeles Times and Times Mirror Corporation.* Washington, D.C.: University Press of America, 1981. 410 p.

LOUISIANA-PACIFIC

Louisiana-Pacific. *The L-P Originals.* Portland, Oreg.: The Company, 1983. 19 p. (Special tenth anniversary issue of *Momentum*, the company magazine.)

LOUISIANA POWER AND LIGHT COMPANY

Louisiana Power and Light Company. *50 Years of Service, 1927-1977.* New Orleans: The Company, 1977. 77 p.

LOUISVILLE AND NASHVILLE RAILROAD COMPANY

Klein, Maury. *History of the Louisville and Nashville Railroad.* New York: Macmillan, 1972. 572 p.

LTV CORPORATION

LTV Corporation. *A History of the LTV Corporation.* Dallas: The Company, 1984. 3 p.

LTV Corporation. *LTV Looking Ahead.* Dallas: The Company, 1980. 71 p.

LUBRIZOL CORPORATION

Smalheer, Calvin V. *The Story of Lubrizol.* Cleveland: The Company, 1972. 88 p.

LUCAS INDUSTRIES

Nockolds, Harold. *Lucas: The First Hundred Years.* North Pomfret, Vt.: David & Charles, 1976-1978. 2 vols.

LUFKIN INDUSTRIES, INC.

Jackson, Elaine. *From Sawdust to Oil; A History of Lufkin Industries, Inc.*

Lufkin, Tex.: Gulf Publishing Company, 1982. 241 p.

Poland, Robert L. *Lufkin Industries, Inc.: Unique in the South.* New York: Newcomen Society in North America, 1972. 31 p. (Newcomen Address.)

LUKENS, INC.

DiOrio, Eugene L. *Lukens: Remarkable Past--Promising Future.* Coatesville, Pa.: The Company, 1985. 31 p.

THE LUNKENHEIMER COMPANY

Laux, James M. "The One and Only Great Name in Valves; A History of the Lunkenheimer Company." *Queen City Heritage* 41 (Spring 1983): 17-38.

MCCLURE'S MAGAZINE

Wilson, Harold S. *McClure's Magazine and the Muckrakers.* Princeton: Princeton University Press, 1970. 347 p.

MCCORMICK AND COMPANY, INC.

McCormick and Company, Inc. *This is McCormick.* Hunt Valley, Md.: The Company, 1984. 5 p.

MCCRORY CORPORATION

Chain Store Age. *Evolution of a Revolution.* New York: Chain Store Age, 1970. 100 p.

MACDONALD (E.F.) COMPANY

MacDonald, Elton F. <u>Money Isn't Everything!: The Story of the E.F. MacDonald Company.</u> New York: Newcomen Society in North America, 1966. 24 p. (Newcomen Address.)

MCDONALD'S CORPORATION

Boas, Max, and Steve Chain. <u>Big Mac: The Unauthorized Story of McDonald's.</u> New York: New American Library, 1977, c1976. 185 p.

Kroc, Ray, with Robert Anderson. <u>Grinding It Out: The Making of McDonald's.</u> Chicago: H. Regenery, 1977. 201 p.

McDonald's Corporation. <u>McDonald's History Listing.</u> Oak Brook, Ill.: The Company, 1985. 6 p.

MCDONNELL DOUGLAS CORPORATION

Francillon, Rene J. <u>McDonnell Douglas Aircraft Since 1920.</u> London: Putnam, 1979. 721 p.

Ingells, Douglas J. <u>The McDonnell Douglas Story.</u> Fallbrook, Calif.: Aero Publishers, 1979.

Pisney, Raymond F. "James S. McDonnell and His Company: A Vision of Flight and Space." <u>Gateway Heritage</u> 2 (June 1981): 2-17.

Yenne, Bill. _McDonnell Douglas: A Tale of Two Giants._ New York: Crescent Books, 1985. 256 p.

MCGRAW-EDISON COMPANY

Williams, Edward Joseph. _Partners in Success: The Story of McGraw-Edison Company._ New York: Newcomen Society in North America, 1978. 20 p. (Newcomen Publication; no. 1072.)

MCGRAW-HILL BOOK COMPANY

McGraw-Hill Book Company. _Imprint: the McGraw-Hill Book Company Story-- Learning, Information, and Entertainment._ New York: The Company, 1967. 55 p.

MACK TRUCKS, INC.

Hansen, Zenon C.R. _The Legend of the Bulldog._ New York: Newcomen Society in North America, 1974. 43 p. (Newcomen Publication; no. 988.)

Montiville, John B. _Mack: a Living Legend of the Highway._ Tucson: Aztex Corporation, 1981. 219 p.

MCKIM, MEAD AND WHITE

Roth, Leland M. _McKim, Mead & White, Architects._ New York: Harper & Row, 1983. 441 p.

MACLEAN-HUNTER

Chalmers, Floyd S. <u>A Gentleman of the Press: The Story of Colonel John Bayne Maclean and the Publishing Empire He Founded.</u> Garden City, N.Y.: Doubleday, 1969. 368 p.

MACMILLAN BLOEDEL LIMITED

MacKay, Donald. <u>Empire of Wood; The MacMillan Bloedel Story.</u> Seattle: University of Washington Press, 1982. 361 p.

MCNALLY PITTSBURGH

McNally, Edward T. <u>The McNally Story.</u> New York: Newcomen Society in North America, 1973. 35 p.

Mahan, Ernest. <u>The History of McNally Pittsburgh.</u> Wichita, Kan.: McCormick-Armstrong Company, 1972. 270 p.

MCRAE'S DEPARTMENT STORES

McRae, Richard Duncan. <u>Main Entrance in Mississippi: The McRae Story.</u> New York: Newcomen Society in North America, 1971. 21 p. (Newcomen Address.)

MACY (R.H.) AND COMPANY, INC.

Johnson, Curtiss S. <u>America's First Lady Boss; A Wisp of a Girl, Macy's and</u>

Romance. New York: Taplinger, 1965. 164 p.

R.H. Macy and Company, Inc. Macy's New York: 125th Anniversary, 1858-1983. New York: The Company, 1983. 4 p.

MADERA SUGAR PINE COMPANY

Johnston, Hank. Thunder in the Mountains; The Life and Times of Madera Sugar Pine. Los Angeles: Trans-Anglo Books, 1968. 128 p.

MADISON BANK AND TRUST COMPANY

Madison Bank & Trust Company. Sesqui-Centennial; 150 Years of Progress in Banking, 1833-1983. Madison, Ind.: The Bank, 1983. 12 p. (Published as a supplement to the Madison Courier, June 21, 1983.)

MAGIC CHEF, INC.

Rymer, S.B. The Magic Chef Story. New York: Newcomen Society in North America, 1979. 24 p. (Newcomen Publication; no. 1117.)

MAIN (C.T.) CORPORATION

Hall, W.M. Chas T. Main, Inc.: A Professional Legacy. New York: Newcomen Society in North America, 1975. 31 p. (Newcomen Publication; no. 1025.)

MAINE CENTRAL RAILROAD

Miller, E. Spencer. Maine Central Railroad, 1940-1978. New York: Newcomen Society in North America, 1979. 52 p. (Newcomen Publication; no. 1110.)

MANHATTAN LIFE INSURANCE COMPANY

Buck, Wendell. From Quill Pens to Computers: An Account of the First One Hundred and Twenty-five Years of the Manhattan Life Insurance Company of New York. New York: The Company, 1975. 156 p.

MANSIONS AND MILLIONAIRES, INC.

Travis, Arlene, and Carole Aronson. Mansions and Millionaires: Their Story, Their Style. Greenvale, N.Y.: The Company, 1983. 119 p.

MANVILLE CORPORATION

Brodeur, Paul. An Industry on Trial. New York: Pantheon Books, 1984.

Goodwin, W. Richard. The Johns-Manville Story. New York: Newcomen Society in North America, 1972. 16 p. (Newcomen Address.)

Johns-Manville Corporation. Johns-Manville People: An Odyssey of Progress. Denver: The Company, 1976. 32 p.

MAPCO, INC.

Jarman, Rufus. <u>The Energy Merchants.</u> New
   York: Rosen Press, 1977. 279 p.

Thomas, Robert E. <u>From a Dream to a
   "Scrappy" Little Pipeline to a
   National Leader in Energy.</u> New York:
   Newcomen Society in North America,
   1976. 19 p. (Newcomen Publication; no.
   1039.)

MARLIN FIREARMS COMPANY

Kenna, Frank. <u>The Marlin Story.</u> New York:
   Newcomen Society in North America,
   1975. 24 p. (Newcomen Publication; no.
   1011.)

MARSH AND MCLENNAN COMPANIES

"Founding Fathers: The History of Marsh
   and McLennan Companies." <u>M 8</u>
   (September 1981): 1-8.

Souder, William F., Jr. <u>Marsh and
   McLennan: A Century of Insurance
   Service 1871-1971.</u> New York: Newcomen
   Society in North America, 1971. 20 p.
   (Newcomen Address.)

MARSH SUPERMARKETS, INC.

<u>Lasting Values: The First Half-Century of
   Marsh Supermarkets, Inc.</u> Yorktown,
   Ind.: The Company, 1984. 214 p.

MARTIN MARIETTA CORPORATION

Cunningham, Mary. <u>Powerplay: What Really Happened at Bendix.</u> New York: Linden Press/Simon & Schuster, 1984. 286 p.

Hartz, Peter F. <u>Merger; The Exclusive Inside Story of the Bendix-Martin-Marietta Takeover War.</u> New York: Morrow, 1985. 418 p.

Lambert, Hope. <u>Till Death Do Us Part: Bendix vs. Martin Marietta.</u> San Diego: Harcourt Brace Jovanovich, 1983. 264 p.

Sloan, Allan. <u>Three Plus One Equals Billions: The Bendix-Martin Marietta War.</u> New York: Arbor House, 1983. 270 p.

MARY KAY COSMETICS

Ash, Mary K. <u>Mary Kay.</u> New York: Harper & Row, 1981. 206 p.

Shook, Robert L. "Mary Kay Ash." In <u>The Entrepreneurs</u>, 103-114. New York: Harper & Row, 1980.

MASCO CORPORATION

Masco Corporation. <u>Masco 50: The First Fifty Years, 1929-79.</u> Taylor, Mich.: The Company, 1979. 15 p.

MASSON (PAUL) VINEYARDS

Balzer, Robert L. <u>Uncommon Heritage; The Paul Masson Story.</u> Los Angeles: Ward Richie Press, 1970. 118 p.

MATSON NAVIGATION COMPANY

Worden, William L. <u>Cargoes: Matson's First Century in the Pacific.</u> Honolulu: University of Hawaii, 1981. 192 p.

MATTEL, INC.

Handler, Elliot. <u>The Impossible Really Is Possible: The Story of Mattel.</u> New York: Newcomen Society in North America, 1968. 28 p. (Newcomen Address.)

MAYER (OSCAR) AND COMPANY

Mayer, Oscar G. <u>Oscar Mayer & Company: From Corner Store to National Processor.</u> New York: Newcomen Society in North America, 1970. 24 p. (Newcomen Address.)

MAYTAG COMPANY

Maytag Company. <u>Brief History of the Maytag Company.</u> Newton, Iowa: The Company, 1985. 3 p.

"Maytag." <u>Merchandiser</u> 27, no.2 (1982) (Anniversary issue.)

MCI COMMUNICATIONS CORPORATION

Kahaner, Larry. On the Line; The Men of MCI--Who Took on AT&T, Risked Everything, and Won. New York: Random House, 1986. 327 p.

Shook, Robert L. "William G. McGowen." In The Entrepreneurs, 139-156. New York: Harper & Row, 1980.

MEAD CORPORATION

Maurer, Herrymon. In Quiet Ways: George H. Mead, the Man and the Company. Dayton, Ohio: The Company, 1970. 307 p.

MEDIA NETWORKS, INC.

Shook, Robert L. "Dale W. Lang." In The Entrepreneurs, 53-65. New York: Harper & Row, 1980.

MEIJER, INC.

Meijer, Hendrik G. Thrifty Years: The Life of Hendrik Meijer. Grand Rapids, Mich.: Erdmans, 1984. 246 p.

MELROE COMPANY

Karolevitz, Robert F. "E.G.," Inventor by Necessity; The Story of E.G. Melroe and the Melroe Company. Aberdeen, S.D.: North Plains Press, 1968. 160 p.

MELVILLE SHOE CORPORATION

Rooney, Francis C., Jr. Creative Merchandising in an Era of Change. New York: Newcomen Society in North America, 1970. 24 p. (Newcomen Address.)

MERCANTILE NATIONAL BANK, DALLAS

Francis, J.D. The Growing Story of the Mercantile National Bank. New York: Newcomen Society in North America, 1972. 20 p. (Newcomen Address.)

MERCANTILE STORES COMPANY, INC.

Newcomb, William A. Mercantile Stores Company, Inc.: A Profile of a Growing Retail Enterprise. Wilmington, Del. Mercantile Stores Co., Inc. 1975. 131 p.

MERCHANTS NATIONAL BANK AND TRUST COMPANY OF INDIANAPOLIS

Frenzel, Otto N., Jr. The City and the Bank 1865-1965: The Story of Merchants National and Trust Company of Indianapolis. New York: Newcomen Society in North America, 1965. 24 p. (Newcomen Address.)

Jarvis, Helen R. The City and the Bank, 1865-1965; The Story of 100 Years in the Life of Indianapolis and the

Merchants National Bank & Trust Company of Indianapolis. Indianapolis: Benham Press, 1965. 114 p.

MERCHANTS NATIONAL BANK AND TRUST COMPANY OF SYRACUSE

Melvin, Crandall. A History of the Merchants National Bank and Trust Company of Syracuse, New York; One Hundred Eighteen Years. Syracuse: Syracuse University, 1969. 158 p.

MERRELL DOW PHARMACEUTICALS

Enck, Henry Snyder. "William Stanley Merrell, Cincinnati Industrialist." Thesis, University of Cincinnati, 1965.

MERRILL BANKSHARES COMPANY

Grant, John F. Merrill Bankshares Company: "--Business Talents and Devotion to Those Highest Commercial Principles which Underlie the Truest and Most Enduring Success." New York, Newcomen Society in North America, 1977. 22 p. (Newcomen Publication; no. 1066.)

MERRILL LYNCH

Regan, Donald T. The Merrill Lynch Story. New York: Newcomen Society in North America, 1981. 22 p. (Newcomen Publication; no. 1142.)

MERRILL TRANSPORT COMPANY

Merrill, Paul E. Forty-six Years a Truckman: The Story of Merrill Transport Company. New York: Newcomen Society in North America, 1975. 26 p. (Newcomen Publication; no. 1023.)

METRO-GOLDWYN-MAYER, INC.

Eames, John Douglas. The MGM Story: The Complete History of Fifty Roaring Years. New York: Crown Publishers, 1975. 400 p.

Easton, Carol. The Search for Sam Goldwyn; A Biography. New York: Morrow, 1976, c1975. 304 p.

Marx, Arthur. Goldwyn: A Biography of the Man Behind the Myth. New York: Norton, 1976. 376 p.

Metro-Goldwyn-Mayer, Inc. Corporate History. Culver City, Calif.: The Company, 1978. 4 p.

METROMEDIA, INC.

Kluge, John W. The Metromedia Story. New York: Newcomen Society in North America, 1974. 18 p.

MIAMI DOLPHINS

McLemore, Morris T. The Miami Dolphins. Garden City, N.Y.: Doubleday, 1972. 343 p.

MICHIGAN NATIONAL BANK

Poll, Richard D. <u>Howard J. Stoddard, Founder, Michigan National Bank.</u> East Lansing: Michigan State University Press, 1980. 257 p.

MIDLAND MUTUAL LIFE INSURANCE COMPANY

McIntosh, James B. <u>The Midland Mutual Life Insurance Company: "The Pearl of the Midwest."</u> New York: Newcomen Society in North America, 1972. 17 p. (Newcomen Address.)

MIDSTATE AIRLINES

Midstate Airlines. <u>Midstate Airlines: More than Two Decades of Service.</u> Stevens Point, Wis.: The Company, 1985. 4 p.

MIDWAY AIRLINES

Midway Airlines. <u>The Midway Story.</u> Chicago: The Company, 1985. 4 p.

MIKE-SELL'S POTATO CHIP COMPANY

Mapp, Leslie C. <u>"A Common Thing Done Uncommonly Well": The Story of the Mike-Sell's Potato Chip Company.</u> New York: Newcomen Society of the United States, 1985. 19 p. (Newcomen Publication; no. 1236.)

MILES LABORATORIES, INC.

Compton, Walter A. Serving Needs in Health and Nutrition: The Story of Miles Laboratories, Inc. New York: Newcomen Society in North America, 1973. 24 p.

Cray, William C. Miles: A Centennial History, 1884-1984. Englewood Cliffs, N.J.: Prentice-Hall, 1984. 277 p.

Miles Laboratories, Inc. Miles: Our First Century, 1884-1984. Elkhart, Ind.: The Company, 1984. 20 p.

MILLER MANUFACTURING COMPANY, INC.

Mattison, Lewis C. Forests, Wood products, and Homes; The Story of the Miller Manufacturing Company, Inc., 1897-1972. Richmond: Whittet and Shepperson, 1972. 56 p.

MILTON BRADLEY COMPANY
See:
BRADLEY (MILTON) COMPANY

MILTON ROY COMPANY

Sheen, Robert T. The Milton Roy Story: From a Basement Workshop to a Professionally Managed Public Company. New York: Newcomen Society in North America, 1972. 28 p. (Newcomen Address.)

MINIATURE PRECISION BEARINGS, INC.

Hill, Evan. <u>Beanstalk; The History of Miniature Precision Bearings, Inc., 1941-1966.</u> Keene, N.H.: The Company, 1966. 188 p.

MINNEAPOLIS STAR AND TRIBUNE COMPANY

Morison, Bradley L. <u>Sunlight on Your Doorsteps: The</u> Minneapolis Tribune<u>'s First Hundred Years, 1867-1967.</u> Minneapolis: Ross & Haines, Inc., 1966. 149 p.

MINNESOTA TRANSFER RAILWAY COMPANY

Stottlemyr, John M. <u>The First 100 Years: A History of the Minnesota Transfer Railway Company.</u> Minneapolis: The Company, 1982. 16 p.

MINNESOTA VIKINGS

Diamond, Jeff. <u>The First Fifteen Years: Vikings, 1961-1975.</u> Minneapolis: Minnesota Vikings, 1976. 76 p.

MINUTE MAID CORPORATION

Harris, Sara, and Robert Francis Allen. <u>The Quiet Revolution: The Story of a Small Miracle in American Life.</u> New York: Rawson Associates Publishers, 1978. 283 p.

MISSISSIPPI POWER COMPANY

Watson, A.J., Jr. Electric Power and People Power: The Story of the Mississippi Power Company. New York: Newcomen Society in North America, 1969. 24 p. (Newcomen Address.)

MISSOURI PACIFIC CORPORATION

Jenks, Downing B. The Missouri Pacific Story. New York: Newcomen Society in North America, 1977. 15 p. (Newcomen Publication; no. 1065.)

Miner, H. Craig. The Rebirth of the Missouri Pacific, 1956-1983. College Station: Texas A&M University Press, 1983. 236 p.

THE MISSOURI PUBLIC SERVICE COMPANY

Green, Richard C. The Missouri Public Service Company: A Saga of Free Enterprise. New York: Newcomen Society in North America, 1967. 28 p. (Newcomen Address.)

MOBIL OIL CORPORATION

Socony Mobil Oil Company, Inc. Mobil Oil Corporation; A Report to the Financial Community. New York, 1966. 60 p.

Warner, Rawleigh, Jr. Mobil Oil: A View from the Second Century. New York: Newcomen Society in North America, 1966. 24 p. (Newcomen Address.)

THE MONARCH MACHINE TOOL COMPANY

The Monarch Machine Tool Company. <u>The Seventy-fifth Year.</u> Sidney, Ohio: The Company, 1984. 8 p.

MONSANTO COMPANY

Forrestal, Dan J. <u>Faith, Hope, and $5,000: The Story of Monsanto: The Trials and Triumphs of the First 75 Years.</u> New York: Simon & Schuster, 1977. 185 p.

Levinson, Harry, and Stuart Rosenthal. "John W. Hanley." In <u>CEO: Corporate Leadership in Action</u>, 137-176. New York: Basic Books, 1984.

MONTANA-DAKOTA UTILITIES COMPANY

Montana-Dakota Utilities Company. <u>The First 50 Years.</u> Bismarck: The Company, 1979. 28 p.

MONTGOMERY WARD AND COMPANY

Herndon, Bootan. <u>Satisfaction Guaranteed; An Unconventional Report to Today's Consumers.</u> New York: McGraw-Hill, 1972. 342 p.

Latham, Frank Brown. <u>1872-1972: A Century of Serving Consumers; The Story of Montgomery Ward.</u> 2nd ed. Chicago: The Company, 1972. 95 p.

MORAN TOWING AND TRANSPORTATION COMPANY, INC.

Moran, Edmond J. The Moran Story. New York: Newcomen Society in North America, 1965. 24 p. (Newcomen Address.)

MORGAN (J.P.) AND COMPANY

Hoyt, Edwin P., Jr. The House of Morgan. New York: Dodd, Mead and Company, 1966. 428 p.

MORGAN STANLEY AND COMPANY, INC.

Morgan Stanley and Company, Inc. Morgan Stanley 1970. New York: The Company, 1971. 83 p.

MORTON THIOKOL, INC.

Morton Thiokol, Inc. The Right Chemistry: A History of Morton Thiokol, Inc. Chicago: The Company, 1985. 15 p.

MOTOROLA, INC.

Colletti, Jerome A. Profit Sharing and Employee Attitudes; A Case Study of the Deferred Profit-Sharing Program at Motorola, Inc. Madison: Center for the Study of Productivity Motivation, University of Wisconsin, 1967. 96 p.

Petrakis, Harry Mark. A Founder's Touch: The Life of Paul Galvin of Motorola. New York: McGraw-Hill, 1965. 240 p.

MOTOWN RECORD CORPORATION

Benjaminson, Peter. The Story of Motown. New York: Grove Press, 1979. 180 p.

Martin, Sandra Pratt. Inside Motown; The Million Dollar Story of the Black Sound. New York: Drake, 1974.

Waller, Don. The Motown Story. New York: Scribner's, 1985. 256 p.

MOUNT HOPE FINISHING COMPANY

Davis, Burke. A Fierce Personal Pride: The History of Mount Hope Finishing Company and Its Founding Family. Butner, N.C.: The Company, 1981. 167 p.

MOUNT WASHINGTON RAILWAY COMPANY

Teague, Ellen C. Mount Washington Railway Company: World's First Cog Railway, Mount Washington, New Hampshire. New York: Newcomen Society in North America, 1970. 28 p.

MOUNTAIN BELL

Harden, H. "100 Years of Service." Telephony 196 (2 April 1979): 50-52

MPI INDUSTRIES, INC.

Ryan, Charles B. Molding Its Future with Wood and Plastic: The Story of MPI

Industries, Inc. New York: Newcomen Society in North America, 1968. 24 p. (Newcomen Address.)

MUNFORD, INC.

Munford, Dillard. Munford, Inc.: A Brief History. New York: Newcomen Society in North America, 1974. 16 p.

MUTUAL BENEFIT LIFE INSURANCE COMPANY

Mutual Benefit Life Insurance Company. A Brief History. Newark: The Company, 1966. 32 p.

NABISCO BRANDS, INC.

Cahn, William. Out of the Cracker Barrel: The Nabisco Story from Animal Crackers to Zuzus. New York: Simon and Schuster, 1969. 367 p.

NALCO CHEMICAL COMPANY

Nalco Chemical Company. 50 years of Progress. Oak Brook, Ill.: The Company, 1978. 13 p.

NASH FINCE COMPANY

Nash Finch Company. 100 Years: 1885-1985. St. Louis Park, Minn.: The Company, 1984. 40 p.

NATIONAL AIRLINES, INC.

Cearley, George Walker, Jr. National "Airlines of the Stars": An Illustrated History. Dallas: G.W. Cearley, Jr., 1985. 96 p.

Williams, Brad. The Anatomy of an Airline. New York: Doubleday, 1970. 233 p.

THE NATIONAL BANK OF COMMERCE OF SEATTLE

Marple, Elliot, and Bruce H. Olson. The National Bank of Commerce of Seattle, 1889-1969; Territorial to Worldwide Banking in Eighty Years, Including the Story of the Marine Bancorporation. Palo Alto, Calif.: Pacific Books, 1972. 277 p.

NATIONAL BANK OF COMMERCE TRUST AND SAVINGS ASSOCIATION

Yaussi, Glenn. National Bank of Commerce: Seventy-five Years of Service to Nebraska. New York: Newcomen Society in North America, 1977. 18 p. (Newcomen Publication; no. 1071.)

NATIONAL BANK OF DETROIT

National Bank of Detroit. History of NBD. Detroit, Mich.: The Bank, 1985. 22 p.

NATIONAL BISCUIT COMPANY

Cahn, William. *Out of the Cracker Barrel: The Nabisco Story from Animal Crackers to Zuzus.* New York: Simon and Schuster, 1969. 367 p.

NATIONAL CAN CORPORATION

Stuart, Robert D. *The National Can Story; in an Historic Industry an Historic Company Organized for the Future.* New York: Newcomen Society in North America, 1971. 28 p. (Newcomen Address.)

NATIONAL CASH REGISTER COMPANY

Allyn, Stanley C. *My Half Century with NCR.* New York: McGraw-Hill, 1967. 209 p.

"Celebrating the Future, 1884-1984." In *NCR Annual Report*, 10-32. Dayton: The Company, 1983.

NATIONAL COMMERCE BANK AND TRUST COMPANY

Herzog, Lester W., Jr. *150 Years of Service and Leadership: The Story of National Commerce Bank and Trust Company.* New York: Newcomen Society in North America, 1975. 25 p. (Newcomen Publication; no. 1018.)

NATIONAL FARMER'S BANK

Millett, Larry. <u>The Curve of the Arch: The Story of Louis Sullivan's Owatonna Bank.</u> St. Paul: Minnesota Historical Society Press, 1985. 248 p.

NATIONAL GRANGE MUTUAL INSURANCE COMPANY

Colby, Kenneth P. <u>From an Idea to Reality: The Story of National Grange Mutual Insurance Company.</u> New York: Newcomen Society in North America, 1973. 22 p.

NATIONAL INTERGROUP, INC.

National Intergroup, Inc. <u>History.</u> Pittsburgh: The Company, 1985. 2 p.

NATIONAL LABORATORIES, LEHN AND FINK DIVISION

"Fred Taylor: 50 Years at Lehn and Fink." <u>Aerosol Age</u> 20 (September 1975): 33+.

NATIONAL LIBERTY CORPORATION

DeMoss, Arthur S. <u>National Liberty Corporation.</u> New York: Newcomen Society in North America, 1978. 14 p. (Newcomen Publication; no. 1079.)

NATIONAL LIFE AND ACCIDENT INSURANCE COMPANY, INC.

Stamper, Powell. <u>The National Life Story: A History of the National Life and</u>

<u>Accident Insurance Company of Nashville, Tennessee.</u> New York: Appleton-Century-Crofts, 1968. 359 p.

NATIONAL RAILROAD PASSENGER CORPORATION
See:
AMTRAK

NATIONAL REVENUE CORPORATION

Shook, Robert L. "Richard D. Schultz." In <u>The Entrepreneurs,</u> 127-137. New York: Harper & Row, 1980.

THE NATIONWIDE INSURANCE COMPANIES

Doss, Bowman. <u>People Working Together: The Story of the Nationwide Insurance Organization.</u> New York: Newcomen Society in North America, 1968. 24 p. (Newcomen Address.)

Jeffers, Dean W. <u>The Nationwide Story, Volume II: A Phenomenal Growth Period.</u> New York: Newcomen Society in North America, 1981. 19 p. (Newcomen Publication; no. 1150.)

NCNB

NCNB. <u>NCNB: A Brief History.</u> Charlotte, N.C.: The Company, 1984. 5 p.

NCR
See:
NATIONAL CASH REGISTER COMPANY

NEEDHAM HARPER WORLDWIDE, INC.

Harper, Paul. <u>Working the Territory: 60 Years of Advertising from the People of Needham Harper Worldwide, Inc.</u> Englewood Cliffs, N.J.: Prentice-Hall, 1985. 127 p.

NEILS (J.) LUMBER COMPANY

Neils, Paul. <u>Julius Neils and the J. Neils Lumber Company.</u> Seattle: F. McCaffrey, 1971. 87 p.

NESTLE COMPANY, INC.

Heer, Jean. <u>World Events--1866-1966: The First Hundred Years of Nestle.</u> White Plains, N.Y.: Nestle Co., Inc., 1966. 226 p.

Wolflisberg, Hans J. <u>A Century of Global Operations; The Flavorful World of Nestle.</u> New York: Newcomen Society in North America, 1966. 28 p. (Newcomen Address.)

NEW ENGLAND MOXIE COMPANY

<u>Moxie Encyclopedia, Vol 1: The History.</u> Vestal, N.Y.: Vestal Press, 1985.

Potter, Frank N. <u>The Moxie Mystique.</u> Virginia Beach, Va: Donning Co., 1981.

NEW ENGLAND MUTUAL LIFE INSURANCE COMPANY

Collier, Abram T. <u>A Capital Ship: New England Life: A History of America's First Chartered Mutual Life Insurance Company, 1835-1985.</u> Boston: The Company, 1985. 336 p.

NEW ENGLAND PATRIOTS

Fox, Larry. <u>The New England Patriots.</u> New York: Atheneum, 1979. 345 p.

McGuane, George. <u>New England Patriots: A Pictorial History.</u> Virginia Beach: JCP Corporation of Virginia, 1980. 208 p.

NEW YORK BANK FOR SAVINGS

New York Bank for Savings. <u>The Story of the New York Bank for Savings: The First 150 Years.</u> New York: The Bank, 1969. 21 p.

NEW YORK DAILY NEWS

McGivena, Leo E. <u>The News: The First Fifty Years of New York's Picture Newspaper.</u> New York: New York Daily News, 1969. 428 p.

NEW YORK GIANTS

Terzian, James P. <u>New York Giants.</u> New York: Macmillan, 1973. 191 p.

Stein, Fred. *Day by Day in Giants History.* New York: Leisure Press, 1985.

NEW YORK ISLANDERS

Wilner, Barry. *The New York Islanders: Countdown to a Dynasty.* New York: Leisure Press, 1983. 208 p.

NEW YORK LIFE INSURANCE COMPANY

Meares, Charles William Victor. *Looking Back; A Memoir of New York Life.* S.l.: s.n., 1985. 162 p.

New York Life Insurance Company. *New York Life: A Company on the Move.* New York: The Company, 1969. 31 p.

NEW YORK METS

D'Agostino, Dennis. *This Date in New York Mets History: A Day by Day Listing of Events in the History of the New York National League Baseball Team.* New York: Stein and Day, 1981. 222 p.

Fishman, Lew. *New York's Mets: Miracle at Shea.* Englewood Cliffs N.J.: Prentice-Hall, 1974. 126 p.

Koppett, Leonard. *The New York Mets; The Whole Story.* Rev. ed. New York: Macmillan, 1974. 384 p.

THE NEW YORK STOCK EXCHANGE

Sobel, Robert. <u>The Last Bull Market: Wall Street in the 1960's.</u> New York: Norton, 1980. 242 p.

Sobel Robert. <u>N.Y.S.E.: A History of the New York Stock Exchange, 1935-1975.</u> New York: Weybright and Talley, 1975. 398 p.

NEW YORK TELEPHONE COMPANY

Ehrenberg, Ronald G. <u>The Regulatory Process and Labor Earnings.</u> New York: Academic Press, 1979. 204 p.

NEW YORK TIMES COMPANY

Levinson, Harry, and Stuart Rosenthal. "Arthur O. Sulzberger." In <u>CEO: Corporate Leadership in Action</u>, 219-258. New York: Basic Books, 1984.

Talese, Gay. <u>The Kingdom and the Power.</u> New York: World Publishing Company, 1969. 555 p.

Talese, Gay. <u>The Kingdom and the Power.</u> Garden City, N.Y.: Anchor Press, Doubleday, 1978. 590 p.

NEW YORK YANKEES

Bove, Vincent. <u>And on the Eight Day God Created the Yankees.</u> Plainfield, N.J.: Haven Books, 1981. 174 p.

Frommer, Harvey. *Baseball's Greatest Rivalry: The New York Yankees and Boston Red Sox.* New York: Atheneum, 1982. 159 p.

Gallagher, Mark. *Day by Day in New York Yankees History.* New York: Leisure Press, 1983. 352 p.

Gallagher, Mark. *Fifty Years of Yankee All-Stars.* New York: Leisure Press, 1984. 224 p.

Honig, Donald. *The New York Yankees: An Illustrated History.* New York: Crown, 1981. 32 p.

Salant, Nathan. *This Date in New York Yankees History.* Rev. ed. New York: Stein & Day, 1983. 418 p.

Sullivan, George, and John Powers. *Yankees: An Illustrated History.* Englewood Cliffs, N.J.: Prentice-Hall, 1982. 312 p.

NEWHALL LAND AND FARMING COMPANY

Dickason, James F. *The Newhall Land and Farming Company: Unlocking the Productivity of the Land.* New York: Newcomen Society in North America, 1983. 24 p. (Newcomen Publication, no. 1210.)

NEWMONT MINING CORPORATION

Ramsey, Robert Henderson. Men and Mines of Newmont; A Fifty-Year History. New York: Octagon Books, 1973. 344 p.

NEWPORT STEEL CORPORATION

Corwin, Nancy. "Industrial Development in Northern Kentucky: The Newport Steel Story." Unpublished paper, 1985. 24 p. (On file at the Newport Steel Corporation.)

NIP MAGAZINE

"30 Years of Publishing: A Legacy of Excellence, 1955-1985." NIP (July 1985): 46-49.

NISSAN MOTOR CORPORATION IN U.S.A.

Egerton, John. Nissan in Tennessee. Smyrna, Tenn.: Nissan Motor Corporation, 1983. 127 p.

Rae, John Bell. Nissan/Datson, A History of Nissan Motor Corporation in U.S.A., 1960-1980. New York: McGraw-Hill, 1982. 331 p.

NL INDUSTRIES

Nestor, Oscar W. The Strike as an Investment to Increase Productivity. New Brunswick, N.J.: Institute of

Management and Labor Relations, Rutgers, State University of New Jersey, 1980. 75 p.

NORRIS INDUSTRIES, INC.

Norris, Kenneth T. The Story of Norris Industries, Inc.: from Job Shop to Industrial Giant. New York: Newcomen Society in North America, 1973. 30 p.

NORTH AMERICAN ROCKWELL CORPORATION

Atwood, John Leland. North American Rockwell, Storehouse of High Technology. New York: Newcomen Society in North America, 1970. 24 p. (Newcomen Address.)

See also: Rockwell International

NORTH CAROLINA MUTUAL LIFE INSURANCE COMPANY

Gloster, Jesse E. North Carolina Mutual Life Insurance Company: Its Historical Development and Current Operations. New York: Arno Press, 1976. 349 p.

Kennedy, William Jesse. The North Carolina Mutual Story; A Symbol of Progress, 1898-1970. Durham: The Company, 1970. 308 p.

Weare, Walter B. Black Business in the New South: A Social History of the

<u>North Carolina Mutual Life Insurance Company.</u> Urbana: University of Illinois Press, 1973. 312 p.

NORTH CAROLINA RAILROAD COMPANY

North Carolina. Department of Transportation. <u>Report on the North Carolina Railroad Company and Atlantic & North Carolina Railroad Company for the General Assembly of North Carolina, December 22, 1976.</u> Raleigh: State of North Carolina, Department of Transportation, 1977. 98 p.

<u>The Tree of Life; A History of the North Carolina Railroad.</u> Compiled and designed by John F. Gilbert. Text by Grady B. Jefferys. Raleigh: North Carolina Railroad Company, 1972. 96 p.

NORTH CENTRAL AIRLINES, INC.

Serling, Robert J. <u>Ceiling Unlimited; The Story of North Central Airlines.</u> Marceline, Mo.: Walsworth Publishing Company, 1973. 245 p.

NORTH-EAST AIRLINES

Larcom, Paul S. "Eastward Ho by Air: A History of Boston-Maine and Central Vermont Airways." (With an Early History of Their Successor North-East Airlines.) <u>American Aviation Historical Society Journal</u> 25, no. 4 (1980): 242-250.

NORTH JERSEY RAPID TRANSIT COMPANY

Quinby, Edwin Jay. *Interurban Interlude; A History of the North Jersey Rapid Transit Company.* Ramsey, N.J.: Model Crafts, 1968. 92 p.

NORTH PACIFIC COAST RAILROAD COMPANY

Dickinson, A. Bray. *Narrow Gauge to the Redwoods; The Story of the North Pacific Coast Railroad and San Francisco Bay Paddle-Wheel Ferries.* Costa Mesa, Calif.: Trans-Angelo Books, 1970. 168 p.

NORTHEAST AIRLINES, INC.

Mudge, Robert W. *Adventures of a Yellowbird: The Biography of an Airline.* Boston: Branden Press, 1969. 374 p.

NORTHERN ILLINOIS GAS COMPANY

Chandler, Marvin. *An Energetic Distributor of the Energy of the Future: The Story of Northern Illinois Gas Company.* New York: Newcomen Society in North America, 1966. 28 p. (Newcomen Address.)

NORTHERN OHIO TRACTION AND LIGHT COMPANY

Blower, James M. *Northern Ohio Traction Revisited.* Akron: The Company, 1968. 181 p.

Blower, James M., and Robert S. Korach. The NOT&L Story. Chicago: Center Electric Railfans Association, 1966. 268 p.

NORTHERN TRUST BANK

"History in the Making: The Northern Trust Marks Its 95th Anniversary." Bank News 37 (14 August 1984): 1-3.

NORTHROP CORPORATION

Northrop Corporation. Northrop Corporation Historical Background. Los Angeles: The Company, 1985. 5 p.

NORTHWEST AIRLINES, INC.

Mills, Stephen E. A Pictorial History of Northwest Airlines. New York: Bonanza Books, 1980, c1972. 192 p.

NORTHWEST BANCORPORATION

Chucker, Harald. Banco at Fifty: A History of Northwest Bancorporation 1929-1979. Minneapolis: The Bank, 1979. 82 p.

NORTHWEST G.F. MUTUAL INSURANCE COMPANY

Fischer, David C. Northwest G.F. Mutual Insurance Company; Eureka, South Dakota, 75th anniversary, 1897-1972. Eureka, S.D.: The Company, 1972. 39 p.

NORTHWESTERN BELL TELEPHONE COMPANY

Rippey, James Crockett. Goodbye, Central--Hello, World: A Centennial History of Northwestern Bell: The Diary of a Dream. Omaha: published for the Telephone Pioneers of America by Northwestern Bell, 1975. 344 p.

NORTON COMPANY

Cheape, Charles W. Family Firm to Modern Multinational: Norton Company, A New England Enterprise. Cambridge: Harvard University Press, 1985. 424 p. (Harvard Studies in Business History; vol. 36.)

Purcell, Theodore Vincent. Institutionalizing Corporate Ethics: Case History. New York: Presidents Association, Chief Executive Officers' Division of American Management Association, 1979. 32 p.

NORTON SIMON, INC.

Mahoney, David J. Growth and Social Responsibility: The Story of Norton Simon, Inc. New York: Newcomen Society in North America, 1973. 23 p. (Newcomen Address.)

NOXELL CORPORATION

Witt, Norbert A. The Noxzema Story. New York: Newcomen Society in North

America, 1967. 24 p. (Newcomen Address.)

NUCOR CORPORATION

Fortney, David. "The Little Steel Mill that Could." <u>Reader's Digest</u> 127 (August 1985): 110-114.

NUCOR Corporation. <u>History of NUCOR Corporation</u>. Charlotte, N.C.: The Company, 1970. 3 p.

OAK INDUSTRIES, INC.

Oak Industries, Inc. <u>Fifty Years.</u> Rancho Bernard, Calif.: The Company, 1982. 16 p.

OAKLAND RAIDERS

Peterson, James A., and Gray L. Miller. <u>The Year of the Raiders.</u> New York: New America Library, 1984. 256 p.

OCCIDENTAL LIFE INSURANCE COMPANY OF CALIFORNIA

Occidental Life Insurance Company of California. <u>A Star in the West; The Occidental Story.</u> Los Angeles: The Company, 1970. 119 p.

OGDEN STANDARD-EXAMINER

Hatch, Wilda Gene. <u>A Pioneer in Communications: The History of</u> Ogden Standard-Examiner <u>and the Electronic</u>

Advancements of the Standard Corporation. New York: Newcomen Society in North America, 1972. 27 p. (Newcomen Address.)

OGLEBAY NORTON COMPANY

Jonovic, Donald J. *Iron Industry and Independence; A Biographical Portrait of Courtney Burton, Jr., American Industrialist and Patriot.* Cleveland: Jamieson Press, 1985. 269 p.

OHIO BELL TELEPHONE COMPANY

Ohio Bell Telephone Company. *A Brief History of the Ohio Bell Telephone Company.* Cleveland: The Company, 1975. 24 p.

OHIO CASUALTY GROUP

"A Story of Success." *Motor Travel* 39 (November 1966): 8-12. (Official publication of the Butler County Automobile Club.)

OHIO FARMERS INSURANCE COMPANY

Condon, George E. *History of Ohio Farmers Insurance Company, 1848-1984.* Westfield Center, Ohio: Westfield Companies, 1985. 275 p.

OHIO VALLEY ELECTRIC CORPORATION

Waterman, Merwin Howe. *Ohio Valley Electric Corporation; A Case Study in*

<u>Developing and Financing Private Power
for a Public Purpose.</u> Ann Arbor,
Mich.: Bureau of Business Research,
Graduate School of Business,
University of Michigan, 1966. 95 p.
(Michigan Business Studies, vol. 17,
no. 3.)

OKLAHOMA GAS AND ELECTRIC COMPANY

Kennedy, Donald S. <u>Pioneers in Public
Service: The Story of Oklahoma Gas and
Electric Company.</u> New York: Newcomen
Society in North America, 1972. 28 p.
(Newcomen Address.)

Oklahoma Gas and Electric Company. <u>The
Story of Oklahoma Gas and Electric
Company, 1902-1983.</u> Oklahoma City: The
Company, 1983. 32 p.

OKLAHOMA PUBLISHING COMPANY

Gaylord, E.K. <u>The Oklahoma Publishing
Company.</u> New York: Newcomen Society in
North America, 1971. 28 p. (Newcomen
Address.)

OKONITE COMPANY

Okonite Company. <u>The Okonite Company,
1878-1978, Our One-Hundredth Year
Serving the Electrical Industry for
Over 100 Years.</u> Ramsey, N.J.: The
Company, 1979. 70 p.

ONEIDA LTD.

Carden, Maren L. *Oneida: Utopian Community to Modern Corporation.* Baltimore: Johns Hopkins University Press, 1969. 228 p.

OPM LEASING SERVICES

Fenichell, Stephen. *Other People's Money; The Rise and Fall of OPM Leasing Services.* Garden City, N.Y.: Doubleday, 1985. 256 p.

Gandossy, Robert P. *Bad Business: The OPM Scandal and the Education of the Establishment.* New York: Basic Books, 1985. 262 p.

OSCAR MAYER AND COMPANY
See:
MAYER (OSCAR) AND COMPANY

OUTBOARD MARINE CORPORATION

Outboard Marine Corporation. *Outboard Marine Corporation.* Waukeegan, Ill.: The Company, 1965.

OWENS-CORNING FIBERGLASS CORPORATION

Owens-Corning Corporation. *The History of Owens-Corning Fiberglass Corporation: A Capsule Look.* Toledo: The Company, 1982. 14 p.

OWENS-ILLINOIS, INC.

Owens-Illinois, Inc. *Brief History of Owens-Illinois, Inc.* Toledo: The Company, 1985. 2 p.

OZARK AIR LINES

Kidd, Glennon. "Wings Over the Ozarks: A History of Ozark Air Lines." *American Aviation Historical Society Journal* 22 (Fall 1977): 181-187.

PACCAR, INC.

"History." In *Paccar, Inc. Annual Report*, 4-17. Bellvue, Wash.: The Company, 1979.

PACIFIC GAS AND ELECTRIC COMPANY

Pacific Gas and Electric Company. *P.G. and E. Country.* San Francisco: The Company, 1966.

PACIFIC LIGHTING CORPORATION

Hornby, Robert A. *Pacific Lighting Corporation: A Giant of Energy.* New York: Newcomen Society in North America, 1968. 24 p. (Newcomen Address.)

PACIFIC LUMBER COMPANY

Wilkerson, Hugh. *Life in the Peace Zone; An American Company Town.* New York: Macmillan, 1971. 158 p.

PACIFIC MUTUAL LIFE INSURANCE COMPANY OF CALIFORNIA

Nunis, Doyce B. Past is Prologue: A Centennial Profile of Pacific Mutual Life Insurance Company. Los Angeles: The Company, 1968. 72 p.

PACIFIC POWER AND LIGHT COMPANY

Dierdorff, John. How Edison's Lamp Helped Light the West; The Story of Pacific Power & Light Company and Its Pioneer Forebears. Portland: The Company, 1971. 313 p.

Pacific Power and Light Company. The Pacific Power Story: 75 Years of Service. Portland: The Company, 1985. 56 p.

PACIFICORP

Frisbee, Don C. The PacifiCorp Story: 75 Years of Service and Partnership. New York: Newcomen Society in the United States, 1985. 24 p. (Newcomen Publication; no. 1232.)

PACKARD MOTOR CAR COMPANY

Aiken, Michael. Economic Failure, Alienation and Extremism. Ann Arbor: University of Michigan Press, 1968. 213 p.

Scott, Michael G. _H. Packard: The Complete Story._ Blue Ridge Summit, Pa.: Tab Books, 1985. 201 p.

Turnquist, Robert E. _The Packard Story; The Car and the Company._ New York: A.S. Barnes, 1965. 286 p.

PACOLET MANUFACTURING COMPANY

Webb, J.A. _The History of New Holland, Georgia, and Pacolet Manufacturing Company._ Roswell, Ga.: W.H. Wolfe Associates, 1985. 445 p.

PAN AMERICAN WORLD AIRWAYS, INC.

Bender, Marylin, and Selig Altschul. _Chosen Instrument: Pan Am, Juan Trippe, The Rise and Fall of an American Enterprise._ New York: Simon and Schuster, 1982. 605 p.

Brock, Horace. _More About Pan Am: A Pilot's Story Continued._ Lunenberg, Vt.: Stinehour Press, 1980. 101 p. (Supplement to _Flying the Oceans: A Pilot's Story of Pan Am, 1935-1955._)

Daley, Robert. _An American Saga; Juan Trippe and His Pan Am Empire._ New York: Random House, 1980. 529 p.

Norris, William. _Willful Misconduct: An Untold Story._ New York: Norton, 1984. 290 p.

PANHANDLE EASTERN PIPELINE COMPANY

Panhandle Eastern Pipeline Company. *Panhandle 50.* Houston: The Company, 1979. 28 p.

PARAMOUNT PICTURES, INC.

Eames, John Douglas. *The Paramount Story.* New York: Crown, 1985. 368 p.

PARKE-DAVIS AND COMPANY

Parke-Davis and Company. *Parke-Davis at 100: Progress in the Past--Promise for the Future.* Detroit: The Company, 1966.

PARKER BROTHERS, INC.

Parker Brothers, Inc. *90 Years of Fun, 1883-1973; The History of Parker Brothers.* Salem, Mass.: The Company, 1973. 71 p.

PARKER DRILLING COMPANY

Parker Drilling Company. *Fifty Years of Drilling, 1934-1984.* Tulsa: The Company, 1984. 16 p.

PARKER HANNIFIN CORPORATION

Parker, Patrick S. *Parker Hannifin Corporation.* New York: Newcomen Society in North America, 1980. 26 p. (Newcomen Publication; no. 1107.)

PARMORAND PUBLICATIONS

Nicolaides, Louis. The Production Company. 2nd ed. Beverly Hills: Parmorand Publications, 1983. 175 p.

PARSER MINERAL CORPORATION

"Parser Mineral Corporation Celebrates 100th Anniversary." Lapidary Journal 32 (July 1978): 986+.

PARSONS AND WHITTEMORE ORGANIZATION

Landegger, Karl F. Growing with the Paper Industry Since 1853: The Parsons and Whittemore Organization and the Black Clawson Company. New York: Newcomen Society in North America, 1968. 24 p. (Newcomen Address.)

PARSONS BRINCKERHOFF, INC.

Bobrick, Benson. Parsons Brinckerhoff: The First 100 Years. New York: Van Nostrand Reinhold, 1985. 276 p.

PARSONS, BRINCKERHOFF, QUADE AND DOUGLAS, INC.

Douglas, Walter S. An Enduring Heritage: Ninety Years of Progress in Engineering, Planning, and Architecture. New York: Newcomen Society in North America, 1975. 17 p. (Newcomen Publication; no. 1019.)

PAUL MASSON VINEYARDS
See:
MASSON (PAUL) VINEYARDS

PEABODY HOLDING COMPANY, INC.

"Peabody Celebrates First 100 Years in the Coal Business." Coal Age 88 (June 1983): 22-23.

PEAT, MARWICK, MITCHELL AND COMPANY

Hanson, Walter E. Peat, Marwick, Mitchell and Company: 80 Years of Professional Growth. New York: Newcomen Society in North America, 1978. 19 p. (Newcomen Publication; no. 1075.)

Wise, T.A. Peat, Marwick, Mitchell & Co.: 85 Years. New York: The Company, 1982. 107 p.

PENN CENTRAL COMPANY

Daughen, Joseph R., and Peter Binzen. The Wreck of the Penn Central. Boston: Little, Brown, 1971. 365 p.

Gartner, Michael. Riding the Pennsy to Ruin; A Wall Street Journal Chronicle of the Penn Central Debacle. Princeton, N.J.: Dow Jones Books, 1971. 90 p.

Salsbury, Stephen. No Way to Run a Railroad: The Untold Story of the Penn Central Crisis. New York: McGraw-Hill, 1982. 363 p.

Sobel, Robert. *The Fallen Colossus: The Penn Central and the Metamorphosis of American Capitalism.* New York: Weybright and Talley, 1976. 370 p.

U.S. Securities and Exchange Commission. *The Financial Collapse of the Penn Central Company; Staff Report to the Special Subcommittee on Investigations of the Committee on Interstate and Foreign Commerce, U.S. House of Representatives.* Washington, D.C.: GPO, 1972. 392 p.

See also: Amtrak

PENN SQUARE BANK

Singer, Mark. *Funny Money.* New York: Knopf, 1985. 256 p.

Zweig, Phillip L. *Belly Up; The Collapse of the Penn Square Bank.* New York: Crown Publishers, 1985. 500 p.

PENNEY (J.C.) COMPANY, INC.

Batten, William M. *The Penney Idea: Foundation for the Continuing Growth of the J.C. Penney Company.* New York: Newcomen Society in North America, 1967. 24 p. (Newcomen Address.)

J. C. Penney Company, Inc. *Background on the J.C. Penney Company, Inc.* New York: The Company, 1985. 10 p.

J. C. Penney Company, Inc. J.C. Penney Milestones. New York: The Company, 1983. 4 p.

PENNSYLVANIA POWER AND LIGHT COMPANY

Nash, John Rumm, and Craig Orr. Pennsylvania Power & Light Company: A Guide to the Records. Wilmington: Hagley Museum and Library, 1985. 226 p.

Pennsylvania Power & Light Company. Pennsylvania Power & Light Company Profile: Statistical Review, 1966-1976. Discussion of Current Issues. Allentown, Pa.: The Company, 1977. 48 p.

PENNSYLVANIA POWER COMPANY

Pennsylvania Power Company. 50 Years, 1931-1981. New Castle, Pa.: The Company, 1981. 23 p.

PENOBSCOT SAVINGS BANK

Penobscot Savings Bank. 100 Years, Penobscot Savings Bank; Bangor and the World, 1869-1969. Bangor, Maine: The Bank, 1969. 23 p.

PENZOIL COMPANY

Meyer, Henry I. Corporate Financial Planning Models. New York: Wiley, 1977. 218 p.

PEOPLE EXPRESS, INC.

Walsh, John. "The People's Co-op Takes Flight." The Director 37, no. 3 (October 1983): 43-44.

PEOPLES BANK OF BLOOMINGTON

Crissey, Elwell. Peoples Bank of Bloomington: First 100 years, 1869-1969. Bloomington, Ill.: Pantagraph Press, 1969. 153 p.

PEOPLE'S SAVING BANK--BRIDGEPORT

Hawley, Samuel W. People's Savings Bank--Bridgeport: A Story of Private Thrift and Public Service. New York: Newcomen Society in North America, 1974. 26 p. (Newcomen Publication; no. 1001.)

PEPSI-COLA COMPANY

Louis, J.C. The Cola Wars. New York: Everest House, 1980. 386 p.

Mack, Walter, and P. Buckley. No Time Lost. New York: Atheneum, 1982. 211 p.

Pepsi-Cola Company. The Pepsi-Cola Story. Purchase, N.Y.: The Company, 1984. 14 p.

PERKIN-ELMER CORPORATION

"History." In <u>Perkin-Elmer Corporation.
Background information</u>, 32-33.
Norwalk, Conn.: The Company, 1985.

PETER PAUL, INC.

Elston, Lloyd W. <u>Peter Paul, Inc.:
Quality Candy Since 1919.</u> New York:
Newcomen Society in North America,
1971. 24 p. (Newcomen Address.)

PETROLANE, INC.

Munzer, R.J. <u>Petrolane, Inc.</u> New York:
Newcomen Society in North America,
1979. 17 p. (Newcomen Publication; no.
1097.)

PFIZER, INC.

Mines, Samuel. <u>Pfizer: An Informal
History.</u> New York: The Company, 1978.
248 p.

THE PHILADELPHIA PHILLIES

Bilovsky, Frank, and Richard Westcott.
<u>The Phillies Encyclopedia.</u> New York:
Leisure Press, 1984. 541 p.

Dolson, Frank. <u>The Philadelphia Story: A
City of Winners.</u> South Bend, Ind.:
Icarus Press, 1981. 318 p.

Lewis, Allen. <u>The Philadelphia Phillies.</u>
New York: Simon and Shuster, 1982.

Lewis, Allen. *The Philadelphia Phillies: A Pictorial History.* Virginia Beach: JCP Corporation of Virginia, 1981. 176 p.

Lewis, Allen. *This Date in Philadelphia Phillies History: A Day by Day Listing of Events in the History of the Philadelphia National League Baseball Team.* New York: Stein and Day, 1979. 273 p.

THE PHILADELPHIA RAPID TRANSIT COMPANY

Cox, Harold E. *Utility Cars of Philadelphia, 1892-1971.* Forty Fort, Pa.: The Company, 1971. 132 p.

THE PHILADELPHIA 76'ERS

Williams, Pat, and Bill Lyons. *We Owed You One: The Uphill Struggle of the Philadelphia 76'ers.* Wilmington, Del.: Tri Mark Publishing Company, 1983. 220 p.

THE PHILADELPHIA STOCK EXCHANGE

Wetherill, Elkins. *The Story of the Philadelphia Stock Exchange.* New York: Newcomen Society in North America, 1976. 19 p. (Newcomen Publication; no. 1036.)

PHILIP MORRIS, INC.

Hunter, Sam. *Art in Business: The Philip Morris Story.* New York: Published Under the Auspices of Business Committee for the Arts by Abrams, 1979. 200 p.

Philip Morris, Inc. *Philip Morris History.* New York: Communications Research Dept., Philip Morris, Inc., 1982. 22 p.

Philip Morris, Inc. *Philip Morris History Highlights.* New York: The Company, 1985. 29 p.

PHILIPS INDUSTRIES, INC.

Philips Industries, Inc. *25th Year; Twenty-five Years of Growth.* Dayton: The Company, 1982. 22 p.

PHILLIPS PETROLEUM COMPANY

Finney, Robert. *Phillips, The First 66 Years.* Bartlesville, Okla.: The Company, 1983. 219 p.

THE PHOENIX GAZETTE

Pulliam, Eugene C. *Is There a Fighter in the House?* New York: Newcomen Society in North America, 1966. 24 p. (Newcomen Address.)

PICKARD, INC.

Platt, Dorothy Pickard. The Story of Pickard China. Hanover, Pa.: Printed by Everybody's Press, 1970. 85 p.

PIEDMONT AIRLINES

Davis, Thomas H. The History of Piedmont: Setting a Special Pace. New York: Newcomen Society in North America, 1982. 24 p. (Newcomen Publication; no. 1160.)

PIEDMONT AND NORTHERN RAILWAY

Fetters, Thomas T., and Peter W. Swanson. The Piedmont and Northern; the Great Electric System of the South. San Marino, Calif: Golden West Books, 1974. 175 p.

THE PILLSBURY COMPANY

Powell, William J. Pillsbury's Best: A Company History from 1869. Minneapolis: The Company, 1985. 252 p.

PINKERTON'S NATIONAL DETECTIVE AGENCY

Glasheen, Leah. "We Never Sleep--Fifty Years of Pinkerton's at the Smithsonian." Security Management 25 (November 1981): 45-6.

Morn, Frank. The Eye that Never Sleeps: A History of the Pinkerton National

Detective Agency. Bloomington: Indiana University Press, 1982. 244 p.

PIONEER NATURAL GAS COMPANY

Pioneer Natural Gas Company. <u>The History of the Pioneer Natural Gas Company.</u> Amarillo, Tex.: The Company, 1965. 6 p.

PIPER AIRCRAFT CORPORATION

Francis, Devon E. <u>Mr. Piper and His Cubs.</u> Ames: Iowa State University Press, 1973. 256 p.

Piper, W.T. <u>From Club to Navajo: The Story of Piper Aircraft Corporation.</u> New York: Newcomen Society in North America, 1970. 31 p. (Newcomen Address.)

PITTSBURGH AND LAKE ERIE RAILROAD

McLean, Harold H. <u>Pittsburgh and Lake Erie R.R.</u> San Marino, Calif.: Golden West Books, 1980. 236 p.

PITTSBURGH-DES MOINES CORPORATION

Versteeg, Jean D. <u>The History of Pittsburgh-Des Moines Corporation, 1892-1982.</u> Pittsburgh: The Company, 1982. 77 p.

PITTSBURGH PIRATES

Eckhouse, Morris, and Carl Mastrocola. <u>This Date in Pittsburgh Pirates History.</u> New York: Stein and Day, 1980. 272 p.

PITTSBURGH STEELERS

Didinger, Ray. <u>Pittsburgh Steelers.</u> New York: Macmillan, 1974. 192 p.

Oates, Bob. <u>Pittsburgh's Steelers: The First Half Century.</u> Los Angeles: published for the Pittsburgh Steelers by Rosebud Books, 1982. 95 p.

PITTSTON COMPANY

Pittston Company. <u>Pittston, Yesterday, Today, and Tomorrow.</u> Greenwich, Conn.: The Company, 1980. 32 p.

PIZZA INN, INC.

Pizza Inn, Inc. <u>Pizza Inn: The First Twenty-five Years.</u> Dallas: The Company, 1984. 9 p.

PLAYBOY ENTERPRISES, INC.

Miller, Russel. <u>Bunny, The Real Story of Playboy.</u> New York: Holt, Rinehart & Winston, 1985, c1984. 352 p.

POLAROID CORPORATION

National Council of the Churches of Christ in the United States of America. Corporate Information Center. <u>The Polaroid "Experiment" in South Africa.</u> New York: Office of Resource Studies, Division of Christian Life and Mission, National Council of Churches, 1971. 14 p.

Polaroid Corporation. <u>Polaroid Corporation: A Chronology.</u> Cambridge, Mass.: The Company, 1983. 10 p.

Olshaker, Mark. <u>Instant Image; The Polaroid Story, Edwin Land and the Polaroid Experience.</u> New York: Stein & Day, 1978. 277 p.

POPULAR SCIENCE PUBLISHING COMPANY

Heyn, Ernest V. <u>A Century of Wonders: 100 Years of Popular Science.</u> New York: Doubleday, 1972. 320 p.

POTLATCH CORPORATION

Madden, Richard B. <u>"Tree Farmers and Wood Converters": The Story of Potlatch Corporation.</u> New York: Newcomen Society in North America, 1975. 24 p. (Newcomen Publication; no. 1010.)

PPG INDUSTRIES

PPG Industries. <u>PPG: A Century of Achievement.</u> Pittsburgh: The Company,

1983. 31 p. (Published as vol. 91, no. 2, of *PPG Products Magazine.*)

THE *PRAIRIE FARMER*

Evans, James F. *Prairie Farmer and WLS: the Burridge D. Butler Years.* Urbana: University of Illinois Press, 1969. 329 p.

PRICE WATERHOUSE AND COMPANY

"Price Waterhouse Review Anniversary Issue Commemorating the Seventy-fifth Anniversary of Price Waterhouse & Company." *Price Waterhouse Review* 10 (Autumn 1965): 1-71.

PROCTER AND GAMBLE COMPANY

Millman, Nancy F. "Saga of P&G's Ivory Soap: Keeping a Brand Afloat 100 Years." *Advertising Age* 50 (2 July 1979): 24-27.

Procter and Gamble Company. *The Story of Procter and Gamble.* Cincinnati: The Company, 1972. 48 p.

Schisgall, Oscar. *Eyes on Tomorrow: the evolution of Procter and Gamble.* Chicago: J.G. Ferguson Publishing Company, 1981. 295 p.

PROTECTIVE LIFE INSURANCE COMPANY

Rushton, William J., III. *A Sense of Quality, A Sense of Protective Life.*

New York: Newcomen Society in North America, 1976. 22 p. (Newcomen Publication; no. 1049.)

PROVIDENT LOAN SOCIETY OF NEW YORK

Schmed, Peter. God Bless Pawnbrokers. New York: Dodd, Mead, 1975. 217 p.

PROVINCETOWN-BOSTON AIRLINE, INC.

"PBA History." Air Transportation World 22 (January 1985): 76-77.

PRUDENTIAL INSURANCE COMPANY OF AMERICA

Carr, William H.A. From Three Cents a Week; The Story of the Prudential Insurance Company of America. Englewood Cliffs, N.J.: Prentice-Hall, 1975. 316 p.

PUBLIC SERVICE COMPANY OF INDIANA

Blanchar, Carroll H. Indiana and the Electric Age: The Story of Public Service Company of Indiana. New York: Newcomen Society in North America, 1969. 28 p. (Newcomen Address.)

Public Service Company of Indiana. Indiana and the Electric Age: the Story of Public Service Indiana. Plainfield, Ind.: The Company, 1982. 20 p.

PUBLIC SERVICE ELECTRIC AND GAS COMPANY

Conniff, James C.G., and Richard Conniff. *The Energy People: A History of PSE&G.* Newark, N.J.: The Company, 1978. 392 p.

Smith, Robert I. *A Cycle of Service: The Story of Public Service Electric and Gas Company.* New York: Newcomen Society in North America, 1980. 24 p. (Newcomen Publication; no. 1121)

PUBLISHERS WEEKLY

Grannis, C.B. "1872-1972; Celebrating 100 Years of Publishers Weekly and the American Book Trade." *Publishers Weekly* 201 (17 January 1972): 28-36.

PUBLIX SUPER MARKETS

Jenkins, George W. *The Publix Story.* New York: Newcomen Society in North America, 1978. 23 p. (Newcomen Publication; no. 1098.)

PULLMAN, INC.

Pullman, Inc. *Portrait at 100.* Chicago: The Company, 1976. 16 p.

QUAKER OATS COMPANY

Marquette, Arthur F. *Brands, Trademarks, and Good Will: The Story of the Quaker Oats Company.* New York: McGraw-Hill, 1967. 274 p.

QUICK FROZEN FOODS

Williams, E.W. "Biography of an Industry and the Magazine that Grew Up with It: The History of Frozen Foods, 1938-1968." Quick Frozen Foods 31 (August 1968): 49-105.

RALSTON PURINA COMPANY

Ralston Purina Company. Ralston Purina Vignettes. St. Louis: The Company, 1970. 9 p.

RAND CORPORATION

Rand Corporation. Rand's 25th Anniversary Volume. Santa Monica, Calif.: The Company, 1973. 239 p.

Smith, Bruce L.R. The Rand Corporation; Case Study of a Nonprofit Advisory Corporation. Cambridge, Mass.: Harvard University Press, 1966. 332 p.

RAYTHEON COMPANY

Scott, Otto J. The Creative Ordeal: The Story of Raytheon. New York: Atheneum, 1974. 429 p.

RCA CORPORATION

Dreher, Carl. Sarnoff: An American Success. New York: Quadrangle/New York Times, 1977. 282 p.

Radio Corporation of America. <u>RCA: A
Historical Perspective.</u> Princeton,
N.J.: The Company, 1985. 86 p.

<u>RCA: A Collection of Five Articles About
RCA.</u> Moorestown, N.J.: The Company,
1971. 36 p.

READER'S DIGEST ASSOCIATION, INC.

Wood, James Playsted. <u>Of Lasting
Interest: The Story of Reader's
Digest.</u> Garden City, N.Y.: Doubleday,
1967. 270 p.

READING COMPANY

Carleton, Paul. <u>Memories of Reading
Company Power, 1833-1976.</u> Dunnellon,
Fla.: D. Carleton Railbooks, 1985. 144
p.

RELIABLE LIFE INSURANCE COMPANY

McMahon, Helen Griffin. <u>Portals to
Protection; A History of the Reliable
Life Insurance Company from the
Perspective of Helen Griffin McMahon.</u>
St. Louis: The Company, 1972. 181 p.

REPUBLIC AIRLINES

"Birth of a Major Airline." <u>Air
International</u> (November 1982): 1-8.

REPUBLIC FINANCIAL SERVICES, INC.

Perry, Russell H. *Republic Financial Services, Inc.: Since 1903--A Story of Progress Under the American Free Enterprise System.* New York: Newcomen Society in North America, 1976. 24 p. (Newcomen Publication; no. 1042.)

REPUBLICBANK CORPORATION

RepublicBank Corporation. *RepublicBank Corporation.* Dallas: The Bank, 1985. 9 p.

RESORTS INTERNATIONAL, INC.

Mahon, Gigi. *The Company that Bought the Boardwalk: A Reporter's Story of How Resorts International Came to Atlantic City.* New York: Random House, 1980. 262 p.

REVLON, INC.

Tobias, Andrew P. *Fire and Ice: The Story of Charles Revlon, The Man Who Built the Revlon Empire.* New York: W. Morrow, 1976. 22 p.

REYNOLDS AND REYNOLDS COMPANY

Meyer, Robert Henry. *The Reynolds and Reynolds Company, "A People's Company."* New York: Newcomen Society in North America, 1973. (Newcomen Address.)

Reynolds and Reynolds Company. <u>Historical Highlights of the Reynolds and Reynolds Company Founded in 1866.</u> Dayton, Ohio: The Company, 1985. 26 p.

REYNOLDS (R.J.) INDUSTRIES, INC.

R.J. Reynolds Industries. <u>Our 100th Anniversary, 1875-1975.</u> Winston-Salem, N.C.: The Company, 1975. 32 p.

Sticht, J. Paul. <u>The RJR Story: The Evolution of a Global Enterprise.</u> New York: Newcomen Society in North America, 1983. 28 p. (Newcomen Publication; no. 1190.)

Tilley, Nannie May. <u>R.J. Reynolds Tobacco Company.</u> Chapel Hill: University of North Carolina Press, 1985. 720 p.

REYNOLDS METALS COMPANY

Reynolds Metals Company. <u>Reynolds Aluminum and the People who Make It.</u> Richmond: The Company, 1975. 24 p.

RICHARDS FARMS, INC.

Shook, Robert L. "William J. Richards." In <u>The Entrepreneurs</u>, 81-91. New York: Harper & Row, 1980.

RICHFIELD OIL CORPORATION

Jones, Charles S. <u>From the Rio Grande to the Arctic; The Story of the Richfield</u>

Oil Corporation. Norman: University of
Oklahoma Press, 1972. 364 p.

RICH'S INC.

Sibley, Celestine. Dear Store: An
Affectionate Portrait of Rich's
Garden City, N.Y.: Doubleday, 1967.
143 p.

RIGGS NATIONAL BANK OF WASHINGTON, D.C.

Carr, Roland T. 32 President's Square.
Foreword by Richard Walsh. Washington,
D.C.: Acropolis Books, 1980.

RKO RADIO PICTURES, INC.

Jewell, Richard B. The RKO Story. New
York: Arlington House, 1982. 320 p.

ROBBINS AND MYERS, INC.

Robbins and Myers, Inc. Highlights from
Our History, 1878-1978. Dayton, Ohio:
The Company, 1978. 11 p.

Wall, Fred G. The Standard of the
Industry: The Story of Robbins and
Myers, Inc. New York: Newcomen Society
in North America, 1978. 16 p.
(Newcomen Publication; no. 1080.)

ROBERTSON (H.H.) COMPANY

Jones, Douglas A. H.H. Robertson: A
Unique International Company. New
York: Newcomen Society in North

America, 1966. 24 p. (Newcomen Address.)

ROBINS (A.H.) COMPANY

A.H. Robins Company. <u>A.H. Robins: 1866-1978.</u> Richmond: The Company, 1978. 32 p.

Englemayer, Sheldon D. <u>Lord's Justice.</u> Richmond: Anchor Press, Doubleday, 1985. 300 p.

Mintz, Morton. <u>At Any Cost: Corporate Greed, Women, and the Dalkon Shield.</u> New York: Pantheon/Random House, 1985. 308 p.

Robins, E. Clairborne. <u>"Making Today's Medicines with Integrity--Seeking Tomorrow's with Persistance": The Story of A.H. Robins Company.</u> New York: Newcomen Society in North America, 1966. 20 p. (Newcomen Address.)

ROBINSON NUGENT, INC.

Robinson Nugent, Inc. <u>In Recognition of J.D. Robinson, 1904-1981: From Local Garage to International Manufacturing Facilities.</u> New Albany, Ind.: The Company, 1983. 6 p.

ROCKWELL INTERNATIONAL

Braband, Ken C. <u>The First 50 Years: A History of Collins Radio Company and</u>

the Collins Divisions of Rockwell International. Cedar Rapids, Iowa: Communications Dept., Avionics Group, Rockwell International, 1983. 218 p.

Rockwell International Corporation. History. Pittsburgh: The Company, 1979. 11 p.

See also: North American Rockwell Corporation

ROCKWELL INTERNATIONAL, GRAPHIC SYSTEMS DIVISION

Kogan, H. "Gross--100 Years of Service to Newspapers." Editor and Publisher Fourth Estate 118 (4 May 1985): 82-83.

RODDIS PLYWOOD CORPORATION

Huston, Harvey. The Roddis Line; the Roddis Lumber & Veneer Company. Railroad and the Dells & Northeastern Railway. Winnetka, Ill.: The Company, 1972. 150 p.

RODDY MANUFACTURING COMPANY

Roddy, Pat. 75 Years of Refreshment. Knoxville: The Company, 1983. 290 p.

ROHM AND HAAS COMPANY

Hochheiser, Sheldon. Rohm and Haas: History of a Chemical Company. Philadelphia: University of Pennsylvania Press, 1985. 300 p.

ROHR CORPORATION

Austin, Edwin T. *Rohr: The Story of a Corporation.* Chula Vista, Calif.: The Company, 1969. 118 p.

ROPER CORPORATION

Roper Corporation. *Roper Corporation 100, 1874-1974: A Century of Quality.* Kankakee, Ill.: The Company, 1974. 9 p.

ROSTENBERG (LEONA)

Rostenberg, Leona, and Madeleine B. Stern. *Old & Rare; Thirty Years in the Book Business.* New York: A. Schram, 1974. 234 p.

ROTARY CLUB, CHARLOTTE, N.C.

Green, Harold K. *The Rotary Club of Charlotte; 50 Years of "Service Above Self."* Charlotte: The Club, 1966. 80 p.

ROTARY CLUB, LAKELAND, FLA.

Lay, Chester Frederic. *Fifty Golden Years, 1918-1968; A Brief History of Lakeland Rotary.* Lakeland, Fla.: The Club, 1968. 69 p.

ROTARY CLUB, OAKLAND, CALIF.

<u>Rotarily Yours; A History of the Rotary Club of Oakland.</u> Oakland, Calif.: The Club, 1969. 224 p.

ROTARY CLUB, PALO ALTO, CALIF.

Rotary Club, Palo Alto, Calif. <u>The First Fifty Years of the Rotary Club of Palo Alto, 1922-1972; A Chronological Narrative of the Palo Alto Rotary Club's Contributions to Group Fellowship, Community Service, Vocational Ethics, and International Understanding.</u> Palo Alto, Calif.: The Club, 1972. 96 p.

ROTARY CLUB, TRENTON, N.J.

<u>History of the Trenton Rotary Club, 1914-1969; Fifty-five Years of Civic and Social Activities.</u> Prepared under the joint authorship of J. Lewis Unsworth and others. Trenton, N.J.: Published under the auspices of the Trenton Historical Society, 1970. 214 p.

ROTARY INTERNATIONAL

Rotary International. <u>The World of Rotary.</u> Edited by Elliott McCleary. Evanston, Ill.: The Club, 1975. 144 p. (Rotary International Publication; no. 88.)

ROUSE COMPANY

Gibbons, Boyd. *Wye Island.* Baltimore: Published for Resources for the Future by Johns Hopkins University Press, 1977. 227 p.

RUST-OLEUM CORPORATION

Edwards, H. Wallace. *Gift o' the sea; The Story of Rust-Oleum.* Evanston, Ill.: The Company, 1971. 151 p.

RYAN AERONAUTICAL COMPANY

Wagner, William. *Ryan, the Aviator: Being the Adventures and Ventures of Pioneer Airman and Businessman T. Claude Ryan.* New York: McGraw-Hill, 1971. 253 p.

SAFECO INSURANCE COMPANIES

Copeland, Sid. *The Safeco Story, 1923-1980.* Seattle: The Companies, 1981. 247 p.

SAFEWAY STORES

"Ending Our Fiftieth Year: The First Decade." *Safeway News* 31 (February/March 1976): 1+.

"Ending Our Fiftieth Year: The Second Decade." *Safeway News* 31 (April 1976): 7-12.

"Ending Our Fiftieth Year: The Third Decade." <u>Safeway News</u> 31 (May/June 1976): 4-10.

"Ending Our Fiftieth Year: The Fourth Decade." <u>Safeway News</u> 31 (July 1976): 8-12.

"Ending Our Fiftieth Year: The Fifth Decade." <u>Safeway News</u> 31 (August/September 1976): 5-9.

"Ending Our Fiftieth Year: The Sixth Decade." <u>Safeway News</u> 31 (October 1976): 1-12.

Safeway Stores, Inc. <u>Our 50th Year.</u> Oakland, Calif.: The Company, 1975. 25 p. (Published as part of the 1975 annual report.)

SAGA CORPORATION

"Corporate History." In <u>Saga Corporation. Fact book</u>, 4-7. Menlo Park, Calif.: The Company, 1984.

ST. LOUIS CAR COMPANY

Lind, Alan R. <u>From Horsecars to Streamliners: An Illustrated History of the St. Louis Car Company.</u> Park Forest, Ill.: Transportation History Press, 1978. 400 p.

ST. LOUIS CARDINALS

Broeg, Bob. Bob Broeg's Redbirds, A Century of Cardinals' Baseball. St. Louis: River City Publishers, 1981.

Leptich, John, and Dave Barnowski. This Date in St. Louis Cardinals History. New York: Stein and Day, 1983. 353 p.

ST. PAUL AND TACOMA LUMBER COMPANY

Morgan, Murray Cromwell. The Mill on the Boot: The Story of the St. Paul and Tacoma Lumber Company. Seattle: University of Washington Press, 1982. 286 p.

ST. REGIS PAPER COMPANY

Amigo, Eleanor, and M. Neuffer. Beyond the Adirondacks: The Story of St. Regis Paper Company. Westport, Conn.: Greenwood Press, 1980. 219 p. (Contributions in Economics and Economic History; no. 35.)

SALT LAKE TRIBUNE

Malmquist, O.N. The First 100 Years: A History of the Salt Lake Tribune, 1871-1971. Salt Lake City: Utah State Historical Society, 1971. 454 p.

SAMBO'S RESTAURANTS, INC.

Bernstein, Charles. Sambo's: Only a Fraction of the Action; The Inside

Story of a Restaurant Empire's Rise
and Fall. Burbank, Calif.: National
Literary Guild, 1984. 197 p.

SAN DIEGO AND CORONADO FERRY COMPANY

San Diego and Coronado Ferry Company.
Pathway Through the Bay. San Diego:
The Company, 1969. 8 p.

SAN DIEGO GAS AND ELECTRIC COMPANY

"Centennial Edition, 1881-1981." News
Meter Quarterly 57, no. 1 (1981): 1-47.

THE SAN FRANCISCO FORTY-NINERS

Sullivan, John. Day by Day in San
Francisco Forty-Niners History. New
York: Leisure Press, 1984. 240 p.

THE SAN FRANCISCO GIANTS

Mandel, Mike. SF Giants, An Oral History.
Santa Cruz, Calif.: Mandel, 1979. 256 p.

Stein, Fred, and Nick Peters. Day by Day
in Giants History. New York: Leisure
Press, 1985. 304 p.

SAN JOAQUIN AND EASTERN RAILROAD

Johnston, Hank. The Railroad that Lighted
Southern California. Los Angeles:
Trans-Anglo Books, 1965. 128 p.

SANDERS ASSOCIATES, INC.

Sanders Associates, Inc. Background Information. South Nashua, N.H.: The Company, 1984. 13 p.

THE SATURDAY EVENING POST

Friedrich, Otto. Decline and Fall: The Struggle for Power at a Great American Magazine, the Saturday Evening Post. New York: Harper and Row, 1970. 499 p.

See also: Curtis Publishing Company

SAUNDERS LEASING SYSTEM, INC.

Saunders, Harris. Top Up or Down? The Origin and Development of the Automobile and Truck Renting and Leasing Industry--56 years, 1916-1972. Birmingham: The Company, 1972. 306 p.

SAVINGS AND LOAN BANK OF THE STATE OF NEW YORK

Eldridge, Charles John Wilson, and Edward H. Leete. The Bank that Led the Way: Savings and Loan Bank of the State of New York; The First Fifty Years, 1915-1965. New York: The Bank, 1966. 258 p.

SAVINGS BANK OF NEW LONDON

Noyes, Gertrude Elizabeth. The Savings Bank of New London at 150, 1827-1977. New London, Conn.: The Bank, 1977. 110 p.

SCHLITZ (JOS.) BREWING COMPANY

Rowen, James. "Corporate Lore: The Case of Schlitz." <u>Across the Board</u> 21 (September 1984): 55-57.

SCHLUMBERGER LIMITED

Auletta, Ken. <u>The Art of Corporate Success: The Story of Schlumberger.</u> New York: Putnam, 1984. 184 p.

SCOTT AVIATION CORPORATION

Scott, Earle M. <u>The Saga of Scott Aviation Corporation.</u> Buffalo: Printed by Artcraft Printers and Lithographers, 1973. 249 p.

SCOTTISH AMERICAN INVESTMENT COMPANY LIMITED

Weir, Ronald B. <u>A History of the Scottish American Investment Company Limited, 1873-1973.</u> Edinburgh: The Company, 1973. 36 p.

SEA ISLAND COMPANY

Gilbert, John. <u>Sea Island Company, 1930-1980: Alfred W. Jones of Sea Island.</u> New York: Newcomen Society in North America, 1981. 32 p. (Newcomen Publication; no. 1132.)

SEABOARD LUMBER AND SHIPPING

Perrault, E.G. Wood & Water: The Story of Seaboard Lumber and Shipping. Seattle: University of Washington Press, 1985. 320 p.

SEABORD AIR LINE RAILWAY

Prince, Richard E. Seabord Air Line Railway: Steam Boats, Locomotives and History. Green River, Wyo.: The Company, 1969. 268 p.

SEALED AIR CORPORATION

Dunphy, Thomas Joseph Dermot. Sealed Air Corporation: "Our Products Protect Your Products": A Story of Modern Day Protective Packaging. New York: Newcomen Society in North America, 1982. 20 p. (Newcomen Publication; no. 1173.)

SEALED POWER CORPORATION

"History--Chronology of Growth." In Sealed Power Corporation. Fact File, 17-18. Muskegon, Mich.: The Company, 1985.

SEARS, ROEBUCK AND COMPANY

Worthy, James C. Shaping an American Institution: Robert E. Wood and Sears, Roebuck. Urbana: University of Illinois Press, 1984. 344 p.

Weil, Gordon Lee. Sears, Roebuck, U.S.A.: The Great American Catalog Store and How It Grew. Briarcliff Manor, N.Y.: Stein and Day, 1977. 277 p.

See also: Allstate Insurance Company

SEATTLE-FIRST NATIONAL BANK

Scates, Shelby. Firstbank: The Story of Seattle-First National Bank. Seattle: The Bank, 1970. 130 p.

SECURITY MUTUAL LIFE INSURANCE COMPANY

Baker, William Gary. "A History of the Security Mutual Life Insurance Company, 1895-1971." Ph.D. diss., University of Nebraska, 1975. 268 p.

SECURITY PACIFIC NATIONAL BANK

Larkin, Frederick G., Jr. Security Pacific Bank's 100 Years of Keeping Faith with the Community. New York: Newcomen Society in North America, 1971. 27 p. (Newcomen Address.)

SECURITY STORAGE COMPANY OF WASHINGTON, D.C.

Gore, Philip Larner. Around the Corner or Around the World--Move with Security: The Story of Security Storage Company of Washington. New York: Newcomen Society in North America, 1976. 23 p. (Newcomen Publication; no. 1054.)

SELZNICK INTERNATIONAL

Behlmer, Rudy. Memo from David O. Selznick. New York: Viking Press, 1972. 549 p.

SHAKLEE CORPORATION

Shook, Robert L. The Shaklee Story. New York: Harper & Row, 1982. 188 p.

SHEARSON LOEB RHOADES

Carrington, Tim. The Year They Sold Wall Street. Boston: Houghton Mifflin, 1985. 384 p.

See also: American Express Company

SHELL OIL COMPANY

Beaton, Kendall. Enterprise in Oil; A History of Shell in the United States. New York: Appleton-Century-Crofts, 1967. 515 p.

Bridges, Harry. The Americanization of Shell: The Beginnings and Early Years of Shell Oil Company in the United States. New York, Newcomen Society in North America, 1972. 26 p. (Newcomen Address.)

Wells, Barbara. Shell at Deer Park: The Story of the First Fifty Years. Houston: The Company, 1972. 139 p.

SHENANDOAH LIFE INSURANCE COMPANY

Herbert, Hiram J. *Shenandoah Life, The First Fifty Years, 1916-1966.* Roanoke, Va.: The Company, 1966. 102 p.

SHERWIN-WILLIAMS COMPANY

Sherwin-Williams Company. *Century Past Century Future.* Cleveland: The Company, 1966.

SHREVE, CRUMP AND LOW COMPANY

Shreve, Crump & Low Co. *Selling Quality Jewels Since 1800; A History of Shreve, Crump & Low Co.* Boston: The Company, 1974. 72 p.

SIFCO INDUSTRIES, INC.

Smith, Charles H. *SIFCO Industries, Inc.: "Forging Ahead."* New York: Newcomen Society in North America, 1984. 23 p. (Newcomen Publication; no. 1204.)

SIMON AND SCHUSTER, INC.

Schwed, Peter. *Turning the Pages: An Insider's Story of Simon & Schuster, 1924-1984.* New York: Macmillan, 1984. 300 p.

SINCLAIR OIL COMPANY

Sinclair Oil Company. *A Great Name in Oil: Sinclair Through Fifty Years.* New York: F.W. Dodge Company, 1966. 102 p.

SKELLY OIL COMPANY

Ironside, Roberta. *An Adventure Called Skelly; A History of Skelly Oil Company Through Fifty Years, 1919-1969.* New York: Appleton-Century-Crofts, 1970. 147 p.

SMITH AND WESSON, INC.

Jinks, Roy G. *History of Smith and Wesson: Nothing of Importance Will Come Without Effort.* North Hollywood, Calif.: Beinfeld Publishing Company, 1977. 290 p.

SMITH, HINCHMAN AND GRYLLS ASSOCIATES, INC.

Meathe, Philip J. *Smith, Hinchman & Grylls Associates, Inc., Architects, Engineers, Planners.* New York: Newcomen Society in North America, 1979. 30 p. (Newcomen Publication; no. 1106.)

SMITHKLINE CORPORATION

Marion, John Francis. *The Fine Old House: SmithKline Corporation's First 150 Years.* Philadelphia: The Company, 1980. 251 p.

SMITH'S TRANSFER CORPORATION

Brown, Charles D. *Fifty Years Down the Road: The Story of Smith's Transfer*

1930-1980. Verona, Va.: McClure Press, 1981. 128 p.

SNAP-ON TOOLS CORPORATION

Snap-on Tools Corporation. <u>Snap-on Tools Corporation, 1920-1980's.</u> Kenosha, Wis.: The Company, 1984. 28 p.

SONOCO PRODUCTS COMPANY

Coker, Charles W. <u>The Story of SONOCO Products Company.</u> New York: Newcomen Society in North America, 1976. 23 p. (Newcomen Publication; no. 999.)

SONOCO Products Company. <u>A Commitment to Values, the SONOCO Tradition.</u> Hartsville, S.C.: The Company, 1985. 15 p.

SOO LINE RAILROAD COMPANY

Abbey, Wallace W. <u>The Little Jewel: Soo Line Railroad Company and the Locomotives That Make It Go.</u> Pueblo, Colo.: Pinion Productions, 1984. 216 p.

SOTHEBY PARKE BERNET, INC.

Herrmann, Frank. <u>Sotheby's: Portrait of an Auction House.</u> New York: Norton, 1981, c1980. 468 p.

Norton, Thomas E. <u>100 Years of Collecting in America; The Story of Sotheby Parke</u>

Bernet. New York: H.N. Abrams, 1984. 240 p.

SOUTH CAROLINA NATIONAL BANK

Lindley, James G. South Carolina National: The First 150 Years. New York: Newcomen Society of the United States, 1985. 24 p. (Newcomen Publication; no. 1245.)

Rogers, George C. The South Carolina National Bank; The First One Hundred and Fifty Years. Columbia, S.C.: The Bank, 1984. 99 p.

SOUTH CENTRAL BELL IN MISSISSIPPI

Edmonds, N. Frank. South Central Bell in Mississippi. New York: Newcomen Society in North America, 1981. 24 p. (Newcomen Publication; no. 1128.)

SOUTHERN BANCORPORATION OF ALABAMA

Gaffey, Guy H., Jr. Southern Bancorporation of Alabama: A Story of Safety, Service, Integrity, Innovation, and Growth. New York: Newcomen Society in North America, 1975. 18 p. (Newcomen Publication; no. 1026.)

SOUTHERN BELL

Southern Bell. Legacy and Promise: The Story of Southern Bell. Atlanta: The Company, 1984. 64 p.

SOUTHERN CALIFORNIA EDISON COMPANY

Myers, William A. Iron Men and Copper Wires: A Centennial History of the Southern California Edison Company. Glendale, Calif.: Trans-Anglo Books, 1983. 255 p.

Whitaker, James B. Strategic Planning in a Rapidly Changing Environment. Lexington, Mass.: Lexington Books, 1978.

THE SOUTHERN COMPANY

Branch, Hallee, Jr. Alabama Power Company and the Southern Company. New York: Newcomen Society in North America, 1967. 24 p. (Newcomen Address.)

THE SOUTHERN RAILWAY COMPANY

Davis, Burke. The Southern Railway: Road of the Innovators. Chapel Hill: University of North Carolina Press, 1985. 309 p.

SOUTHERN SAW SERVICE, INC.

Brown, Edmund D. 1594 Evans Drive, S.W.: A History of Southern Saw Service, Inc., and the Atlanta Saw Service. Atlanta: The Company, 1983. 213 p.

SOUTHERN UNION GAS COMPANY

Chesnutt, N.P. Southern Union. El Paso: Mangan Books, 1979. 216 p.

SOUTHLAND CORPORATION

Liles, Allen. Oh Thank Heaven! The Story of the Southland Corporation. Dallas: The Company, 1977. 264 p.

SOUTHWEST AIRLINES

Southwest Airlines. Southwest Airlines History. Dallas: The Company, 1984. 31 p.

SOUTHWIRE COMPANY

Richards, Roy. A Southern Adventure in Free Enterprise: The Story of Southwire Company. New York: Newcomen Society in North America, 1966. 24 p. (Newcomen Address.)

SPARKMAN AND STEPHENS

Kinney, Francis S. "You Are First": The Story of Olin and Rod Stephens of Sparkman & Stephens, Inc. New York: Dodd, Mead, 1978. 327 p.

SPENCER STUART AND ASSOCIATES

Stuart, Spencer R. Spencer Stuart & Associates, 25 Years of Professional Leadership in Executive Search Consulting. New York: Newcomen Society in North America, 1982. 24 p. (Newcomen Publication; no. 1163.)

SPIEGEL, INC.

Cornell, James, Jr. <u>The People Get the Credit: The First One Hundred Years of the Spiegel Story, 1865-1965.</u> Chicago: The Company, 1965. 171 p.

Smalley, Orange A. <u>The Credit Merchants; A History of Spiegel, Inc.</u> Introduction by: Harold F. Williamson. Carbondale: Southern Illinois University Press, 1973. 336 p.

SPIRAL PRESS, INC.

Pierpont Morgan Library. <u>The Spiral Press Through four Decades; an Exhibition of Books and Ephemera; With a Commentary by Joseph Blumenthal.</u> New York: Pierpont Morgan Library, 1966. 66 p.

SPRINGS INDUSTRIES, INC.

"Colonel's Different Kind of Company." <u>Textile World</u> 125 (December 1975): 51+.

SQUARE D COMPANY

Square D Company. <u>About Square D.</u> Paletine, Ill.: The Company, 1985. 20 p.

SQUIBB CORPORATION

Furlaud, Richard M. <u>Squibb Corporation: Its First Four Years.</u> New York: The Company, 1971.

STALEY (A.E.) MANUFACTURING COMPANY

Forrestal, Dan J. <u>The Kernal and the Bean: The 75-year Story of the Staley Company.</u> New York: Simon & Schuster, 1982. 315 p.

STANDARD CORPORATION, OGDEN, UTAH

Hatch, Wilda Gene. <u>A Pioneer in Communications; The History of the</u> Ogden Standard-Examiner <u>and the Electronic Advancements of the Standard Corporation.</u> New York: Newcomen Society in North America, 1972. 27 p.

STANDARD FRUIT AND STEAMSHIP COMPANY

Karnes, Thomas L. <u>Tropical Enterprise: The Standard Fruit and Steamship Company in Latin America.</u> Baton Rouge: Louisiana State University Press, 1978. 332 p.

See also: Castle and Cooke, Inc.

STANDARD LIFE INSURANCE COMPANY

Newman, W.R., III. <u>"Bucking Like a Mule": The Story of Standard Life.</u> New York:

Newcomen Society in North America, 1972. 24 p. (Newcomen Address.)

STANDARD OIL COMPANY

Destler, Chester McArthur. Roger Sherman and the Independant Oil Men. Ithaca: Cornell University Press, 1967. 305 p.

Gray, Edmund R., and C. Ray Gullett. Employee Representation at Standard Oil Company of New Jersey: A Case Study. Baton Rouge: Division of Research, College of Business Administration, Louisiana State University, 1973. 40 p.

STANDARD OIL COMPANY OF CALIFORNIA

Haynes, Harold J. Standard Oil Company of California: 100 Years Helping to Create the Future. New York: Newcomen Society in North America, 1980. 22 p. (Newcomen Publication; no. 1115.)

Standard Oil Company of California. The First 100 Years. San Francisco: The Company, 1979. 10 p.

STANDARD OIL COMPANY OF INDIANA

Dedmon, Emmett. Challange and Response; A Modern History of the Standard Oil Company (Indiana). Chicago: Mobium Press, 1984. 324 p.

STANDARD OIL COMPANY OF NEW JERSEY

Gray, Edmund R., and C. Ray Gullett. <u>Employee Representation at Standard Oil Company of New Jersey: A Case Study.</u> Baton Rouge: Division of Research, College of Business Administration, Louisiana State University, 1973. 40 p.

Wall, Bennett H., and George S. Gibb. <u>Teagle of Jersey Standard.</u> New Orleans, La.: Tulane University, 1974. 386 p.

STANDARD RATE AND DATA SERVICE, INC.

Myers, Kenneth H. <u>SRDS: The National Authority Serving the Media-buying Function.</u> Evanston, Ill.: Northwestern University Press, 1968. 335 p.

STANDARD SCREW COMPANY

Taylor, James A. <u>"Minding Our Business": The Story of Standard Screw Company.</u> New York: Newcomen Society in North America, 1969. 32 p. (Newcomen Address.)

THE STANLEY WORKS

Davis, Donald W. <u>The Stanley Works: A 125 Year Beginning.</u> New York: Newcomen Society in North America, 1969. 24 p. (Newcomen Address.)

STAR PIN COMPANY OF SHELTON, CONN.

Heusser, Audrey E. "The First One-hundred Years of a People Oriented Company." Connecticut Industry 44 (September 1966): 6-7+.

STATE AUTOMOBILE MUTUAL INSURANCE COMPANY

Gingher, Paul R. Running Mates: The Story of State Automobile Mutual Insurance Company and Columbus Mutual Life Insurance Company. New York: Newcomen Society in North America, 1978. 30 p. (Newcomen Publication; no. 1090.)

STATE NATIONAL BANK OF EL PASO

Sonnichsen, Charles Leland. The State National Since 1881: the Pioneer Bank of El Paso. El Paso: Texas Western Press, 1971. 171 p.

STEVENS (J.P.) AND COMPANY

Conway, Mimi. Rise Gonna Rise: A Portrait of Southern Textile Workers. Garden City, N.Y.: Anchor Press, 1979. 228 p.

Ferguson, Lloyd C. From Family Firm to Corporate Giant; J.P. Stevens and Company, 1813-1963. Braintree, Mass.: D.H. Mark Publishing Company, 1970. 33 p.

STONE CONTAINER CORPORATION

Stone, Marvin N. Stone Container Corporation: A Story of Growth in the American Tradition. New York: Newcomen Society in North America, 1975. 24 p. (Newcomen Publication; no. 1004.)

STONE MANUFACTURING COMPANY

Stone, Eugene E. Stone Manufacturing Company: The First Half-century of Clothing a Changing World. New York: Newcomen Society in North America, 1985. 22 p. (Newcomen Publication; no. 1222.)

STORY MAGAZINE

Foley, Martha. The Story of Story Magazine: A Memoir. New York: Norton, 1980. 288 p.

STP CORPORATION

Brufke, Edward F. The Racer's Edge; Andy Granatelli and the STP Corporation. Braintree, Mass.: D.H. Mark Publishing Company, 1971. 28 p.

STRAUS-FRANK COMPANY

Lanzone, John A. Horse, Next to Woman, God's Greatest Gift to Man; A History of the Straus-Frank Company. San Antonio, Tex.: The Company, 1970. 72 p.

STRAWBRIDGE AND CLOTHIER

Lief, Alfred. *Family Business: A Century in the Life and Times of Strawbridge and Clothier.* New York: McGraw-Hill, 1968. 343 p.

Veale, Frank R. *Family Business: Strawbridge and Clothier; the Momentous Seventies.* Philadelphia: The Company, 1981. 224 p.

STUDEBAKER CORPORATION

Cannon, William A. *Studebaker: The Complete Story.* Blue Ridge Summit, Pa.: Tab Books, 1981. 368 p.

Hall, Asa E., and Richard M. Langworth. *The Studebaker Century: A National Heritage.* Contoocook, N.H.: Dragonwyck Publications, 1983. 192 p.

Langworth, Richard M. *Studebaker: The Postwar Years.* Osceola, Wis.: Motorbooks International, 1979. 195 p.

SUBURBAN PROPANE GAS CORPORATION

Anton, Mark J. *Suburban Propane Gas Corporation: The Development of a Selectively Positioned Energy Company.* New York: Newcomen Society in North America, 1982. 20 p. (Newcomen publication; no. 1167.)

SUBURBAN TRUST COMPANY

Sherwood, J. Robert. The Story of Suburban Trust Company: A Bank with Vision. New York: Newcomen Society in North America, 1968. 28 p. (Newcomen Address.)

SUN OIL COMPANY

Johnson, Arthur M. The Challenge: The Sun Oil Company, 1947-1977. Columbus: Ohio State University Press, 1983. 481 p.

SUNDSTRAND CORPORATION

Sundstrand Corporation. A History of the Company. Rockford, Ill.: The Company, 1985. 10 p.

SUNDT (M.M.) CONSTRUCTION COMPANY

Sundt, M. Eugene, and W. E. Naumann. M.M. Sundt Construction Company: "From Small Beginnings--." New York: Newcomen Society in North America, 1975. 36 p. (Newcomen Publication; no. 993.)

SUNFLOWER FOOD STORES

Lewis, Morris, Jr. Wholesaler--Retailer: The Story of Lewis Grocer Company and the Sunflower Food Stores. New York: Newcomen Society in North America, 1975. 21 p. (Newcomen Publication; no. 1021.)

SUNSWEET GROWERS, INC.

Couchman, Robert. *The Sunsweet Story; A History of the Establishment of the Dried Fruit Industry in California and of the 50 Years of Service of Sunsweet Growers, Inc.* San Jose: The Company, 1967. 139 p.

SUPERMARKETS GENERAL CORPORATION

"Happy Birthday, Everybody! Pathmark is Ten years Old." *Pathmark News* (September 1978): 1-4.

SUPREME LIFE INSURANCE COMPANY

Puth, Robert C. *Supreme Life: The History of a Negro Life Insurance Company.* New York: Arno Press, 1976, c1968. 293 p. (Originally presented as the author's thesis, Northwestern University, 1967.)

SVERDRUP CORPORATION

Franzwa, Gregory M. *Legacy, The Sverdrup Story.* St. Louis: The Company, 1978. 286 p.

SYSCO CORPORATION

Sysco Corporation. *The Sysco Story.* Houston: The Company, n.d. 16 p.

SYSCO/FROST-PACK FOOD SERVICES, INC.

Geelhoed, E. Bruce. <u>The Thrill of Success: The Story of SYSCO/Frost-Pack Food Services, Inc.</u> Muncie, Ind.: Bureau of Business Research, College of Business and Department of History, Ball State University, 1983. 96 p. (Ball State University Business History Series; no. 2.)

SYSTEM DEVELOPMENT CORPORATION

Baum, Claude. <u>The System Builders: The Story of SDC.</u> Santa Monica, Calif.: The Company, 1981. 302 p.

TAFT BROADCASTING COMPANY

Taft Broadcasting Company. <u>History of Taft Broadcasting Company.</u> Cincinnati: The Company, 1985. 16 p.

TANDY CORPORATION

West, James L. <u>Tandy Corporation: "Start on a Shoe String."</u> New York: Newcomen Society in North America, 1968. 24 p. (Newcomen Address.)

TANNER (O.C.) COMPANY

Tanner, Obert C. <u>Commitment to Beauty.</u> New York: Newcomen Society in North America, 1982. 23 p. (Newcomen Publication; no. 1146.)

TDK USA CORPORATION

"TDK; Portrait of a Company in Fast Forward." <u>Audio</u> 68 (August 1984). (Special advertising supplement.)

TEC, INC.

TEC, Inc. <u>Background of TEC, Inc.</u> Tucson: The Company, 1981. 4 p.

TENNECO, INC.

Tenneco, Inc. <u>Tenneco's First 35 Years.</u> Houston: The Company, 1978. 16 p.

TEXACO, INC.

Texaco, Inc. <u>A Short History of Texaco, Inc., 1902-1984.</u> White Plains, N.Y.: The Company, 1984. 33 p.

TEXAS EASTERN CORPORATION

Bufkin, I. David. <u>Texas Eastern Corporation, "A Pioneering Spirit."</u> New York: Newcomen Society in North America, 1983. 24 p. (Newcomen Publication; no. 1187.)

TEXAS GULF SULPHUR COMPANY, INC.

Shulman, Morton. <u>The Billion Dollar Windfall.</u> New York: Morrow, 1970, c1969. 239 p.

TEXAS INSTRUMENTS

Bagamery, Ann. "Texas Instruments in Mid-life." *Forbes* 129 (15 March 1982): 64-69.

Texas Industrial Commission. *Texas Instruments: Global Growth from Seismology to Space Age Technology.* Dallas: The Company, 1971.

Texas Instruments. *A Brief History of Texas Instruments.* Dallas: The Company, 1982. 3 p.

TEXASGULF

Fogarty, Charles F. *The Story of Texasgulf: A Story of People Dedicated to Finding, Developing, and Conserving Natural Resources Essential to a Higher Standard of Living for Everyone.* New York: Newcomen Society in North America, 1976. 40 p. (Newcomen Publication; no. 1033.)

TEXTRON, INC.

Eisenhauer, Robert S. *Textron--From the Beginning.* Providence, R.I.: The Company, 1979. 147 p.

Little, Royal. *How to Lose $100,000,000 and Other Valuable Advice.* Boston: Little, Brown, 1979. 334 p.

Textron, Inc. *The Royal Little Story.* Providence, R.I.: The Company, 1966.

THOMAS (S.N.) SONS

Thomas, Leon S. _S.N. Thomas' Sons and Norman Shirtmakers: "A Family Affair."_ New York: Newcomen Society in North America, 1979. 20 p. (Newcomen Publication; no. 1105.)

TICOR

Loebbecke, Ernest J. _Serving the Nation's Needs for Diversified Financial Services: The Story of the T.I. Corporation of California._ New York: Newcomen Society in North America, 1973. 23 p. (Newcomen Publication; no. 983.)

TIDY CAR, INC.

Shook, Robert L. "Gary Goranson." In _The Entrepreneurs_, 93-101. New York: Harper & Row, 1980.

TIFFANY AND COMPANY

Purtell, Joseph. _The Tiffany Touch._ New York: Pocket Books, 1973. 390 p.

TIGER INTERNATIONAL, INC.

"The First Thirty Years." _Tiger Spirit_ 1 (April 1978): 11-27.

TIME, INC.

Byron, Christopher. *The Fanciest Drive: What Happened When the Media Empire of Time/Life Leaped Without Looking into the Age of High-Tech.* New York: W.W. Norton, 1986. 280 p.

TIMES MIRROR CORPORATION

Hart, Jack R. *The Information Empire: The Rise of the Los Angeles Times and Times Mirror Corporation.* Washington, D.C.: University Press of America, 1981. 410 p.

THE TIMKEN COMPANY

The Timken Company. *History of the Timken Company.* Canton, Ohio: The Company, 1978. 22 p.

TODD SHIPYARDS CORPORATION

Gilbride, John L. *Todd Shipyards: In Peace and War.* New York: Newcomen Society in North America, 1966. 28 p. (Newcomen Address.)

Mitchell, C. Bradford. *Every Kind of Shipwork: A History of Todd Shipyards Corporation, 1916-1981.* New York: The Company, 1981. 320 p.

TORCHMARK CORPORATION

Samford, Frank Park. *Torchmark Corporation: A History of a New*

Company. New York: Newcomen Society in North America, 1984. 26 p. (Newcomen Publication; no. 1226.)

TOYOTA MOTOR SALES, U.S.A.

Toyota Motor Sales, U.S.A. Toyota USA: The First Fifteen Years. Torrance, Calif.: The Company, 1973. 48 p.

TRACY COLLINS BANK AND TRUST COMPANY

Arrington, Leonard J. Tracy Collins Bank & Trust Company: A Record of Responsibility, 1884-1984. Midvale, Utah: Eden Hill, 1984. 252 p.

TRAILER TRAIN COMPANY

Buford, Curtis D. Trailer Train Company: A Unique Force in the Railroad Industry. New York: Newcomen Society in North America, 1982. 24 p. (Newcomen Publication; no. 1159.)

TRANS WORLD AIRLINES, INC.

Serling, Robert J. Howard Hughes' Airline: An Informal History of TWA. New York: St. Martin's/Marek, 1983. 338 p.

Tinn, David B. Just About Everybody vs. Howard Hughes. Garden City, N.Y.: Doubleday, 1973. 462 p.

Trans World Airlines, Inc., Flight Operations Department. Legacy of

Leadership: A Pictorial History of Trans World Airlines. Marceline, Mo.: Walsworth Publishing Company, 1971. 224 p.

See also: Hughes Aircraft Company

TRANSCONTINENTAL GAS PIPELINE CORPORATION

Transcontinental Gas Pipeline Corporation. *History of Transcontinental.* Houston: The Company, 1968. 18 p.

THE TRAVELERS INSURANCE COMPANIES

Beach, Morrison H. *"A Century of Security": The Story of the Travelers Insurance Companies.* New York: Newcomen Society in North America, 1973. 29 p. (Newcomen Address.)

The Travelers Insurance Company. *The History of Insurance in America Reads Like a History of the Travelers.* Hartford: The Company, 1981. 37 p.

TREND LINE CORPORATION

Hogg, William T. *In the Sun Belt--at the Right Time--with the Right People: The Story of Trend Line in Central Mississippi.* New York: Newcomen Society in North America, 1977. 20 p. (Newcomen Publication; no. 1063.)

THE TRUMP GROUP, INC.

Tuccille, Jerome. <u>Trump, The Saga of America's Most Powerful Real Estate Baron.</u> New York: Donald I. Fine, 1985. 243 p.

TRW

Mettler, Ruben F. <u>The Little Brown Hen That Could: The Growth Story of TRW, Inc.</u> New York: Newcomen Society in North America, 1982. 24 p. (Newcomen Publication; no. 1172.)

TRW. <u>The Little Brown Hen That Could.</u> Cleveland, Ohio: The Company, 1984. 24 p.

TRW--REDA PUMP DIVISION

TRW--Reda Pump Division. <u>Memories, A Story of People and a Company Called TRW Reda.</u> Bartlesville, Okla.: The Division, 1980. 126 p.

TURNER BROADCASTING SYSTEMS, INC.

Williams, Christian. <u>Lead, Follow or Get Out of the Way: The Story of Ted Turner.</u> New York: Times Books, 1981. 282 p.

See also: Atlanta Braves

TWENTIETH CENTURY-FOX FILM CORPORATION

Dunne, John Gregory. The Studio. New York: Farrar, Straus & Giroux, 1969. 255 p.

Thomas, Tony, and Aubrey Solomon. The Films of 20th Century-Fox: A Pictorial History. Secaucus, N.J.: Citadel Press, 1985. 492 p.

TWIN CITY RAPID TRANSIT COMPANY

Lowry, Goodrich. Streetcar Man: Tom Towry and the Twin City Rapid Transit Company. Minneapolis: Lerner Publications, 1979. 177 p.

TYSON FOODS, INC.

"Doing Business Just for You: Yesterday." In Annual Report, 4-8. Springdale, Ark.: The Company, 1984.

UAL, INC.

Carlson, Edward E. UAL, Inc.: United Airlines and Western International Hotels: Partners in Travel. New York: Newcomen Society in North America, 1975. 15 p. (Newcomen Publication; no. 1030.)

UNC RESOURCES

UNC Resources. UNC Resources History. Falls Church, Va.: The Company, 1983. 10 p.

UNION BANK, LOS ANGELES

Volk, Harry J. Union Bank: Sixty Years of Quality Banking. New York: Newcomen Society in North America, 1974. 23 p. (Newcomen Publication; no. 1006.)

UNION CARBIDE CORPORATION

Union Carbide Corporation. Our History. Danbury, Conn.: The Company, 1976. 15 p.

UNION CENTRAL LIFE INSURANCE COMPANY

Union Central Life Insurance Company. Splendid Century; A Centennial History of the Union Central Life Insurance Company of Cincinnati, Ohio 1867-1967. Cincinnati: The Company, 1967. 161 p.

UNION ELECTRIC COMPANY

Union Electric Company. A History of Union Electric Company. St. Louis: The Company, 1984. 5 p.

UNION MUTUAL LIFE INSURANCE COMPANY

Lane, Carleton G. A Maine Heritage: A Brief History of Union Mutual Life Insurance Company, 1848-1968. New York: Newcomen Society in North America, 1968. 28 p. (Newcomen Address.)

UNION NATIONAL BANK AND TRUST COMPANY OF SOUDERTON

Ruth, John L. The History of the Indian Valley and Its Bank. Souderton, Pa.: The Bank, 1976. 209 p.

THE UNION NATIONAL BANK, LOWELL, MASSACHUSETTS

Bourgeois, Homer W. The Union National Bank: The Story of an All American Bank in an All American City. New York: Newcomen Society in North America, 1972. 24 p. (Newcomen Address.)

UNION OIL COMPANY OF CALIFORNIA

Hartley, Fred L. "The Spirit of 76": The Story of the Union Oil Company of California. New York: Newcomen Society in North America, 1976. 20 p. (Newcomen Publication; no. 1053.)

Hutchinson, William Henry. Oil, Land, and Politics: The California Career of Thomas Robert Bard. Norman: University of Oklahoma Press, 1965. 2 v.

Union Oil Company of California. Sign of the 76: The Fabulous Life and Times of the Union Oil Company of California. Los Angeles: The Company, 1976. 424 p.

Wetly, Earl M. The 76 Bonanza: The Fabulous Life and Times of the Union Oil Company of California. Menlo Park,

Calif.: Lane Magazine and Book Company, 1966. 351 p.

UNION PACIFIC CORPORATION

Cook, William Sutton. <u>Building the Modern Union Pacific.</u> New York: Newcomen Society of the United States, 1984. 24 p. (Newcomen Publication; no. 1228.)

Union Pacific Corporation. <u>Union Pacific Corporation: Energy, Transportation, Natural Resources.</u> New York: The Company, 1979. 28 p.

UNION PACIFIC RAILROAD COMPANY

Ames, Charles E. <u>Pioneering the Union Pacific; A Reappraisal of the Builders of the Railroads.</u> New York: Appleton, 1969. 608 p.

Athearn, Robert G. <u>Union Pacific Country.</u> Chicago: Rand McNally, 1971. 480 p.

Baily, Edd H. <u>The Century of Progress: A Heritage of Service. Union Pacific, 1869-1969.</u> New York: Newcomen Society in North America, 1969. 24 p. (Newcomen Address.)

UNION TRUST COMPANY OF MARYLAND

Cooper, Elliot T. <u>A Documentary History of the Union Trust Company of Maryland, Baltimore, and Its Predecessor Institutions: Bank of Baltimore and the National Bank of</u>

Baltimore, 1795-1969. Baltimore: The Company, 1970. 281 p.

UNIROYAL, INC.

Vila, George R. The Story of UNIROYAL: 75 Years of Progress. New York: Newcomen Society in North America, 1968. 24 p. (Newcomen Address.)

UNITED AIRLINES, INC.

Carlson, Edward E. UAL, Inc.: United Airlines and Western International Hotels, Partners in Travel. New York: Newcomen Society in North America, 1975. 15 p. (Newcomen Publication; no. 1030.)

Johnson, Robert Elliott. Airway One: A Narrative of United Airlines and Its Leaders. Chicago: The Company, 1974. 208 p.

Taylor, Frank J. "Pat" Patterson. Menlo Park, Calif.: Lane Magazine and Book Company, 1967. 160 p.

UNITED ARTISTS

Balio, Tino. United Artists: The Company Built by the Stars. Madison: University of Wisconsin Press, 1976. 323 p.

UNITED BANK OF ARIZONA

Simmons, James P. Banking on Arizona's Future: The Story of United Bank of Arizona. New York: Newcomen Society in North America, 1980. 27 p. (Newcomen Publication; no. 1124.)

UNITED BANKS OF COLORADO, INC.

Hart, N. Berne. United Banks of Colorado, Inc.: A Proud History of Service to Colorado. New York: Newcomen Society in North America, 1981. 19 p. (Newcomen Publication; no. 1139.)

UNITED FRUIT COMPANY

McCann, Thomas P. An American Company: The Tragedy of United Fruit. New York: Crown, 1976. 244 p.

UNITED PARCEL SERVICE OF AMERICA

United Parcel Service of America. This is United Parcel Service. Greenwich, Conn.: The Company, 1976. 36 p.

UNITED PRESS INTERNATIONAL, INC.

Quigg, H.D. "UPI; As It Was and As It Is." Editor and Publisher, the Fourth Estate 115 (25 September 1982): 16-18.

USAIR

USAir. USAir History. Pittsburgh: The Company, 1980. 3 p.

U.S. BORAX AND CHEMICAL CORPORATION

Travis, Norman J. <u>The Tinical Trail: A History of Borax.</u> London: Harrap, 1984. 311 p.

Travis, Norman J., and C.L. Randolph. <u>United States Borax & Chemical Corporation: The First One Hundred Years.</u> New York: Newcomen Society in North America, 1973. 24 p.

U.S. INDUSTRIAL CHEMICALS COMPANY

Barnes, Harry C. <u>From Molasses to the Moon: The Story of U.S. Industrial Chemicals Company.</u> New York: The Company, 1975. 160 p.

UNITED STATES RUBBER COMPANY

Babcock, Glenn D. <u>History of the United States Rubber Company: A Case Study in Corporate Management.</u> Bloomington, Ind.: Bureau of Business Research, Graduate School of Business, Indiana University, 1966. 495 p.

UNITED STATES SAVINGS BANK OF NEWARK, N.J.

United States Savings Bank of Newark, N.J. <u>History of the United States Savings Bank of Newark, N.J.</u> Newark: The Bank, 1976. 92 p.

UNITED STATES STEEL CORPORATION

Voorhees, Enders McClumpha. *Financial Policy in a Changing Economy.* Lebanon, Pa.: Sowers Printing Company, 1970. 232 p.

UNITED STATES SUGAR CORPORATION

McGovern, Joseph J. *United States Sugar Corporation: The First Fifty Years.* Clewiston, Fla.: The Company, 1981. 45 p.

UNITED TECHNOLOGIES CORPORATION

Fernandez, Ronald. *Excess Profits; The Rise of United Technologies.* Reading, Mass.: Addison-Wesley, 1983. 320 p.

UNITED TELECOMMUNICATIONS, INC.

Henson, Paul H. *United Telecommunications, Inc.: A Rose by Any Other Name--.* New York: Newcomen Society in North America, 1972. 22 p. (Newcomen Address.)

UNITED TILE COMPANY OF DALLAS

United Tile Company of Dallas. *Dependability for Twenty Years, 1947-1967.* Dallas: The Company, 1967.

UNIVERSAL FOODS CORPORATION

Universal Foods Corporation. *Universal Foods: The First 100 Years.* Milwaukee: The Company, 1982. 46 p.

UNIVERSAL PICTURES COMPANY, INC.

Fitzgerald, Michael G. *Universal Pictures: A Panoramic History in Words, Pictures, and Filmographies.* New Rochelle, N.Y.: Arlington House, 1976. 766 p.

UOP (UNIVERSAL OIL PRODUCTS COMPANY)

Logan, John O. *UOP--Technology in Action.* New York: Newcomen Society in North America, 1975. 16 p. (Newcomen Publication; no. 1017.)

USLIFE CORPORATION

Crosby, Gordon E., Jr. *USLIFE Corporation: Meeting Changing Consumer Needs Through Diversified Financial Services.* New York: Newcomen Society in North America, 1972. 19 p. (Newcomen Address.)

USM CORPORATION

Brewster, William S. *USM Corporation: Our First 75 Years.* New York: Newcomen Society in North America, 1974. 20 p. (Newcomen Publication; no. 989.)

UTAH-IDAHO SUGAR COMPANY

Arrington, Leonard J. *Beet Sugar in the West, A History of the Utah-Idaho Sugar Company, 1891-1966.* Seattle: University of Washington Press, 1966. 234 p.

VICTOR COMPTOMETER CORPORATION

Darly, Edwin. *It All Adds Up; The Growth of Victor Comptometer Corporation.* Chicago: The Company, 1968. 243 p.

VIRGINIA ELECTRIC AND POWER COMPANY

Will, Erwin H. *The Past--Interesting, The Present--Intriguing, The Future--Bright: A Story of Virginia Electric and Power Company.* New York: Newcomen Society in North America, 1965. 24 p. (Newcomen Address.)

VULCAN MATERIALS COMPANY

Blount, W. Houston. *The Past as a Challenge to the Future.* New York: Newcomen Society in the United States, 1984. 20 p. (Newcomen Publication; no. 1184.)

WACHOVIA CORPORATION

Wachovia Corporation. *Wachovia: 1879-1979.* Winston-Salem: The Company, 1979. 21 p.

WACO AIRCRAFT COMPANY

Brandly, Raymond H. <u>Waco Airplanes: Ask Any Pilot: The Authentic History of Waco Airplanes and the Biographies of the Founders, Clayton J. Bruckner and Elwood J. Sam Junkin.</u> Dayton: R.H. Brandly, 1979. 163 p.

Schreiner, Herm. "The Waco Story, Part I: Clayton Bruckner and the Founding Years." <u>American Aviation Historical Society Journal</u> 25 (Winter 1980): 281-299.

WAKEFIELD SEAFOODS

Blackford, Mansel G. <u>Pioneering a Modern Small Business: Wakefield Seafoods and the Alaskan Frontier.</u> Greenwich, Conn.: JAI Press, 1979. 210 p. (Industrial Development and the Social Fabric; vol. 6.)

WAL-MART STORES, INC.

Wal-Mart Stores, Inc. <u>Wal-Mart Stores Fact Sheet.</u> Bentonville, Ariz.: The Company, 1985. 3 p.

WALDEN BOOK COMPANY, INC.

Frank, Jerome P. "Waldenbooks at 50." <u>Publishers Weekly</u> 223 (29 April 1983): 36-41.

WALGREEN COMPANY

"Seventy-five Years of Walgreen Progress." <u>Walgreen World</u> 43 (September-October 1976): 1-28. (75th anniversary issue.)

WALL DRUG STORES

Jennings, Dana Close. <u>Free Ice Water; The Story of Wall Drug.</u> Aberdeen, S.D.: North Plains Press, 1969. 95 p.

WALL STREET JOURNAL

Caliam, Carnegie Samuel. <u>The Gospel According to the</u> Wall Street Journal. Atlanta: John Knox Press, 1975. 114 p.

Neilson, Winthrop, and Frances Neilson. <u>What's News--Dow Jones: Story of the Wall Street Journal.</u> Radnor, Pa.: Chilton Book Company, 1973. 171 p.

Rosenberg, Jerry M. <u>Inside the Wall Street Journal: The History and the Power of Dow Jones & Company and America's Most Influential Newspaper.</u> New York: Macmillan, 1982. 328 p.

Wendt, Lloyd. <u>The Wall Street Journal: The Story of Dow Jones & the Nation's Business Newspaper.</u> Chicago: Rand McNally, 1982. 448 p.

See also: Dow, Jones and Company

WALLACE-MURRAY CORPORATION

Raach, Fred R. Wallace-Murray Corporation. New York: Newcomen Society in North America, 1972. 23 p. (Newcomen Address.)

WALTERS (JIM) CORPORATION

Williams, Randall and Hilda Dent. "Billion Dollar Shell Game." Southern Exposure 8, no. 1 (1980): 86-91.

WARNER BROTHERS COMPANY

Higham, Charles. Warner Brothers. New York: Scribner's, 1975. 232 p.

Silke, James R. Here's Looking at You, Kid: 50 Years of Fighting, Working and Dreaming at Warner Bros. Boston: Little, Brown, 1976. 317 p.

WARREN RUPP COMPANY

Rupp, Warren E. The Warren Rupp Company: Innovative Pumps Foster Success. New York: Newcomen Society in North America, 1983. 23 p. (Newcomen Publication; no. 1195.)

WASHINGTON GAS LIGHT COMPANY

Bittinger, Donald S. Washington Gas Light Company: A Potpourri of Past, Present, and Future. New York: Newcomen Society in North America, 1971. 24 p. (Newcomen Address.)

WASHINGTON NATIONAL CORPORATION

Washington National Corporation. The People Business: A Brief History of the Washington National Organization. Evanston, Ill.: The Company, 1978. 12 p.

WASHINGTON REDSKINS

Denlinger, Ken. Redskin Country: From Baugh to the Super Bowl. New York: Leisure Press, 1983. 224 p.

Denlinger, Ken. Washington Redskins; The Allen Triumph. Englewood Cliffs, N.J.: Prentice-Hall, 1973. 144 p.

Denlinger, Ken, and Paul Allner. Day by Day in Washington Redskins History. New York: Leisure Press, 1984. 320 p.

WASHINGTON STATE FERRIES

Demoro, Harre W. The Evergreen Fleet: A Pictorial History of Washington State Ferries. San Marino, Calif.: Golden West Books, 1971. 136 p.

WASHINGTON STEEL CORPORATION

Fitch T.S. Washington Steel Was Born South of Columbus. New York: Newcomen Society in North America, 1967. 24 p. (Newcomen Address.)

WEAN UNITED, INC.

Wean, R.J., Jr. *Teamwork and Technology: The Story of Wean United.* New York: Newcomen Society in North America, 1969. 24 p. (Newcomen Address.)

WEATHERHEAD COMPANY

Grabner, George J. *The Weatherhead Company; A Cycle Completed--A Commitment to the Future.* New York: Newcomen Society in North America, 1970. 20 p. (Newcomen Address.)

WEBSTER INDUSTRIES, INC.

Nordholt, John B., Jr. *Webster Industries, Inc.: One Hundred Years of Trail, Travail, and Triumph.* New York: Newcomen Society in North America, 1976. 22 p. (Newcomen Publication; no. 1044.)

WEIL BROTHERS COTTON

Bush, George S. *An American Harvest: The Story of Weil Brothers Cotton.* Englewood Cliffs, N.J.: Prentice-Hall, 1982. 495 p.

WELCH GRAPE JUICE COMPANY, INC.

Chazanof, William. *Welch's Grape Juice: From Corporation to Co-operative.* Syracuse: Syracuse University Press, 1977. 407 p.

WELLS FARGO AND COMPANY

Jackson, William Turrentine. <u>Portland: Wells Fargo's Hub for the Pacific Northwest.</u> Portland: Oregon Historical Society, 1985. 36 p. (Reprinted from the <u>Oregon Historical Quarterly</u>, Fall 1985.)

Loomis, Noel M. <u>Wells Fargo.</u> New York: Clarkson N. Potter, Inc., 1968. 340 p.

<u>Under Cover for Wells Fargo: The Unvarnished Recollections of Fred Dodge.</u> Boston: Houghton Mifflin, 1969. 280 p.

Wells Fargo and Company. <u>In July 1852 a "Newcomer" Made Its Appearance on Montgomery Street in San Francisco.</u> San Francisco: The Company, 1977. 17 p.

WENDY'S INTERNATIONAL, INC.

Wendy's International, Inc. <u>Wendy's: A Tradition of Quality.</u> Dublin, Ohio: The Company, 1984. 99 p.

WEST PENN POWER COMPANY

Van Atta, Robert B. <u>50 Years--At Your Service: The Origins and Development of West Penn Power Company.</u> Greensburgh, Pa.: The Company, 1965. 64 p.

WEST POINT-PEPPERELL, INC.

West Point-Pepperell, Inc. <u>The History of West Point-Pepperell.</u> West Point, Ga.: The Company, 1984. 6 p.

WESTERN AIRLINES, INC.

Serling, Robert J. <u>The Only Way to Fly: The Story of Western Airlines, America's Senior Air Carrier.</u> Garden City, N.Y.: Doubleday, 1976. 494 p.

WESTERN COMPANY OF NORTH AMERICA

Chiles, H.E. <u>The Western Company of North America: 44 years of Pacesetting in the Oil Business.</u> New York: Newcomen Society in North America, 1984. 28 p. (Newcomen Publication; no. 1205.)

WESTERN ELECTRIC COMPANY

Balzer, Richard. <u>Clockwork: Life in and Outside an American Factory.</u> Garden City, N.Y.: Doubleday, 1976. 333 p.

Gorman, Paul A. <u>Century One--A Prologue.</u> New York: Newcomen Society in North America, 1969. 24 p.

McKinsey and Company. <u>A Study of Western Electric's Performance; A Report.</u> New York: AT&T, 1969. 251 p.

Smith, George David. <u>Anatomy of a Business Strategy: Bell, Western Electric and the Origins of the</u>

American Telephone Industry. Baltimore: Johns Hopkins University Press, 1985. 237 p.

See also: American Telephone and Telegraph Company

WESTERN GEAR CORPORATION

Bannan, Thomas J. From Cogwheels to Space-Age Systems: The Story of Western Gear Corporation. New York: Newcomen Society in North America, 1969. 24 p. (Newcomen Address.)

WESTERN INTERNATIONAL HOTELS, INC.

Carlson, Edward E. UAL, Inc.: United Airlines and Western International Hotels: Partners in Travel. New York: Newcomen Society in North America, 1975. 15 p. (Newcomen Publication, no. 1030.)

WESTERN PACIFIC RAILROAD

Perlman, Alfred E. Western Pacific Railroad: "The Feather River Route." New York: Newcomen Society in North America, 1975. 16 p. (Newcomen Publication; no. 1014.)

WESTERN SAVINGS AND LOAN ASSOCIATION

Driggs, Douglas H. The Path We Came By: The Story of Western Savings and Loan Association. New York: Newcomen

Society in North America, 1969. 32 p. (Newcomen Address.)

WESTERN UNION CORPORATION

Western Union Corporation. <u>Western Union: From Wire to Westar.</u> Upper Saddle River, N.J.: The Company, 1985. 20 p.

WESTERN UNION INTERNATIONAL, INC.

Gallagher, Edward A. <u>Getting the Message Across: The Story of Western Union International, Inc.</u> New York: Newcomen Society in North America, 1971. 24 p. (Newcomen Address.)

WESTERN UNION TELEGRAPH CORPORATION

McFall, Russell W. <u>Making History by Responding to Its Forces.</u> New York: Newcomen Society in North America, 1971. 20 p. (Newcomen Address.)

WESTFIELD COMPANIES

Condon, George E. <u>History of Ohio Farmers Insurance Company, 1848-1984.</u> Westfield Center, Ohio: The Company, 1985. 274 p.

WESTINGHOUSE ELECTRIC CORPORATION

Schatz, Ronald W. <u>The Electrical Workers: A History of Labor at General Electric and Westinghouse, 1923-1960.</u> Urbana: University of Illinois Press, 1983. 279 p.

WEYERHAEUSER COMPANY

Jones, Alden H. From Jamestown to Coffin Rock; A History of Weyerhaeuser Operations in Southwest Washington. Tacoma, Wash.: The Company, 1974. 346 p.

Weyerhaeuser, George H. "Forests for the Future": The Weyerhaeuser Story. New York: Newcomen Society in North America, 1981. 24 p. (Newcomen Publication; no. 1141.)

WHITE CASTLE SYSTEM, INC.

Gelfand, M. Howard. "One Square Burger that's Gotten Around: Since 1921 White Castle has Warmed the Heart's and Plates of Many." Advertising Age 54 (21 November 1983): sec. 2, M24-M25.

WICKES CORPORATION

Bush, George. The Wide World of Wickes: An Unusual Story of an Unusual Growth Company. New York: McGraw-Hill, 1976. 486 p.

WILEY (JOHN) AND SONS, INC.

Anthony, Carolyn T. "John Wiley at 175." Publishers Weekly 222 (24 September 1982): 42-46.

Moore, John Hammond. *Wiley: One Hundred Seventy Five Years of Publishing.* New York: Wiley, 1982. 279 p.

WILLAMETTE INDUSTRIES, INC.

Baldwin, Catherine A. *Making the Most of the Best: Willamette Industries' Seventy-five Years.* Portland: The Company, 1982. 172 p.

WINNEBAGO INDUSTRIES, INC.

Winnebago Industries, Inc. *Winnebago: A Proud History, A Dynamic Future.* Forest City, Iowa: The Company, 1981. 8 p.

WISCONSIN POWER AND LIGHT COMPANY

"WP&L's 60th Anniversary." *Concepts for Employees of Wisconsin Power and Light Company* 10 (Spring 1984): 1-27.

WITCO CHEMICAL CORPORATION

Wishnick, William. *The Witco Story.* New York: Newcomen Society in North America, 1976. 34 p. (Newcomen Publication; no. 1029.)

WIX CORPORATION

Sims, Allen H., and L.G. Alexander. *Wix Corporation.* New York: Newcomen Society in North America, 1974. 32 p. (Newcomen Address.)

WLS (RADIO STATION) CHICAGO

Evans, James F. *Prairie Farmer and WLS: The Burridge D. Butler Years.* Urbana: University of Illinois Press, 1969. 329 p.

WOODSTOCK AND SYCAMORE TRACTION COMPANY

Robertson, William E. *The Woodstock and Sycamore Traction Company.* Delavan, Wis.: National Bus Trader, 1985. 56 p.

WOOLWORTH (F.W.) COMPANY

Brough, James. *The Woolworth's.* New York: McGraw-Hill, 1982. 224 p.

F.W. Woolworth Company. **100th Anniversary: 1879-1979.** New York: The Company, 1979. 55 p.

Nichols, John Peter. *Skyline Queen and the Merchant Prince; The Woolworth Story.* New York: Trident Press, 1973. 144 p.

WORCESTER COUNTY NATIONAL BANK

Tymeson, Mildred McClary. *Worcester Bankbook: From County Barter to County Bank, 1804-1966.* Worcester, Mass.: The Bank, 1966. 183 p.

WORCESTER TELEGRAM AND GAZETTE

Stoddard, Robert W. *The Evening Gazette: 100 Years--A Consistent Story.* New

York: Newcomen Society in North America, 1966. 24 p.

WORLD JOURNAL TRIBUNE

Sage, Joseph. *Three to Zero: The Story of the Birth and Death of the* World Journal Tribune. New York: American Newspaper Publishers Association, 1967. 82 p.

WORTHEN BANK AND TRUST COMPANY

Walsh, Mary Phyllis. *In the Vaults of Time.* Little Rock: The Bank, 1976. 179 p.

WORTHINGTON FOODS, INC.

Worthington Foods, Inc. *Putting Good Taste into Good Nutrition; Yesterday and Today.* Worthington, Ohio: The Company, 1984. 12 p.

WORTHINGTON INDUSTRIES

McConnell, John H. *"--And We've Only Scratched the Surface": The Growth Story of Worthington Industries.* New York: Newcomen Society in North America, 1981. 20 p. (Newcomen Publication; no. 1138.)

WQXR (RADIO STATION) NEW YORK CITY

Sanger, Elliot M. *Rebel in Radio; The Story of WQXR.* New York: Hastings House, 1973. 190 p.

WRIGLEY (WM.), JR., COMPANY

Angle, Paul McClelland. Philip K. Wrigley: A Memoir of a Modest Man. Chicago: Rand McNally, 1975. 192 p.

WVLK (RADIO STATION) LEXINGTON, KY.

"WVLK: Central Kentucky's No. 1 Radio Station for 28 Years." Kincaid Towers (1980): 32-35.

WWL (RADIO STATION) NEW ORLEANS

Pusateri, C. Joseph. Enterprise in Radio: WWL and the Business of Broadcasting in America. Washington, D.C.: University Press of America, 1980. 336 p.

WYLE LABORATORIES

Graybill, Harry G., ed. The Wyle Companies. El Segundo, Calif.: The Company, 1972.

WYLY CORPORATION

Voth, Ben. A Piece of the Computer Pie. Houston: Gulf Publishing Company, 1974. 182 p.

WYMAN-GORDON COMPANY

Carter, Joseph R. Wyman-Gordon Company: 100 Years Committed to Challenge and Leadership. New York: Newcomen Society

in North America, 1983. 22 p.
(Newcomen Publication; no. 1194.)

XEROX CORPORATION

Brooks, John. "Story of the Xerox
Corporation." In *Business Adventures*,
145-175. New York: Weybright and
Tally, 1969.

Dessauer, John H. *My Years with Xerox:
The Billions Nobody Wanted.* New York:
Doubleday, 1971. 239 p.

Xerox Corporation. *The Story of
Xerography.* Stamford, Conn.: The
Company, 1978. 9 p.

YARNALL, BIDDLE AND COMPANY

West, Harold A. *Two Hundred Years, 1764-
1964: The Story of Yarnall, Biddle and
Company, Investment Bankers.*
Philadelphia: The Company, 1965. 82 p.

YELLOW FREIGHT SYSTEMS, INC.

Filgas, James F. *Yellow in Motion: A
History of Yellow Freight System, Inc.*
Bloomington: Indiana University Press,
1971. 144 p.

THE ZALE CORPORATION

Stringer, Tommy Wayne. "The Zale
Corporation: A Texas Success Story."
Ph.D. diss., North Texas State
University, 1984. 229 p.

ZIONS FIRST NATIONAL BANK

Simmons, Roy W. Zions First National Bank: Growing into Its Second Hundred Years. New York: Newcomen Society in North America, 1974. 23 p. (Newcomen Publication; no. 979.)

ZONDERVAN CORPORATION

Ruark, James E., and T.W. Engstrom. The House of Zondervan. Grand Rapids, Mich.: The Company, 1981. 162 p.

ZURN INDUSTRIES, INC.

Zurn, Everett F., and F.W. Zurn. Zurn Industries, Inc.: The Evolution of Environmentalism. New York: Newcomen Society in North America, 1973. 22 p. (Newcomen Address.)

INDEX BY INDUSTRY

ACCOUNTING

Anderson (Arthur) and Company 18
Haskins and Sells 133
Peat, Marwick, Mitchell and Company 213
Price Waterhouse and Company 224

ADVERTISING

Benton and Bowles, Inc. 36
Burnett (Leo) Company 47
Needham Harper Worldwide, Inc. 193

AIR CONDITIONING, HEATING and REFRIGERATION

Carrier Corporation 51
Garrett Corporation 114

AIRCRAFT

Alexander Aircraft Company 7
Atlantic Aviation Corporation 25
Beech Aircraft Corporation 34
Boeing Company 40
California Aero Company 49
Consolidated Aircraft Corporation 72
Douglas Aircraft Company 88
General Dynamics Corporation 115

Grumman Corporation 128
Hughes Aircraft Company 139
Lockheed Aircraft Corporation 164
McDonnell Douglas Corporation 169-170
Piper Aircraft Corporation 221
Rockwell International 232-233
Rohr Corporation 234
Ryan Aeronautical Company 236
United Technologies Corporation 275
Waco Aircraft Company 278

AIRLINES

Air Florida 5
Alaska Airlines 6
American Airlines, Inc. 10-11
Braniff Airways 43
Comair, Inc. 71
Command-Aire Corporation 71
Continental Airlines Corporation 74-75
Delta Airlines, Inc. 83
Eastern Airlines, Inc. 93-94
Frontier Airlines 113
Laker Airways 158
Midstate Airlines 181
Midway Airlines 181
National Airlines, Inc. 189
North Central Airlines, Inc. 200
North-East Airlines 200
Northeast Airlines, Inc. 201
Northwest Airlines, Inc. 202
Ozark Air Lines 208
Pan American World Airways, Inc. 210
People Express, Inc. 216
Piedmont Airlines 220
Provincetown-Boston Airline, Inc. 225
Republic Airlines 228
Southwest Airlines 250

Tiger International, Inc. 263
Trans World Airlines, Inc. 265-266
United Airlines, Inc. 272
USAir 273
Western Airlines, Inc. 284

APPAREL

Cluett, Peabody and Company, Inc. 67
Genesco, Inc. 121
Kellwood Company 153
Levi Strauss and Company 161
Stone Manufacturing Company 256
Thomas (S.N.) Sons 263
West Point-Pepperell, Inc. 284

AUCTION HOUSES

Sotheby Parke Bernet, Inc. 247-248

AUTOMOTIVE SERVICES

Tidy Car, Inc. 263

BANKING

Alabama Bancorporation 6
Amarillo National Bank 10
Arizona Bank 21
BancOhio Corporation 29
Bank of Boston Corporation 30
Bank of New Mexico 30
Bank of Virginia 30
Bankers Trust Company 31
Barnett Bank of Jacksonville 31
Bowery Savings Bank 42
Buffalo Savings Bank 46
Caldwell and Company 49

Casco Northern Bank, N.A.   51
Central National Bank of Cleveland   53
Chase Manhattan Corporation   56
Chemical Bank   56
Citicorp   63-64
City National Bank and Trust Company of
  Rockford   64-65
Clark County State Bank   65
Commerce Trust Company   71
Deposit Guarantee Bank and Trust Company of
  Jackson   85
Depositors Corporation   85
Detroit Bank and Trust Company   85
East River Savings Bank   93
Farmers and Mechanics National Bank, Frederick,
  Md.   99
Farmers and Merchants Bank of Los Angeles   99
Fidelity-Philadelphia Trust Company   101
Financial General Bankshares, Inc.   103
First Alabama Bancshares   103
First and Merchants National Bank, Richmond   103
First Bank System, Inc.   104
First Fidelity Bancorporation   105
First Hawaiian Bank   105
First Mississippi Corporation   105
First National Bank and Trust Company of
  Wyoming   105
First National Bank in Houston   105
First National Bank of Belleville   106
First National Bank of Biloxi   106
First National Bank of Commerce   106
First National Bank of Denver   106
First National Bank of Fargo   106
First National Bank of Fort Worth   107
First National Bank of Geneva   107
First National Bank of Grand Island   107
First National Bank of Mobile   107
First National Bank of Platteville   107

First National Bank of Tuscaloosa   107-108
First National City Bank   108
First Pennsylvania Bank, N.A.   108
First Security Corporation   108-109
First Trust and Deposit Company, Syracuse,
   N.Y.   109
First Union Corporation   109
Fort Worth National Bank   112
Fourth National Bank and Trust Company   112-113
Franklin National Bank   113
Grenada Bank   127
Hamilton County State Bank   130
Harris Trust and Savings Bank   132
Harter Bank and Trust Company   132
Hartford National Bank and Trust Company   132
Huntington Bancshares, Inc.   140
Huntington National Bank of Columbus   140
Idaho First National Bank   141
Industrial National Bank of Rhode Island   143
Irwin Union Bank and Trust Company   148
Key Banks, Inc.   156
Littleton Savings Bank   164
Madison Bank and Trust Company   172
Merchants National Bank and Trust Company of
   Indianapolis   178-179
Merchants National Bank and Trust Company of
   Syracuse   179
Merrill Bankshares Company   179
Michigan National Bank   181
Morgan (J.P.) and Company   186
National Bank of Commerce of Seattle   189
National Bank of Commerce Trust and Savings
   Association   189
National Bank of Detroit   189.
National Commerce Bank and Trust Company   190
National Farmer's Bank   191
NCNB   192
New York Bank for Savings   194

Northern Trust Bank   202
Northwest Bancorporation   202
Penn Square Bank   214
Penobscot Savings Bank   215
Peoples Bank of Bloomington   216
People's Savings Bank--Bridgeport   216
RepublicBank Corporation   229
Riggs National Bank of Washington, D.C.   231
Savings and Loan Bank of the State of New York   240
Savings Bank of New London   240
Seattle-First National Bank   243
South Carolina National Bank   248
Southern Bancorporation of Alabama   248
State National Bank of El Paso   255
Suburban Trust Company   258
Tracy Collins Bank and Trust Company   265
Union Trust Company of Maryland   271-272
United Bank of Arizona   273
United Banks of Colorado, Inc.   273
United States Savings Bank of Newark, N.J.   274
Wachovia Corporation   277
Wells Fargo and Company   283
Worcester County National Bank   289
Worthen Bank and Trust Company   290
Zions First National Bank   293

BEVERAGES

American Distilling Company   12
Brown-Forman Distillers Corporation   44
Coca-Cola Company   68
Coors (Adolph) Company   76
Dr. Pepper Company   90
Heileman (G.) Brewing Company, Inc.   133
Hills Brothers Coffee, Inc.   135
Hudepohl Brewing Company   139
Leisy Brewing Company   161
Masson (Paul) Vineyards   176

Pepsi-Cola Company 216
Roddy Manufacturing Company 233
Schlitz (Jos.) Brewing Company 241

BOOK STORES

Rostenberg (Leona) 234
Walden Book Company, Inc. 278

BUILDING MATERIALS

Certain-Teed Corporation 54
Manville Corporation 173
Masco Corporation 175
Owens-Corning Fiberglass Corporation 207
Robertson (H.H.) Company 231-232
Wallace-Murray Corporation 280
Walters (Jim) Corporation 280

CABLE and PAY TV SYSTEMS

Oak Industries, Inc. 204

CEMENT, GYPSUM and MASONRY

Gifford-Hill and Company, Inc. 123
Hummel Industries, Inc. 140

CHEMICAL PRODUCTS

Air Products and Chemicals, Inc. 5
Alco Standard Corporation 7
Allied Corporation 8
Cabot Corporation 49
Cargill, Inc. 51
Celanese Corporation of America 52
Chevron Chemical Company-Ortho Division 58
Dexter Corporation 86

Dow Chemical Company 88-89
Du Pont de Nemours (E.I.) and Company 91-92
Ethyl Corporation 98
Farmland Industries, Inc. 100
GAF Corporation 114
Grace (W.R.) and Company 125
Halcon International, Inc. 130
Hercules, Inc. 134
International Minerals and Chemical
  Corporation 146
Loctite Corporation 165
Lord Corporation 165
Lubrizol Corporation 167
Monsanto Company 185
Morton Thiokol, Inc. 186
Nalco Chemical Company 188
PPG Industries 223-224
Rohm and Haas Company 233
STP Corporation 256
U.S. Borax and Chemical Corporation 274
U.S. Industrial Chemicals Company 274
Witco Chemical Corporation 288

CLUBS and PROFESSIONAL ORGANIZATIONS

Automobile Club of Southern California 26
Cincinnati Country Club 62
East Texas Chamber of Commerce 93
Rotary Club, Charlotte, N.C. 234
Rotary Club, Lakeland, Fla. 234
Rotary Club, Oakland, Calif. 235
Rotary Club, Palo Alto, Calif. 235
Rotary Club, Trenton, N.J. 235
Rotary International 235

COAL

Eastern Gas and Fuel Associates 94
Mapco, Inc. 174
Peabody Holding Company, Inc. 213
Pittston Company 222

COMPUTER SERVICES

AccuRay Corporation 3
Computer Sciences Corporation 72
Context Management Corporation 74
Electronic Data Systems Corporation 95
OPM Leasing Services 207
System Development Corporation 260
Wyly Corporation 291

COMPUTERS

Amdahl Corporation 10
Apple Computers 20
Atari, Inc. 24
Burroughs Corporation 47
Data General Corporation 80
Digital Equipment Corporation 87
Honeywell, Inc. 137
International Business Machines Corporation 144-145
Lear Siegler, Inc. 160
National Cash Register Company 190
TEC, Inc. 261

CONGLOMERATES

Alco Standard Corporation 7
Amfac, Inc. 16
Carborundum Company 50
Figgie International Holdings, Inc. 102

Fuqua Industries, Inc. 113
Greyhound Corporation 127
Gulf and Western Industries 128
IC Industries 141
Litton Industries, Inc. 164
Martin Marietta Corporation 175
RCA Corporation 227-228
Tenneco, Inc. 261
Textron, Inc. 262
TRW 267
Vulcan Materials Company 277

CONSTRUCTION

Associated General Contractors of America 23
Austin Bridge Company 26
Austin Company 26
Bechtel Corporation 33
Blount, Inc. 39
Centex Corporation 52
Champion Bridge Company 55
Cianbro Corporation 61
Foster Wheeler Corporation 112
Harbert Corporation 131
Hubbard Construction Company 138
Jones (J.A.) Construction Company 150
Kiewit (Peter) Sons, Inc. 156
Sundt (M.M.) Construction Company 258

CONSUMER CREDIT

American Express Company 12
Associates Corporation of North America 23
Associates Investment Company 23
Beneficial Corporation 36
C.I.T. Financial Corporation 63
Gulf and Western Industries 128
Household Finance Corporation 138

Kentucky Finance Company, Inc.   154
Provident Loan Society of New York   225

CONTAINERS

Anchor Hocking Glass Corporation   18
Brockway Glass Company, Inc.   43
Clark (J.L.) Manufacturing Company   65
National Can Corporation   190
Owens-Illinois, Inc.   208

COSMETICS and TOILETRIES

Arden (Elizabeth), Inc.   20
Chesebrough-Pond's, Inc.   57
Jergens (Andrew) Company   149
Lauder (Estee)   159
Mary Kay Cosmetics   175
Noxell Corporation   203-204
Revlon, Inc.   229

DEFENSE SYSTEMS

General Dynamics Corporation   115
Ling-Temco-Vought, Inc.   163
Lockheed-Georgia Company   164
Northrop Corporation   202
Raytheon Company   227
Scott Aviation Corporation   241

DEPARTMENT STORES, DRUG, and SPECIALTY STORES

Allied Stores Corporation   8
Bloomingdale's   39
Federated Department Stores   101
Ivey (J.B.) and Company   149
Kresge (S.S.) Company   157
Limited, Inc.   162

McCrory Corporation   168
McRae's Department Stores   171
Macy (R.H.) and Company, Inc.   171-172
Meijer, Inc.   177
Mercantile Stores Company, Inc.   178
Montgomery Ward and Company   185
Penney (J.C.) Company, Inc.   214-215
Rich's, Inc.   231
Sears, Roebuck and Company   242-243
Strawbridge and Clothier   257
Tandy Corporation   260
Wal-Mart Stores, Inc.   278
Walgreen Company   279
Wall Drug Stores   279
Woolworth (F.W.) Company   289

DRUGS

Abbott Laboratories   3
Burroughs Wellcome Company   48
Dorsey Laboratories   88
Gilpin (Henry B.) Company   124
Lilly (Eli) and Company   162
Miles Laboratories, Inc.   182
Parke-Davis and Company   211
Pfizer, Inc.   217
Robins (A.H.) Company   232
SmithKline Corporation   246
Squibb Corporation   252

ELECTRIC & GAS UTILITIES

American Electric Power Company   12
Arizona Public Service Company   21
Atlanta Gas Light Company   24
Central Hudson Gas and Electric Corporation   53
Central Illinois Public Service Company   53
Central Power and Light Company   53

Central Vermont Public Service Corporation   54
Cincinnati Gas and Electric Company   62
Citizens Gas and Coke Utility   64
Columbus and Southern Ohio Electric Company   70
Consolidated Edison Company of New York, Inc.   73
Consumers Power Company   74
Detroit Edison Company   85
Duke Power Company   92
Florida Power Corporation   109
Illinois Power Company   142
Indianapolis Power and Light Company   142
International Utilities Corporation   147
Kansas Power and Light Company   152
Louisiana Power and Light Company   167
Mississippi Power Company   184
Missouri Public Service Company   184
Montana-Dakota Utilities Company   185
Northern Ohio Traction and Light Company   201-202
Ohio Valley Electric Corporation   205-206
Oklahoma Gas and Electric Company   206
Pacific Gas and Electric Company   208
Pacific Lighting Corporation   208
Pacific Power and Light Company   209
PacifiCorp   209
Pennsylvania Power and Light Company   215
Pennsylvania Power Company   215
Public Service Company of Indiana   225
Public Service Electric and Gas Company   226
San Diego Gas and Electric Company   239
Southern California Edison Company   249
Southern Company   249
Virginia Electric and Power Company   277
Washington Gas Light Company   280
West Penn Power Company   283
Wisconsin Power and Light Company   288

ELECTRIC EQUIPMENT and SUPPLIES

Anderson Electric Corporation   19
Chance (A.B.) Company   55
Cutler-Hammer, Inc.   79
Emerson Electric Company   96
General Electric Company   116
Gould, Inc.   125
Grainger (W.W.), Inc.   126
McGraw-Edison Company   170
Robbins and Myers, Inc.   231
Square D Company   251
Union Electric Company   269
Westinghouse Electric Corporation   286

ELECTRONIC COMPONENTS

General Radio Company   120-121
Robinson Nugent, Inc.   232
TDK USA Corporation   261
Texas Instruments   262
Wyle Laboratories   291

ENGINEERING

Albert Kahn Associates, Inc.   6
Benham-Blair and Affiliates, Inc.   36
Black and Veatch, Inc.   38
Bovay Engineers, Inc.   42
Camp Dresser and McKee, Inc.   50
Day and Zimmermann, Inc.   80
Freese and Nichols, Inc.   113
Gibbs and Hill, Inc.   123
Harza Engineering Company   132-133
Henningson, Durham and Richardson   134
Jacobs Engineering Group, Inc.   149
Main (C.T.) Corporation   172
McKim, Mead and White   170

Parsons Brinckerhoff, Inc. 212
Parsons, Brinckerhoff, Quade and Douglas, Inc. 212
Smith, Hinchman and Grylls Associates, Inc. 246
Sverdrup Corporation 259

ENGINES

Baldwin-Lima-Hamilton Corporation 28
Baldwin Locomotive Works 28
Boeing Company 40
Briggs and Stratton Corporation 43
Continental Motors Corporation 75
Fairbanks-Morse Corporation 99

ENTERTAINMENT

Corporation for Entertainment and Learning 77
Disney (Walt) Productions 87
Motown Record Corporation 187
Playboy Enterprises, Inc. 222

FARMS

Bob Evans Farms 39
Grove Farm Company, Inc. 128
Richards Farms, Inc. 230

FEEDS and FEED INGREDIENTS

Agway, Inc. 5
Central Soya Company, Inc. 54

FINANCIAL SERVICES

American Stock Exchange 14
Associates Corporation of North America 23
Associates Investment Company 23
AVCO Corporation 26

Baldwin (D.H.) Company 27-28
Deak-Perera Group 82
National Revenue Corporation 192
New York Stock Exchange 196
Philadelphia Stock Exchange 218
Republic Financial Services, Inc. 229
TICOR 263

FLOOR COVERING

Armstrong World Industries, Inc. 22
United Tile Company of Dallas 275

FOOD and FOOD PROCESSING

Amfac, Inc. 16
Anderson, Clayton and Company 18-19
Archer Daniels Midland Company 20
Beatrice Food Company 33
Bob Evans Farms 39
Bryan Foods, Inc. 45
Campbell Soup Company 50
Carnation Company 51
Castle and Cooke, Inc. 51
Consolidated Foods 73
Del Monte Corporation 83
Di Giorgio Fruit Corporation 86
Famous Amos Chocolate Chip Company 99
Foremost-McKeeson, Inc. 111
General Foods Corporation 117
General Mills, Inc. 117
Gerber Products Company 122
Heinz (H.J.) Company 133
Hershey Foods Corporation 134
Kellogg Company 153
Lance, Inc. 158
Land O'Lakes Creameries, Inc. 159
Lepage (F.R.) Bakery, Inc. 161

McCormick and Company, Inc.   168
Mayer (Oscar) and Company   176
Mike-Sell's Potato Chip Company   181
Minute Maid Corporation   183
Nabisco Brands, Inc.   188
Nestle Company, Inc.   193
Norton Simon, Inc.   203
Peter Paul, Inc.   217
Pillsbury Company   220
Quaker Oats Company   226
Ralston Purina Company   227
Richards Farms, Inc.   230
Staley (A.E.) Manufacturing Company   252
Standard Fruit and Steamship Company   252
Sunsweet Growers, Inc.   259
Sysco Corporation   259
Trend Line Corporation   266
United Fruit Company   273
Universal Foods Corporation   276
Wakefield Seafoods   278
Welch Grape Juice Company, Inc.   282
Worthington Foods, Inc.   290

FOOTWEAR

Barry (R.G.) Corporation   31-32
Brown Group, Inc.   44
Endicott Johnson Corporation   96
Interco, Inc.   144
Melville Shoe Corporation   178

FOREST PRODUCTS

Anderson-Tully Company   19
Boise Cascade Corporation   41
Diamond Match Company   86-87
Georgia-Pacific Corporation   122
Kellogg (L.D.) Lumber Company   153

Louisiana-Pacific   166
Mead Corporation   177
Miller Manufacturing Company, Inc.   182
Neils (J.) Lumber Company   193
Pacific Lumber Company   208
Potlatch Corporation   223
Roddis Plywood Corporation   233
St. Paul and Tacoma Lumber Company   238
Seaboard Lumber and Shipping   242
Weyerhaeuser Company   287
Willamette Industries, Inc.   288

FREIGHT TRANSPORTATION

Consolidated Freightways, Inc.   73-74
Emery Air Freight Corporation   96
Federal Express Corporation   100
United Parcel Service of America   273
Yellow Freight System, Inc.   292

FUEL and ICE DEALERS

Brown (K.J.) and Company   44-45

FURNITURE

Hill-Rom Company   135
Keller Manufacturing Company   153
Levitz Furniture Corporation   161
MPI Industries, Inc.   187-188
Wickes Corporation   287

GROCERY and CONVENIENCE STORES

Acme Markets, Inc.   4
Alpha Beta Company   9
Associated Grocers, Inc.   23
Great Atlantic and Pacific Tea Company   126

Jitney Jungle Stores of America   149
Kroger Company   157
Lewis Grocer Company   161
Marsh Supermarkets, Inc.   174
Munford, Inc.   188
Publix Super Markets   226
Safeway Stores   236-237
Southland Corporation   250
Sunflower Food Stores   258
Supermarkets General Corporation   259

HARDWARE

Ace Hardware Corporation   3
Atlanta Saw Company   24
Black and Decker Manufacturing Company   38
Hoe (R.) and Company   135
Kenrick (Archibald) and Sons   154
Knox Industrial Supplies   156
Southern Saw Service, Inc.   249
Standard Screw Company   254
Stanley Works   254

HOME BUILDERS

Champion Home Builders Company   55
Kaufman and Broad, Inc.   152

HOSPITALS

Alachua General Hospital, Inc.   6

HOTELS

Broadmoor Hotel, Inc.   43
Grand Hotel   126
Holiday House   135
Holiday Inns of America, Inc.   136

Inter-Continental Hotels   144
Western International Hotels, Inc.   285

HOUSEHOLD PRODUCTS

Amway Corporation   17-18
Hoover Company   137
Magic Chef, Inc.   172
Maytag Company   176
Norris Industries, Inc.   199
Oneida Ltd.   207
Pickard, Inc.   220
Roper Corporation   234
Shaklee Corporation   244

INSURANCE

Aetna Life and Casualty   4
Allstate Insurance Company   8-9
American General Insurance Company   12
American International Group, Inc.   13
Atlantic Mutual Insurance Company   25
Bankers Security Life Insurance Society   30
Business Men's Assurance Company of America   48
Cincinnati Financial Corporation   62
Columbus Mutual Life Insurance Company   70
Combined Insurance Company of America   71
Confederation Life Insurance Company   72
Connecticut Mutual Life Insurance Company   72
Continental Insurance Company   75
CUNA Mutual Insurance Society   78
East Augusta Mutual Fire Insurance Company   92-93
Employers Insurance of Wausau Mutual Company   96
Equitable Life Assurance Society of the United
  States   97
Equitable Life Insurance Company of Iowa   97
Erie Insurance Exchange   97
Federal Deposit Insurance Corporation   100

Fidelity Union Life Insurance Company   102
Government Employees Insurance Company   125
Guarantee Mutual Life Company   128
Hartford Steam Boiler Inspection and Insurance
  Company   132
Home Insurance Company   136
Hospital Corporation of America   138
Independent Life and Accident Insurance
  Company   142
Insurance Company of North America   144
Kemper Group   153
Kentucky Central Life Insurance Company   154
Liberty Corporation   162
Life Insurance Company of Virginia   162
Manhattan Life Insurance Company   173
Marsh and McLennan Companies   174
Midland Mutual Life Insurance Company   181
Mutual Benefit Life Insurance Company   188
National Grange Mutual Insurance Company   191
National Liberty Corporation   191
National Life and Accident Insurance Company,
  Inc.   191-192
Nationwide Insurance Companies   192
New England Mutual Life Insurance Company   194
New York Life Insurance Company   195
North Carolina Mutual Life Insurance Company   199-200
Northwest G.F. Mutual Insurance Company   202
Occidental Life Insurance Company of
  California   204
Ohio Casualty Group   205
Ohio Farmers Insurance Company   205
Pacific Mutual Life Insurance Company of
  California   209
Protective Life Insurance Company   224-225
Prudential Insurance Company of America   225
Reliable Life Insurance Company   228
Safeco Insurance Companies   236

Security Mutual Life Insurance Company 243
Shenandoah Life Insurance Company 245
Standard Life Insurance Company 252-253
State Automobile Mutual Insurance Company 255
Supreme Life Insurance Company 259
Torchmark Corporation 264-265
Travelers Insurance Companies 266
USLIFE Corporation 276
Washington National Corporation 281
Westfield Companies 286

INVESTMENT

Affiliated Fund, Inc. 5
Babson (David L.) and Company, Inc. 27
Brown Brothers, Harriman and Company 44
Butcher and Company 48
Drexel Burnham Lambert 91
Fiduciary Trust Company of New York 102
Garrett (Robert) and Sons, Inc. 114
Investors Overseas Services 148
Kidder, Peabody, and Company 156
Kuhn, Loeb and Company 157
Lehman Brothers Kuhn Loeb 160
Lord, Abbet and Company 165
Merrill Lynch 179
Morgan Stanley and Company, Inc. 186
Scottish American Investment Company Limited 241
Shearson Loeb Rhoades 244
Yarnall, Biddle and Company 292

JEWELERS

Caldwell (J.E.) and Company 49
Shreve, Crump and Low Company 245
Tanner (O.C.) Company 260
Tiffany and Company 263
Zale Corporation 292

LAW and LEGAL SERVICES

Cummings and Lockwood   78
Gaston, Snow and Ely, Bartlett   115

LEASING

Leasco Data Processing Equipment Corporation   160
Saunders Leasing Systems, Inc.   240

LEISURE TIME

Brunswick Corporation   45
Dickerson (Charles W.) Field Music, Inc.   87
Kentucky Hills Industries   155
Lionel Train Company   163
Resorts International, Inc.   229

MACHINE TOOLS

Acme-Cleveland Corporation   4
Cincinnati Milacron   62
Monarch Machine Tool Company   185

MACHINERY and EQUIPMENT

Allis-Chalmers Corporation   8
Babcock and Wilcox Company   27
Baker International Corporation   27
Barber-Greene Company   31
Black Clawson Company   38
Bodine Corporation   40
Briggs and Stratton Corporation   43
Bucyrus-Erie Company   46
Caterpillar Tractor Company   52
Clark Equipment Company   65
Colt Industries, Inc.   69
Combustion Engineering, Inc.   71

Cooper Industries   76
Deere and Company   82-83
Ex-Cell-O Corporation   98
Fellows Gear Shaper Company   101
Ferracute Machine Company   101
Figgie International Holdings, Inc.   102
Harnischfeger Corporation   131
Joy Manufacturing Company   151
McNally Pittsburgh   171
Melroe Company   177
Miniature Precision Bearings, Inc.   183
Norton Company   203
Parker Hannifin Corporation   211
Sundstrand Corporation   258
TRW-Reda Pump Division   267
USM Corporation   276
Warren Rupp Company   280
Wean United, Inc.   282
Western Gear Corporation   285
Wyman-Gordon Company   291-292

MAIL ORDER

Bean (L.L.), Inc.   32
Berry (L.M.) and Company   36
Horchow Collection   137
Montgomery Ward and Company   185
Penney (J.C.) Company, Inc.   214-215
Sears, Roebuck and Company   242-243
Spiegel, Inc.   251

MANAGEMENT SERVICES

ARA Services, Inc.   20
Equifax, Inc.   97
Gelco Corporation   115
Spencer Stuart and Associates   250-251

MEASURING and CONTROL

Cutler-Hammer, Inc.   79
Fluke (John) Manufacturing Company, Inc.   110
Perkin-Elmer Corporation   217

MEAT PACKING and PROCESSING

Bob Evans Farms   39
Darling-Delaware Company, Inc.   80
Hormel (George A.) and Company   137
Iowa Beef Processors, Inc.   148
Mayer (Oscar) and Company   176
Tyson Foods, Inc.   268

MEDICAL and DENTAL EQUIPMENT and SUPPLIES

Abbott Laboratories   3
Alcon Laboratories, Inc.   7
American Hospital Supply Corporation   13
Johnson and Johnson, Inc.   150
Milton Roy Company   182

METAL PRODUCTS

Charlotte Pipe and Foundry Company   55
Clow Corporation   66
Eastern Company   94
Elano Corporation   95
Gilbert and Bennett Manufacturing Company   123
Illinois Tool Works, Inc.   142
International Silver Company   146
Kaman Corporation   151
Kennametal, Inc.   153
Kerite Company   155
Lunkenheimer Company   168
Marlin Firearms Company   174
Okonite Company   206

SIFCO Industries, Inc.   245
Southwire Company   250
Victor Comptometer Corporation   277

MINING and MINERALS

Aluminum Company of America   9
AMAX, Inc.   10
American Brass Company   11
American Zinc Company   16
Anglo American Corporation of South Africa,
   Ltd.   19
Calumet and Hecla, Inc.   50
Chisos Mining Company   59-60
Cleveland-Cliffs Iron Company   66
Cold Spring Granite Company   68
Copper Range Company   76
Dixon (Joseph) Crucible Company   88
Homestake Mining Company   136-137
Hunt International Resources Corporation   140
Kaiser Industries Corporation   151
Kerr-McGee Nuclear Corporation   155
Newmont Mining Corporation   198
Oglebay Norton Company   205
Parser Mineral Corporation   212
Reynolds Metals Company   230
Texas Gulf Sulphur Company, Inc.   261
Texasgulf   262

MOBIL HOMES

Coachmen Industries, Inc.   67
Fuqua Industries, Inc.   113
Winnebago Industries, Inc.   288

MOTION PICTURE and THEATRE

Columbia Pictures Industries   70
Disney (Walt) Productions   87
Metro-Goldwyn-Mayer, Inc.   180
Paramount Pictures, Inc.   211
Twentieth Century-Fox Film Corporation   268
United Artists   272
Universal Pictures Company, Inc.   276
Warner Brothers Company   280

MOTOR VEHICLE PARTS

Arvin Industries, Inc.   22
Bearings, Inc.   32
Bendix Corporation   35
Boyertown Auto Body Works   42
Budd Company   46
Dana Corporation   80
Eaton Corporation   94
Eaton Yale and Towne, Inc.   94
Echlin, Inc.   95
Lamson and Sessions Company   158
Lucas Industries   167
Sealed Power Corporation   242
Straus-Frank Company   256
Timken Company   264
Weatherhead Company   282
Wix Corporation   288

MOTOR VEHICLES

American Motors Corporation   14
Chrysler Corporation   60-61
De Lorean Motor Company   81-82
Ford Motor Company   110-111
Fruehauf Corporation   113
General Motors Corporation   117-120

Harley-Davidson Motor Company   131
International Harvester Company   145-146
Mack Trucks, Inc.   170
Nissan Motor Corporation in U.S.A.   198
Paccar, Inc.   208
Studebaker Corporation   257
Packard Motor Car Company   209-210
Toyota Motor Sales, U.S.A.   265

NATURAL GAS

American Natural Resources Company   14
Columbia Gas System Service Corporation   70
Consolidated Natural Gas Company   74
Delta Natural Gas Company, Inc.   84
Indiana Gas Company   142
Lone Star Gas Company   165
Northern Illinois Gas Company   201
Panhandle Eastern Pipeline Company   211
Pioneer Natural Gas Company   221
Southern Union Gas Company   250
Suburban Propane Gas Corporation   257
Texas Eastern Corporation   261
Transcontinental Gas Pipeline Corporation   266

NEWSPAPERS

Arizona Republic   21
Birmingham News   38
Boston Globe   41
Chicago Tribune   59
Cincinnati Enquirer   62
Cincinnati Post   63
Evening Gazette (Worchester, MASS.)   98
Fort Worth Star-Telegram   112
Kansas City Star   152
Los Angeles Times   166
Minneapolis Star and Tribune Company   183

New York Daily News 194
New York Times Company 196
Ogden Standard-Examiner 204-205
Phoenix Gazette 219
Salt Lake Tribune 238
Wall Street Journal 279
Worcester Telegram and Gazette 289-290
World Journal Tribune 290

OFFICE EQUIPMENT and FURNITURE

Addressograph Multigraph Corporation 4
Art Metal, Inc. 22
Bruning (Charles) Company 45
Reynolds and Reynolds Company 229-230
Xerox Corporation 292`

OIL

Arabian American Oil Company 20
Ashland Oil and Refining Company, Inc. 23
Atlantic Richfield Company 25
Charter Company 55-56
Continental Oil Company 75
Diamond Shamrock 87
Exxon Corporation 98
Getty Oil Company 122
Gulf Oil Corporation 129
Home-Stake Production Company 136
Hudson Oil Company 139
Husky Oil Company 141
Kerr-McGee Corporation 155
Kewanee Oil Company 156
Mobil Oil Corporation 184
Penzoil Company 215
Phillips Petroleum Company 219
Shell Oil Company 244
Sinclair Oil Company 245

Standard Oil Company   253-254
Sun Oil Company   258
Texaco, Inc.   261
Union Oil Company of California   270-271

OIL SERVICE and EQUIPMENT

Dresser Industries, Inc.   91
Foster Wheeler Corporation   112
Hughes Tool Company   140
Lufkin Industries, Inc.   167-168
NL Industries   198-199
Parker Drilling Company   211
Petrolane, Inc.   217
Pullman, Inc.   226
Schlumberger Limited   241
UOP (Universal Oil Products Company)   276
Western Company of North America   284

PACKAGING

Garlock Packing Company   114
Sealed Air Corporation   242

PAINT

Rust-Oleum Corporation   236
Sherwin-Williams Company   245

PAPER

Chesapeake Corporation of Virginia   57
Crown Zellerbach Corporation   77
Federal Paper Board Company, Inc.   101
Hammermill Paper Company   130
MacMillan Bloedel Limited   171
Parsons and Whittemore Organization   212
St. Regis Paper Company   238

SONOCO Products Company 247
Stone Container Corporation 256

PERIODICALS

Buildings; the Construction and Building Management Journal 47
Cornell Hotel and Restaurant Administration Quarterly 76
Electronic News 95
Forbes Magazine 110
McClure's Magazine 168
NIP Magazine 198
Popular Science Publishing Company 223
Prairie Farmer 224
Publishers Weekly 226
Quick Frozen Foods 227
Reader's Digest Association, Inc. 228
Saturday Evening Post 240
Story Magazine 256

PHOTO and OPTICAL

Bell and Howell Company 34
Kodak (Eastman) Company 157
Polaroid Corporation 223

POLLUTION CONTROL

Browning-Ferris Industries 45
Zurn Industries, Inc. 293

PRINTING and ENGRAVING

American Greetings Corporation 13
Beck Engraving Company, Inc. 33
Gibson Greeting Cards, Inc. 123
Hallmark Cards, Inc. 130

Hederman Brothers 133
Hennegan Company 134
Krueger (W.A.) Company 157
Kwik-Kopy Corporation 158
Lasky Company 159

PUBLISHING

Able (Richard) and Company 3
Bantam Books, Inc. 31
Bobbs-Merrill Company 40
Coward, McCann and Geoghegan 77
Curtis Publishing Company 78-79
Dartnell Corporation 80
Donnelley (R.R.) and Sons 88
Dow, Jones and Company 89-90
Field Enterprises Educational Corporation 102
Grolier, Inc. 127
Harper and Row, Publishers, Inc. 131
Hearst Corporation 133
Houghton, Mifflin Company 138
Lane Publishing Company 159
Lea and Febiger 159
Lee and Shepard, Publishers 160
Lippincott (J.B.) Company 163
McGraw-Hill Book Company 170
Maclean-Hunter 171
Media Networks, Inc. 177
Oklahoma Publishing Company 206
Parmorand Publications 212
Simon and Schuster, Inc. 245
Spiral Press, Inc. 251
Standard Rate and Data Service, Inc. 254
Time, Inc. 264
Times Mirror Corporation 264
Wiley (John) and Sons, Inc. 287-288
Zondervan Corporation 293

RADIO and TELEVISION

American Broadcasting Company   11
Columbia Broadcasting System, Inc.   70
Cox Broadcasting Corporation   77
Metromedia, Inc.   180
RKO Radio Pictures, Inc.   231
Taft Broadcasting Company   260
Turner Broadcasting Systems, Inc.   267
United Press International, Inc.   273
WLS (Radio Station) Chicago   289
WQXR (Radio Station) New York City   290
WVLK (Radio Station) Lexington, Ky.   291
WWL (Radio Station) New Orleans   291

RAILROADS

Amtrak   17
Baltimore and Ohio Railroad Company   28-29
Bessemer and Lake Erie Railroad Company   37
Burlington Northern, Inc.   47
Central Pacific Railway Company   53
Chesapeake and Ohio Railway   56
Chessie System, Inc.   58
Chicago, Burlington and Quincy Railroad Company   58
Delaware and Hudson Railroad   83
Duluth, Missable and Iron Range Railway Company   92
GATX Corporation   115
Hagerstown and Frederick Railway Company   129
Illinois Central Railroad   141
Jonesboro, Lake City and Eastern Railroad   150
Kansas City Southern Railway Company   152
Louisville and Nashville Railroad Company   167
Maine Central Railroad   173
Minnesota Transfer Railway Company   183
Missouri Pacific Corporation   184
Mount Washington Railway Company   187
North Carolina Railroad Company   200

North Pacific Coast Railroad Company 201
Penn Central Company 213-214
Piedmont and Northern Railway 220
Pittsburgh and Lake Erie Railroad 221
Reading Company 228
San Joaquin and Eastern Railroad 239
Seabord Air Line Railway 242
Soo Line Railroad Company 247
Southern Railway Company 249
Trailer Train Company 265
Union Pacific Railroad Company 271
Western Pacific Railroad 285

REAL ESTATE

Coldwell Banker Real Estate Group, Inc. 68
Galbreath (John W.) and Company 114
Leavell Company 160
Newhall Land and Farming Company 197
Rouse Company 236
Sea Island Company 241
Trump Group, Inc. 267

RECORDING

Atlantic Recording Corporation 25
Motown Record Corporation 187

RECREATION

Coleman Company, Inc. 69
Delta Queen Steamboat Company 84
Outboard Marine Corporation 207
Parker Brothers, Inc. 211
Sparkman and Stephens 250

RESEARCH AND DEVELOPMENT

American Institute of Steel Construction, Inc.   13
Batelle Memorial Institute   32
Beckman Instruments, Inc.   33
Rand Corporation   227

RESTAURANTS

Benihana National Corporation   36
Kentucky Fried Chicken   154
McDonald's Corporation   169
Pizza Inn, Inc.   222
Saga Corporation   237
Sambo's Restaurants, Inc.   238-239
Wendy's International, Inc.   283
White Castle System, Inc.   287

RESTORATION

Bedford-Stuyvesant Restoration Corporation   34
Mansions and Millionaires, Inc.   173

SAVINGS AND LOAN

Buckeye Federal Savings and Loan Association   46
California Federal Savings and Loan Association   50
Citizens Federal Savings and Loan Association of Dayton   64
First Federal Savings and Loan Association of Jackson   104
First Federal Savings and Loan Association of Minneapolis   104
First Federal Savings and Loan Association of St. Petersburg   104
Gibraltar Savings and Loan Association   123
Glendale Federal   124
Western Savings and Loan Association   285-286

SECURITY SERVICES

Pinkerton's National Detective Agency   220-221

SHIP BUILDING and SHIPPING

American Ship Building Company   14
Cunard Steamship Company, Ltd.   78
Delta Steamship Lines   84
Ellam (Patrick), Inc.   96
Howard Ship Yard and Dock Company   138
Matson Navigation Company   176
Todd Shipyards Corporation   264

SOAPS and CLEANERS

Armour and Company   21
Clorox Company   66
Colgate-Palmolive Company   69
Economics Laboratory, Inc.   95
Procter and Gamble Company   224

SPORTS

Atlanta Braves   24
Baltimore Orioles   29
Boston Celtics   41
Boston Red Sox   41-42
California Angels   49
Chicago Bears   58
Chicago Cubs   58-59
Chicago White Sox   59
Cincinnati Bengals   61
Cincinnati Reds   63
Cleveland Browns   65-66
Cleveland Indians   66
Dallas Cowboys   79
Denver Broncos   84

Detroit Tiers   86
Green Bay Packers   126
Kansas City Chiefs   151
Los Angeles Dodgers   165-166
Los Angeles Rams   166
Miami Dolphins   180
Minnesota Vikings   183
New England Patriots   194
New York Giants   194-195
New York Islanders   195
New York Mets   195
New York Yankees   196-197
Oakland Raiders   204
Philadelphia Phillies   217-218
Philadelphia 76'ers   218
Pittsburgh Pirates   222
Pittsburgh Steelers   222
St. Louis Cardinals   238
San Francisco Forty-Niners   239
San Francisco Giants   239
Washington Redskins   281

STEEL

Armco Steel Corporation   21
Atlantic Steel Company   26
Bethlehem Steel Corporation   37
Bliss and Laughlin Industries   39
CF&I Steel Corporation   54
Dayton Malleable, Inc.   81
Fansteel, Inc.   99
Inland Steel Company   143
LTV Corporation   167
Lukens, Inc.   168
National Intergroup, Inc.   191
Newport Steel Corporation   198
NUCOR Corporation   204
Pittsburgh-Des Moines Corporation   221

United States Steel Corporation   275
Washington Steel Corporation   281
Worthington Industries   290

SUGAR and CONFECTIONARY PRODUCTS

American Crystal Sugar Company   11
Peter Paul, Inc.   217
United States Sugar Corporation   275
Utah-Idaho Sugar Company   277

TELECOMMUNICATIONS

ALLTEL Corporation   9
American Telephone and Telegraph Company   15-16
Bell Telephone Laboratories, Inc.   34-35
Chesapeake and Potomac Telephone Company   56-57
Cincinnati Bell, Inc.   61
Collins Radio Company   69
Communications Satellite Corporation   71-72
Continental Telephone Corporation   75
General Telephone Company of Florida   121
General Telephone Directory Company   121
International Telephone and Telegraph
  Corporation   146-147
Lincoln Telephone and Telegraph Company   163
MCI Communications Corporation   177
Mountain Bell   187
New York Telephone Company   196
Northwestern Bell Telephone Company   203
Ohio Bell Telephone Company   205
South Central Bell in Mississippi   248
Southern Bell   248
United Telecommunications, Inc.   275
Western Electric Company   284-285
Western Union   286

TEXTILES

Amoskeag Manufacturing Company   16
Avondale Mills   27
Bancroft (Joseph) and Sons Company   30
Burlington Industries, Inc.   47
Dan River, Inc.   79
Fieldcrest Mills, Inc.   102
Glen Raven Mills, Inc.   124
Greenwood Mills   126-127
Mount Hope Finishing Company   187
New England Moxie Company   193
Springs Industries, Inc.   251
Stevens (J.P.) and Company   255
Webster Industries, Inc.   282
Weil Brothers Cotton   282

TIRES and RUBBER GOODS

Armstrong Rubber Company   22
Cooper Tire and Rubber Company   76
Dayco Corporation   81
Firestone Tire and Rubber Company   103
General Tire and Rubber Company   121
Goodyear Tire and Rubber Company   125
UNIROYAL, Inc.   272
United States Rubber Company   274

TOBACCO

American Tobacco Company   16
Liggert Group, Inc.   162
Philip Morris, Inc.   219
Reynolds (R.J.) Industries, Inc.   230

TOYS

Bradley (Milton) Company 43
Coleco Industries, Inc. 68
Lionel Train Company 163
Mattel, Inc. 176

TRADE

Amtorg Trading Corporation 17
Gross, Kelly and Company, Inc. 127-128

TRANSPORTATION

Dayton, Covington, and Piqua Traction Company 81
Denver Tramway Corporation 84
Greyhound Corporation 127
Ithaca Street Railway Company 148
North Jersey Rapid Transit Company 201
Philadelphia Rapid Transit Company 218
Twin City Rapid Transit Company 268
Woodstock and Sycamore Traction Company 289

TRUCKING

Aero Mayflower Transit Company, Inc. 4
Consolidated Freightways, Inc. 73-74
Merrill Transport Company 180
Security Storage Company of Washington, D.C. 243
Smith's Transfer Corporation 246-247

WASTE MANAGEMENT, REFUSE, and SEWERAGE

Browning-Ferris Industries 45
Combustion Engineering, Inc. 71
Industrial Services of America, Inc. 143

WATER TRANSPORTATION

Alexander and Baldwin, Inc. 7
Goodrich Transit Company 124-125
Joy Line 150
Moran Towing and Transportation Company, Inc. 186
San Diego and Coronado Ferry Company 239
Washington State Ferries 281

WATER UTILITY

Hackensack Water Company 129
Indianapolis Water Company 143

WINDOWS

Anderson Corporation 19

INDEX BY AUTHOR

Abbey, Wallace W. 247
Abodaher, David J. 60
Ackerman, Martin S. 78
Adams, Eugene H. 106
Adams, Russell B. 124
Ahrens, Art 58
Aiken, Michael 209
Alberts, Robert C. 133
Alexander, L.G. 288
Alexander, Robert D. 7
Allen, James Elbert 124
Allen, Robert Francis 183
Allner, Paul 281
Allyn, Stanley C. 190
Altschul, Selig 210
Ames, Charles E. 271
Amigo, Eleanor 238
Amos, Wally 99
Anderson, George 46
Anderson, John F. 100
Anderson, Robert 169
Anderson, Roy A. 164
Anderson, Sparky 63
Angle, Paul McClelland 291
Anthony, Carolyn T. 287
Anton, Mark J. 257

Armstrong, Arthur S. 4
Aronson, Carole 173
Arrington, Leonard J. 265, 277
Ash, Mary K. 175
Athearn, Robert G. 271
Atwood, John Leland 199
Auletta, Ken 160, 240
Austin, Edwin T. 234
Axelrod, Regina S. 73
Azzato, Louis E. 112

Babcock, Glenn D. 274
Babson, David L. 27
Bagamery, Ann 262
Baily, Edd H. 271
Bain, Trevor 139
Baird, Nancy Disher 140
Baldwin, Catherine A. 288
Balio, Tino 272
Ballou, Ellen B. 138
Balzar, Richard 284
Balzer, Robert L. 176
Banks, Howard 158
Bannan, Thomas J. 285
Barnes, Harry C. 274

Barnowski, Dave 238
Batten, William M. 214
Baum, Claude 260
Beach, Morrison H. 266
Bean, G. Clarke 21
Beargie, T. 84
Beaton, Kendall 244
Beaver, Roy C. 37
Beck, George P. 33
Beckman, Arnold O. 33
Behlmer, Rudy 244
Bender, Marylin 210
Benham, David Blair 36
Benjaminson, Peter 187
Berger, Harvey 74
Berke, Art 59
Bernstein, Charles 238
Berry, Bryan H. 117
Berry, Loren M. 36
Best, Gerald M. 53
Beynon, H. 110
Bias, Charles V. 28, 56, 58
Bilovsky, Frank 217
Binzen, Peter 213
Bisheff, Steve 166
Bittinger, Donald S. 280
Blackford, Mansel G. 46, 278
Blanchar, Carroll H. 225
Blount, W. Houston 277
Blount, Winton M. 39
Blower, James M. 201, 202
Bluhdorn, Charles G. 128

Boas, Max 169
Bobrick, Benson 212
Boddie, David L. 87
Bodine, Richard P. 40
Boe, Archie R. 8
Boehm, George A. 32
Bolling, George 15
Bond, Lewis H. 112
Booth, John M. 30
Boschken, Herman L. 41
Boulton, David 164
Boulware, Lemuel R. 115
Bourgeois, Homer W. 270
Bovay, Harry E., Jr. 42
Bove, Vincent 196
Boyd, James 76
Braband, Ken C. 69, 232
Bradley, Rodger 17
Brady, Maxine 39
Branch, Hallee, Jr. 249
Brandly, Raymond H. 278
Braznell, William 83
Brecher, Jeremy 11
Brewster, Gordon E., Jr. 276
Bricker, William H. 87
Brickey, Homer 34
Bridges, Harry 244
Briggs, Don F. 121
Brock, Horace 210
Brodeur, Paul 173
Broeg, Bob 238
Broehl, Wayne G. 82
Brooks, John 15
Brooks, John 238, 292
Brooks, John G. 160
Brough, James 289
Brown, Charles D. 246

Brown, Edmund D. 24, 249
Brown, Russell R. 12
Brown, Stanley H. 163
Brown, Werner C. 134
Bruening, Joseph M. 32
Brufke, Edward F. 256
Bryan, George W. 45
Bryan, Jacob F. 142
Bryant, Keith L. 152
Buck, Wendell 173
Buckley, P. 216
Bufkin, I. David 261
Buford, Curtis D. 265
Burley, Roscoe Carlyle 97
Burns, Thomas S. 145
Bush, George 74, 287
Bush, George S. 282
Bussy, R. Kenneth 159
Butcher, Jonathan 48
Butterfield, Stephen 17
Byrne, John J. 125
Byron, Christopher 264

Cahn, Louis F. 99
Cahn, William 72, 188, 190
Caliam, Carnegie Samuel 89, 279
Cameron, Charles Clifford 109
Cannon, William A. 257
Cantor, Bert 148
Carden, Maren L. 207
Carleton, Paul 228
Carlson, Edward E. 268, 272, 285
Carmichael, O.C., Jr. 23
Carosso, Vincent P. 156
Carr, Roland T. 231
Carr, William H.A. 144, 225
Carrington, Tim, 12, 244
Carter, Joseph R. 291
Case, George S., Jr. 158
Case, Weldon W. 9
Casey, E.P. 98
Cash, Joseph H. 136
Cearley, George Walker 11, 93, 189
Chain, Steve 169
Chalmers, Floyd S. 171
Chance, F. Gano 55
Chandler, Alfred D. 91
Chandler, Marvin 201
Chaney, Lindsay 133
Chazanof, William 282
Cheape, Charles W. 203
Cheatham, Owen R. 122
Chesnutt, N.P. 250
Chiles, H.E. 284
Chucker, Harold 202
Church, Roy A. 154
Cianchette, Ival R. 61
Cieply, Michael 133
Clark, Ellery H. 41
Clark, Wilfred A. 30
Clary, Jack T. 65
Cleland, Robert Glass 99

Cleveland, Harold Van B. 63
Coe, Fred A. 48
Coffin, David Linwood 86
Cohen, Scott 24
Coker, Charles W. 247
Colby, Gerald 91
Colby, Kenneth P. 191
Collett, Ritter 61, 63
Colletti, Jerome A. 186
Collier, Abraham T. 194
Comparato, Frank E. 135
Compton, Walter A. 182
Condon, George E. 205, 286
Conley, Eugene A. 128
Conn, Charles P. 18
Conner, Floyd 61, 63
Conniff, James C.G. 226
Conniff, Richard 226
Connor, Dick 84, 151
Conway, Mimi 255
Cook, William Sutton 271
Coons, Coke 22
Cooper, Dennis R. 121
Cooper, Elliot T. 271
Copeland, Sid 236
Cornell, James, Jr. 251
Corwin, Nancy 198
Cosgrove, John N. 25
Couchman, Robert 259
Cox, Arthur J. 101
Cox, Harold E. 218
Cramer, Esther R. 9
Cray, Ed 117, 161
Cray, William C. 182

Cree, Albert A. 54
Crissey, Elwell 216
Cromwell, Joseph H. 56, 57
Crosby, Gordon E., Jr. 276
Cross, Malcolm A. 79
Cull, George E. 49
Culligan, Mathew J. 78
Cummings, Nathan 73
Cunningham, Bill 16
Cunningham, Mary 8, 35, 175
Curry, Robert P. 62

D'Agostino, Dennis 195
Daigle, John M. 51
Dainty, Ralph B. 80
Daley, Robert 210
Dalglish, Garven 135
Dammann, George H. 60, 119
Danzig, Fred 36
Darly, Edwin 279
Daughen, Joseph R. 213
Davenport, Joe 139
Davidson, J. Craig 72
Davidson, Lorimer A. 125
Davies, Ronald E.G. 74
Davis, Burke 187, 249
Davis, Donald W. 254
Davis, Thomas H. 220
Davisson, Budd 71
De Vries, John A. 7
Deak, Nicholas L. 82
Dedmon, Emmett 253

DeLorean, John Z. 81, 117
Demoro, Harre W. 281
DeMoss, Arthur S. 191
Denlinger, Ken 281
Dent, Hilda 280
Dessauer, John H. 292
Destler, Chester McArthur 253
Diamond, Jeff 183
Dickason, James F. 197
Dickinson, A. Bray 201
Didinger, Ray 222
Dierdorff, John 209
Dill, Alonzo Thomas 57
DiOrio, Eugene L. 168
Dobson, Linda 107
Dolson, Frank 217
Dolzall, Gary W. 28
Dolzall, Stephen F. 28
Dominik, John J. 68
Donahue, John D. 60
Donnelley, Gaylord 88
Dorin, Patrick C. 47, 58
Doss, Bowman 192
Dougherty, Richard 137
Douglas, Walter S. 212
Dowdy, Auburn W. 105
Drain, James A. 151
Drake, Philip M. 78
Dreher, Carl 227
Drew, Lee A. 150
Driggs, Douglas H. 285
Driscoll, Robert S. 5, 165
Drosnin, Michael 139

Duerksen, Christopher J. 88
Duke, Marc 91
Dunbaugh, Edwin 150
Dunham, Terry B. 119
Dunne, John Gregory 258
Dunphy, Thomas Joseph Dermot 242
Durham, Charles W. 134

Eames, Alfred W. 83
Eames, John Douglas 180, 211
Easton, Carol Douglas 180
Eccles, George S. 108
Eckhouse, Morris 66, 222
Edgerton, J. Howard 50
Edmonds, N. Frank 248
Edmonson, Herald A. 17
Edwards, H. Wallace 236
Edwards, Raymond D. 124
Egerton, John 198
Eglin, Roger 158
Ehrenberg, Ronald G. 196
Eikel, Charles F. 78
Eisenhauer, Robert S. 262
Eldridge, Charles John Wilson 240
Ellam, Patrick 96
Elliot, James L. 124
Ellis, Harry E. 90
El-Messidi, Kathy G. 118

Elston, Lloyd W.   217
Elwart, J.P.   61
Enck, Henry Snyder   179
Enders, Ostrom   132
Englemayer, Sheldon D.   232
Engstrom, T.W.   293
Erwin, Paul F.   149
Evans, James F.   224, 289
Exman, Eugene   131
Ezell, John Samuel   155

Fallon, Ivan   82
Falls, Joe   86
Fawcett, Sherwood L.   32
Feinstein, J.M.   17
Feldman, Joan M.   100
Fenichell, Stephen   207
Ferguson, James Leonard   117
Ferguson, Lloyd C.   255
Fernandez, Ronald   275
Fetters, Thomas T.   220
Fielder, Mildred   136
Fields, Robert A.   24
Filgas, James F.   292
Finney, Robert   219
Fischer, David C.   202
Fishbaugh, Charles Preston   138
Fisher, David G.   81
Fisher, Franklin M.   144
Fishman, Katherine Davis   144
Fishman, Lew   195
Fishman, William S.   20

Fitch, T.S.   281
Fite, Gilbert Courtland   100
Fitzgerald, Michael G.   276
Fleming, Al   118, 120
Fleming, Lamar   19
Floros, Leo   4
Flour, J. Robert   109
Fogarty, Charles F.   262
Foltz, N.   108
Foley, Martha   256
Fontaine, A.P.   35
Forrestal, Dan J.   185, 252
Fortney, David   204
Foster, David R.   69
Fowler, Harry W.   102
Fox, Larry   194
Foy, Nancy S.   145
Foye, Arthur B.   133
Francillon, René J.   169
Francis, Devon E.   221
Francis, J.D.   178
Frank, Jerome P.   278
Franzwa, Gregory M.   259
Freedman, Russell   135
French, Robert W.   65
Frenzel, Otto N., Jr.   178
Friedman, Henry   110
Friedrich, Otto   78, 240
Frisbee, Don C.   209
Frommer, Harvey   41, 197
Fultz, Claire E.   140
Fuqua, J.B.   113
Furlaud, Richard M.   252

Gaffey, Guy H., Jr.   248
Galarza, Ernesto   86
Gallagher, Edward A.   286
Gallagher, Mark   197
Gallaway, Edward A.   60
Gandossy, Robert P.   207
Gant, Margaret Elizabeth   124
Garden, Maren L.   207
Gardner, Leo R.   58
Garson, Bill   64
Gartner, Michael   213
Garvey, William P.   85
Gawronski, Francis   119
Gawronski, Frank W.   110, 119
Gaylord, E.K.   206
Geelhoed, E. Bruce   44, 260
Geis, Joseph   59
Geist, James E.   163
Gelfand, M. Howard   287
Getty, Jean Paul   122
Gewecke, Clifford George   165
Gibb, George S.   254
Gibbons, Boyd   236
Gibbs, Patikii   137
Giblin, Edward J.   98
Giffin, Marjie G.   143
Gifford, P.W.   123
Gilbert, John   241
Gilbride, John L.   264
Gillett, Charlie   25
Gillette, Leslie H.   13
Gingher, Paul R.   70, 255

Glasberg, Davita Silfen   56, 160
Glasheen, Leah   220
Gloster, Jesse E.   199
Gold, Eddie   58
Goodwin, Jacob B.   115
Goodwin, W. Richard   173
Goolrick, Robert M.   146
Gordon, Maynard M.   60, 110
Gordon, William Reed   81
Gore, Philip Larner   243
Gorman, Leon A.   32
Gorman, Paul A.   284
Gottlieb, Robert   166
Gottschalk, Alfred   101
Goulden, Joseph C.   15, 79
Grabner, George J.   282
Grangier, M.   25
Grannis, C.B.   226
Grant, Ellsworth S.   165
Grant, Fred A.   32
Grant, John F.   179
Grant, W.J.   74
Grant, William Downing   48
Gray, Edmund R.   253, 254
Graybill, Harry G.   291
Green, Harold K.   234
Green, Joseph Hugh   49
Green, Richard C.   184
Greene, Letha C.   84
Greenwood, Ronald G.   116
Gregor, Arthur   34
Greif, Martin   26

Grether, E.T.   161
Groner, A.   32
Gullett, C. Ray   253, 254
Gushman, John L.   18
Guston, L.R.   118
Guthrie, William S.   46

Haddad, William F.   82
Hafer, Erminie Shaeffer   42
Haffner, Gerald O.   65
Hall, Asa E.   257
Hall, Floyd D.   93
Hall, Joyce C.   130
Hall, Richard W.   52
Hall, W.M.   172
Hampton, Max   144
Handler, Elliot   176
Hansen, Zenon C.R.   170
Hanson, Clarence B., Jr.   38
Hanson, Walter E.   213
Harbert, John M., III   131
Harden, H.   187
Harder, William H.   46
Hardy, Michael John   40
Hareven, Tamara K.   16
Harlow, Howard Reed   141
Harper, Paul   193
Harris, Sara   183
Harrison, Desales   67
Harrison, H. Stuart   66
Hart, Jack R.   166, 264
Hart, N. Berne   273
Hartley, Fred L.   270

Hartz, Peter F.   35, 175
Harwood, Herbert H.   29
Harwood, Herbert H., Jr.   129
Haselton, Wallace M.   85
Hatch, Wilda Gene   204, 252
Hawkins, John C.   29, 86
Hawley, Samuel W.   216
Haynes, Harold J.   253
Heavrin, Charles A.   19
Hederman, Robert M., Jr.   133
Hedrick, Frank E.   34
Heer, Jean   193
Heiney, J.W.   142
Helzer, Albert M.   65
Hendon, Booton   111
Hennessy, Edward L.   8
Henry, Waights G.   67
Henshaw, Tom   41
Henson, Paul H.   275
Herbert, Hiram J.   245
Herndon, Bootan   185
Herrmann, Frank   247
Herzog, Lester W., Jr.   190
Heusser, Audrey E.   255
Heyn, Ernest V.   223
Higham, Charles   280
Hill, Evan   183
Hilton, George Woodman   17, 59
Hipp, Francis M.   162
Hirt, A. Orth   97
Hochheiser, Sheldon   233
Hodgson, G.   148
Hoffman, William   68

Hogg, William T. 265
Hollander, Ron 162
Holman, William H. 149
Holt, Hazel 106
Holt, Patricia 159
Honig, Donald 197
Horn, Carol 92
Hornby, Robert A. 208
Howard, Herbert H. 77
Hoyt, Edwin P. 126
Hoyt, Edwin P., Jr. 186
Hunter, Sam 219
Hurt, Harry 140
Huston, Harvey 233
Hutchinson, Robert A. 64
Hutchinson, William Henry 270
Hyde, Francis Edwin 78
Hyman, Sidney 108

Iacocca, Lee A. 60
Ingells, Douglas J. 88, 169
Ingram, Robert Lockwood 33
Ironside, Roberta 246
Ivey, George M. 149

Jabbonsky, Larry 90
Jackson, Carlton 127
Jackson, Elaine 167
Jackson, William Turrentine 283
Jacobs, Donald 163
Jacobs, Joseph J. 149

Jarman, Rufus 174
Jarman, W. Maxey 121
Jarvis, Helen R. 178
Jeffers, Dean W. 192
Jeffrey, Balfour S. 152
Jenkins, George W. 226
Jenks, Downing B. 184
Jennings, Dana Close 279
Jewell, Richard B. 231
Jinks, Roy G. 246
Johnson, Arthur M. 258
Johnson, Barclay G. 123
Johnson, Curtiss S. 171
Johnson, Jerry W. 137
Johnson, Robert Elliott 272
Johnson, William B. 141
Johnston, Hank 172, 239
Jollie, Rose Marie 53
Jones, Alden H. 287
Jones, Arthur 110
Jones, Charles S. 25, 230
Jones, Douglas A. 231
Jones, Edwin L. 150
Jones, Lawrence M. 69
Jonovic, Donald J. 205

Kahaner, Larry 15, 177
Kahn, E.J. 162
Kaman, Charles H. 151
Kanner, Barbara 100
Karnes, Thomas L. 252
Karolevitz, Robert F. 177
Kaufman, Charles N. 153

Kelchburg, Ann 75
Keller, David N. 76
Kellogg, Walter W. 153
Kelly, Daniel T. 127
Kemper, James M. 71
Kenna, Frank 174
Kennedy, Donald S. 206
Kennedy, Gerald S. 117
Kennedy, John R. 101
Kennedy, William J. 20, 199
Kennington, Robert E. 127
Kerby, Jerry L. 64
Kerr, Richard D. 148
Kidd, Glennon 208
Kidder, Tracy 80
Kilgour, Raymond Lincoln 160
Kimes, Beverly Rae 120
Kincade, Arthur W. 112
King, Frank A. 92
King, Jenny L. 119
King, Sol 6
Kinney, Francis S. 250
Kirkland, John F. 28, 99
Kirkland, William A. 105
Klaus, Robert A. 157
Klein, Maury 167
Kleinfield, Sonny 15
Kluge, John W. 180
Knepper, M. 82
Knowles, Phillip H. 80
Koether, George 143
Kogan, H. 233
Kogan, Herman 3, 138

Kohn, Howard 155
Koppett, Leonard 195
Kouwenhoven, John A. 44
Krauss, Bob 128
Krebs, M. 95
Kresge, Stanley Sebastian 157
Kroc, Ray 169
Kuniansky, Harry R. 26
Kurstedt, Harold A. 3

Lambert, Hope 35, 175
Lamm, John 82
Lancaster, Robert B. 162
Landau, Ralph 130
Landegger, Karl F. 38, 212
Lane, Carleton G. 269
Lane, L.W., Jr. 159
Langford, Jim 58
Langworth, Richard M. 60, 257
Lanners, Fred T. 95
Lanzone, John A. 256
Larcom, Paul S. 200
Larkin, Fredrick G., Jr. 243
Lasky, Victor 111
Laslie, Donald S. 130
Latham, Frank Brown 185
Lauder, Estee 159
Laux, James M. 168
Lavin, Joseph J. 88
Lawler, Joseph C. 50
Lawrence, Joanne T. 26
Lay, Beirne 164

Lay, Chester Frederic 234
Laycock, George 157
Leete, Edward H. 240
Leiby, Adrian Coulter 129
Leinsdorf, David 108
Leisy, Bruce R. 161
Lenzner, Robert 122
Lepage, Regis A. 161
Leptich, John 238
Levin, Hillel 82
Levinson, Harry 10, 64, 116, 145, 185, 196
Levy, Jo Ann L. 68
Levy, William V. 66
Lewis, Alfred A. 20
Lewis, Allen 217
Lewis, Leslie L. 80
Lewis, Morris, Jr. 161, 258
Lewis, Walter David 83
Liebhafsky, H.A. 116
Lief, Alfred 257
Liles, Allen 250
Limprecht, Hollis 156
Lind, Alan R. 237
Lindberg, Richard 59
Lindley, James G. 248
Little, Royal 262
Loebbecke, Ernest J. 263
Logan, John O. 276
Lombardi, Jerry 11
Loomis, Noel M. 283
Lord, Thomas 165
Louis, J.C. 68, 216
Lowry, Goodrich 268

Lucas, Lydia A. 11
Lucas, William F. 44
Luce, Charles F. 73
Ludvigsen, E.L. 94
Lund, Doniver Adolph 104, 107
Luskey, Sam 84
Lynde, Bill 160
Lyons, Bill 218
Lyons, Louis M. 41

McCallum, Jack 36
McCann, Thomas P. 273
McCarthy, Walter J. 85
McCleary, Elliott 235
McClintick, David 70, 136
McCloy, John Jay 129
McConnell, John H. 290
McDaniel, William Herbert 34
MacDonald, Elton F. 169
MacDonald, Ray W. 47
McFall, Russell W. 286
McFerrin, John Berry 49
McGee, Dean A. 155
McGivena, Leo E. 194
McGovern, Joseph J. 275
McGuane, George 194
McIntosh, James B. 181
Macioce, Thomas M. 8
Mack, Walter 216
MacKay, Donald 171
McKenna, Donald C. 153
McLaughlin, Ambrose P. 164
McLean, Harold H. 221

McLemore, Morris T. 180
McMahon, Helen Griffin 228
McMillan, Harold W. 54
McMillen, Russell G. 94
McMullan, W.P. 85
McNally, Edward T. 171
McPherson, Rene C. 80
McQuillen, Michael J. 130
McRae, Richard Duncan 171
Madden, Richard B. 223
Mahan, Ernest 171
Mahon, Gigi 229
Mahoney, David J. 203
Malik, Rex 145
Malim, Thomas 101
Malmquist, O.N. 238
Mancheski, Frederick J. 95
Mandel, Mike 239
Mansfield, Harold 40
Mapp, Leslie C. 181
Marder, William 114
Marion, John Francis 246
Marple, Elliot 189
Marquette, Arthur F. 226
Marsh, Barbara 145
Martin, Edmund F. 37
Martin, Sandra Pratt 187
Martindale, Wight 161
Marx, Arthur 180
Mason, Paul 107
Mason, Raymond K. 55

Mastrocola, Carl 222
Mathews, Charles Elijah 107
Mathison, Richard R. 26
Matters, Marion E. 11
Mattison, Lewis C. 182
Maurer, Herrymon 177
Mayer, Oscar G. 176
Meares, Charles William Victor 195
Meathe, Philip J. 246
Meek, Phillip J. 112
Meijer, Hendrik G. 177
Mellander, Deane 29
Mellow, Craig 51
Melvin, Crandall 179
Meredeen, Sander 72
Merrill, Paul E. 180
Mettler, Ruben F. 267
Metz, Robert 70
Meyer, Henry I. 215
Meyer, Malcolm 54
Meyer, Robert Henry 229
Meyers, Jeff 79
Miars, David H. 55
Miller, E. Spencer 173
Miller, Edward W. 101
Miller, Gray L. 204
Miller, Harold T. 138
Miller, Raymond Curtis 85, 123
Miller, Russel 222
Miller, Shannon 26
Millett, Larry 191
Millman, Nancy F. 224
Mills, Stephen E. 202
Miner, H. Craig 184
Mines, Samuel 217

Minor, R.S. 80
Mintz, Morton 232
Miske, Jack C. 81
Mitchell, C. Bradford 264
Montgomery, M.R. 32
Montiville, John B. 170
Mooney, Booth 23
Moore, John Hammond 288
Moran, Edmond J. 186
Morgan, Monty Brown 90
Morgan, Murray Cromwell 238
Morison, Bradley L. 183
Morison, William W. 111
Moritz, Michael 20, 60
Morn, Frank 220
Morton, Jack Andrew 35
Mosley, Leonard 87, 91
Mudge, Robert W. 201
Mueller, Robert W. 126
Muir, D.T. 92
Mullins, Ronald G. 75
Mundt, R.B. 7
Munford, Dillard 188
Munson, Kenneth G. 40
Munyan, Mary G. 91
Munzer, R.J. 217
Murphy, Austin S. 93
Murphy, H. Lee 45
Myers, Kenneth H. 254
Myers, William A. 249

Nance, John J. 43
Nash, John Rumm 215
Naumann, William L. 52
Neils, Paul 193

Neilson, Frances 89, 279
Neilson, Winthrop 89, 279
Nelson, William C. 65
Nestor, Oscar W. 198
Neuffer, M. 238
Neville, Dorothy 102
Nevins, Allan 131
Newcomb, William A. 178
Newhan, Ross 49
Newlin, Lyman 3
Newman, W.R., III 252
Newton, Wesley Phillips 83
Nicholas, James R. 113
Nichols, John Peter 289
Nicholson, Arnold 4
Nicolaides, Louis 212
Nielsen, M. 27
Nockolds, Harold 167
Norbye, Jan P. 60
Nordholt, John B., Jr. 282
Norris, James D. 16
Norris, Kenneth T. 199
Norris, William 40, 210
Norton, Thomas E. 247
Novak, W. 60
Noyes, Gertrude Elizabeth 240
Nunis, Doyce B. 209
Nutler, Ervin J. 95

Oates, Bob 222
O'Bar, Jack 40

Olmsted, George Hamden 103
Olsen, Kenneth H. 87
Olshaker, Mark 223
Olson, Bruce H. 189
Olson, Robert A. 152
O'Neill, Dennis J. 121
Onigman, Marc 24
O'Reilly, Maurice 125
Orr, Craig 215
Ozanne, Robert 145

Page, B. 148
Pale, Francis L. 62
Palmer, Peggy 158
Parker, Patrick S. 211
Parsons, Al 109
Patterson, Ted 29
Payne, Darwin 91
Payne, Walter A. 52
Pearce, John E. 44, 154
Pease, George Sexton 97
Perlman, Alfred E. 285
Perrault, E.G. 242
Perry, Russell H. 229
Persinos, John F. 6
Peters, Nick 239
Peterson, Clarence 31
Peterson, James A. 204
Peterson, R.L. 148
Peterson, Walter F. 8
Petrakis, Harry Mark 186
Phalin, Howard V. 102
Phillips, Bert E. 65
Phillips, John Patrick 15

Piper, W.T. 221
Pisney, Raymond F. 169
Pitrone, Jean M. 61
Platt, Dorothy Pickard 220
Plummer, Frank 103
Poland, Robert L. 168
Poll, Richard D. 181
Ponder, Ronny 100
Post, James E. 4
Potter, Frank N. 193
Powell, William J. 220
Powers, John 197
Powers, Ormund 138
Prince, Richard E. 242
Pulliam, Eugene C. 21, 219
Purcell, Theodore Vincent 203
Purtell, Joseph 263
Pusateri, C. Joseph 291
Puth, Robert C. 259
Putnam, Frank B. 99

Quigg, H.D. 273
Quinby, Edwin Jay 200
Quinlan, Sterling 11

Raach, Fred R. 280
Rae, John Bell 198
Ragsdale, Kenneth Baxter 59
Ramsey, Robert Henderson 198
Randolph, C.L. 274
Rashke, Richard L. 155

Rathbun, Frank F. 6
Rathgeber, Bob 63
Raw, Charles B. 148
Regan, Donald T. 179
Reich, Robert B. 60
Reilly, William P. 21
Rice, Berkely 164
Richard, Gilbert F. 46
Richards, Roy 250
Rinehart, Raymond G. 66
Rippey, James Crockett 203
Ritchie, B. 158
Robbins, Frederic J. 39
Robert, Joseph C. 98
Robertson, William E. 289
Robins, E. Clairborne 232
Robinson, Jack Fay 34
Robinson, Leroy 99
Robinson, Thomas B. 38
Robson, Paul W. 50
Roddy, Pat 233
Rodgers, William 145
Rogers, George C. 248
Rooney, Francis C., Jr. 178
Root, John B. 132
Rosenberg, Jerry M. 89, 279
Rosenthal, Stuart 10, 64, 116, 145
Ross, John R. 122
Ross, Smith G. 155
Rosser, Howard W. 93
Rostenberg, Leona 234
Roth, Leland M. 170
Rowand, Roger 120, 143
Rowen, James 241
Ruark, James E. 293
Ruble, Kenneth Douglas 19, 159
Rudd, Theodore O. 155
Ruderman, Gary S. 115
Rumer, Thomas A. 64
Rupp, Warren E. 280
Rushton, William J., III 224
Ruth, John L. 270
Ryan, Charles B. 187
Rymer, S.B. 172

Sage, Joseph 290
Salant, Nathan 197
Salsbury, Stephen 91, 213
Samford, Frank Park 264
Sampson, Anthony 147
Sanders, Harland 154
Sanford, James K. 162
Sanger, Elliot M. 290
Santry, Arthur J. 71
Satterfield, Archie 6
Saunders, Harris 240
Scamehorn, Howard Lee 54
Scanlin, J.R. 115
Scates, Shelby 243
Schatz, Ronald W. 116, 286
Schiff, John J. 62
Schisgall, Oscar 42, 127, 224

Schlueter, Clyde F.   96
Schmed, Peter   225
Schmitt, Paul   59
Schoenberg, Robert J.   147
Scholl, Robert R.H.   114
Schonerberger, William A.   114
Schoor, Gene   166
Schramm, Henry W.   109
Schreiner, Herm   278
Schuler, John Hamilton   19
Schultz, Leslie P.   30
Schwed, Peter   245
Scobel, Donald N.   94
Scott, David Charles   8
Scott, Earle M.   241
Scott, Michael   210
Scott, Otto J.   23, 38, 227
Scott, Tom B.   104
Seabrook, John M.   147
Seaman, B.   60
Searle, Philip F.   29
Seder, Arthur R.   14
Seldow, Leona   9
Serling, Robert J.   11, 74, 93, 200, 265, 284
Serrin, William   118
Seward, William   88
Shaner, J. Richard   25
Shea, James J., Jr.   43
Sheen, Robert T.   182
Sherwood, J. Robert   258
Shetterly, Robert B.   66
Shirk, Charles A.   26

Shook, Robert L.   71, 82, 114, 128, 137, 139, 175, 177, 192, 230, 244, 263
Shulman, Morton   261
Shultz, George Pratt   21
Sibley, Celestine   231
Silke, James R.   280
Simmons, James P.   273
Simmons, Roy W.   293
Simpich, Frederick, Jr.   16
Sims, Allen H.   288
Sinclair, Donald B.   120
Singer, Mark   214
Sloan, Allan   35, 175
Smalheer, Calvin V.   167
Smalley, Orange A.   251
Smith, Beth Laney   55
Smith, Bruce L.R.   227
Smith, Charles H.   245
Smith, Frank K.   94
Smith, George David   15, 284
Smith, George F.   139
Smith, James C.   27
Smith, Robert I.   226
Smith, Roger B.   119
Snead, William Scott   96
Snyder, John   61, 63
Sobel, Robert   14, 145, 147, 196, 214
Solomon, Aubrey   268
Sonnichsen, Charles Leland   255
Sorenson, Lorin   111
Sorey, Gordon Kent   89
Sorge, Marjorie   95, 120

Souder, William F., Jr. 174
Spero, Joan Edelman 113
Stakhouse, Jan 11
Stamper, Powell 191
Steel, George, 5
Stein, Barry 34
Stein, Fred 195, 239
Stein, Mirriam 74
Stephens, Harrison 33
Stephens, Kent 86
Stern, Madeleine B. 234
Stevens, George E. 63
Stevens, Mark 39
Sticht, J. Paul 230
Stoddard, Robert W. 98, 289
Stone, Eugene E. 256
Stone, Marvin N. 256
Stoner, J.F. 29
Stottlemyr, John M. 183
Stover, John F. 141
Stowers, Carlton 79
Stringer, Tommy Wayne 292
Strobel, Lee Patrick 111
Strodes, J. 82
Stuart, Reginald 61
Stuart, Robert D. 190
Stuart, Spencer R. 250
Sturdivant, Frederick D. 13
Sullivan, George 86, 197
Sullivan, John 239
Sundt, M. Eugene 258
Swanson, Peter W. 220

Talbot, Allan R. 73
Talese, Gay 196
Tankersley, G.J. 74
Tanner, Obert C. 260
Taylor, Frank J. 51, 272
Taylor, Graham D. 92
Taylor, James A. 254
Tate, James H. 24
Teague, Ellen C. 187
Tennyson, Jon R. 99
Terzian, James P. 194
Thiessen, Arthur E. 121
Thomas, Bob 87
Thomas, Leon S. 263
Thomas, Robert E. 174
Thomas, Tony 268
Thompson, Layton S. 37
Thompson, Morley P. 27
Thompson, Stanley J. 89
Thompson, Thomas Hazzard 10
Thomson, Lila 104
Thruelsen, Richard 128
Tilley, Nannie May 230
Tinn, David B. 265
Tinstman, Dale C. 148
Tobias, Andrew P. 229
Todd, Zone G. 142
Toffler, Alvin 15
Torinus, John B. 126
Torley, John F. 81
Travis, Arlene 173
Travis, Norman J. 274
Tuccille, Jerome 140, 267

Tullis, Robert H.   136
Turnquist, Robert E.   210
Tutt, William Thayer   43
Tymeson, Mildred McClary   289

Unworth, J. Lewis   235

Valenti, Dan   42
Van Atta, Robert B.   283
Van Every, Philip Lance   158
Vanderberg, Bob   59
Veale, Frank R.   257
Veale, Tinkham   7
Verity, C. William   21
Versteeg, Jean D.   221
Vila, George R.   272
Volk, Harry J.   269
Voorhees, Enders McClumpha   275
Voth, Ben   291

Waddell, Harry   100
Wagner, Richard M.   81
Wagner, William   72, 75, 236
Wall, Bennett H.   254
Wall, Fred G.   231
Waller, Don   187
Walsh, Jack   120
Walsh, James A.   22
Walsh, John   216
Walsh, Mary Phyllis   290

Walton, Ed.   42
Waples, R.M., Jr.   114
Waples, R.M., Sr.   114
Ware, Thomas M.   146
Warner, Rawleigh, Jr.   184
Waterman, Merwin Howe   205
Watson, A.J., Jr.   184
Watters, Pat   68
Wean, R.J., Jr.   282
Weare, Walter B.   199
Weaver, John Downing   51
Webb, J.A.   210
Weil, Gordon Lee   243
Weil, Ulric   145
Weir, Ronald B.   241
Weiss, Morry   13
Wells, Barbara   244
Wells, Frederick Arthur   136
Wells, Robert W.   157
Wendel, C.H.   145
Wendel, William H.   50
Wendt, Lloyd   59, 90, 279
Wessells, John H.   30
West, Harold A.   292
West, James L.   260
Westcott, Richard   217
Westing, Fred   28
Weston, Frank   143
Wetherill, Elkins   218
Wetly, Earl M.   270
Weyerhaeuser, George H.   287
Weyr, Thomas   77
Whitaker, James B.   249

White, Eli G. 96
White, Joseph C. 106
White, W.S. 12
Whitehead, Don 89
Whitman, Edmund S. 117
Whittingham, Richard
  58, 79, 166
Wideman, Frank J. 126
Wilde, Wilson 132
Wilkerson, Hugh 208
Will, Erwin H. 277
Williams, Ben A. 30
Williams, Brad 189
Williams, Christian 267
Williams, E.W. 227
Williams, Edward Joseph
  170
Williams, Frances Leigh
  103
Williams, George M. 36
Williams, Harold A. 114
Williams, J. Kelly 105
Williams, Jon M. 92
Williams, Pat 218
Williams, Randall 280
Wilner, Barry 195
Wilson, Charles John
  240
Wilson, Harold S. 168
Wilson, Kemmons 136
Wilson, Robert Laurence
  69
Wilson, Thomas Carroll
  135
Wilson, William L. 63
Wingate, Phillip Jerome
  92

Wise, George 116
Wise, T.A. 213
Wishnick, William 288
Witt, Norbert A. 203
Wolflisberg, Hans J.
  193
Wolt, Irene 166
Wood, James Playsted
  79, 228
Wood, William C. 107
Woodfill, W. Stewart
  126
Woodford, Arthur 85
Woods, John W. 6
Woodson, Benjamine W.
  12
Woodworth, Constance 20
Worden, William L. 176
Worthy, James C. 242
Wright, David 131
Wright, Richard J. 14

Yahn, Mildred L. 22
Yausi, Glenn 189
Yenne, Bill 170
Ylvisaker, William T.
  125
Yoh, Harold L. 80

Zilg, Gerald C. 92
Zimmermann, Karl R. 83
Zurn, Everett F. 293
Zurn, F.W. 293
Zweig, Phillip L. 214